John Cheever Revisited

Twayne's United States Authors Series

Frank Day, Editor
Clemson University

TUSAS 647

JOHN CHEEVER. © NANCY CRAMPTON.

John Cheever Revisited

Patrick Meanor

State University of New York
College at Oneonta

Twayne Publishers • New York
Maxwell Macmillan Canada • Toronto
Maxwell Macmillan International • New York Oxford Singapore Sydney

John Cheever Revisited
Patrick Meanor

Copyright © 1995 by Twayne Publishers

Twayne Publishers
Macmillan Publishing Company
866 Third Avenue
New York, New York 10022

Maxwell Macmillan Canada, Inc.
1200 Eglinton Avenue East
Suite 200
Don Mills, Ontario M3C 3N1

Library of Congress Cataloging-in-Publication Data

Meanor, Patrick.
  John Cheever revisited / Patrick Meanor.
      p. cm.—(Twayne's United States authors series; TUSAS 647)
  Includes bibliographical references and index.
  ISBN 0-8057-3999-8
  1. Cheever, John—Criticism and interpretation. I. Title. II. Series.
PS3505.H6428Z77 1994
813.'52—dc20   94-11347
                                                                                                    CIP

The paper used in this publication meets the minimum requirements of American
National Standard for Information Sciences—Permanence of Paper for Printed Library
Materials, ANSI Z39.48-1984. ∞ ™

10 9 8 7 6 5 4 3 2 1

Printed in the United States of America.

In loving memory of

my mother, Thelma Caygill Meanor (1902–1986),
who first told me how good John Cheever was

my father, Albert W. Meanor (1908–1984),
who first took me to the Elyria, Ohio, Library when I was a child

and my nephew, Christopher Martin Meanor (1961–1991),
who was the real artist in the family

Contents

Publisher's Note

John Cheever Revisited by Patrick Meanor draws on new materials made available since the 1979 publication of *John Cheever* by Lynne Waldeland. Twayne Publishers is pleased to offer this new critical study.

Preface

John Cheever Revisited proposes that John Cheever is a considerably more serious artist than his reputation as the archetypal *New Yorker* writer has allowed. Because of the publication of Scott Donaldson's excellent biography in 1988, the appearance of *The Letters of John Cheever,* edited by his son, Benjamin Cheever, in the same year as the biography, and, most significantly, the stunning revelations of *The Journals of John Cheever,* edited by Robert Gottlieb and published in 1991, much of the background of Cheever's daily life has been uncovered. This book is the first full-length critical study of Cheever's work informed by the biography, the letters, and the journals, invaluable sources that intimate both the spiritual and psychological genesis of much of his work. While his novels and stories dramatize and, indeed, document the socioeconomic manners and morals of middle-class urban and suburban life from the 1930s through the 1970s, they also demonstrate, when read alongside the letters and journals, precisely how Cheever created, mythopoeically, as complete a world as Faulkner's Yoknapatawpha County or John Updike's Rabbit's world. Cheever fashioned at least seven mythopoeic communities throughout his novels and short stories: St. Botolphs, Bullet Park, Talifer, Remsen Park, Proxmire Manor, Shady Hill, and Gorey Brook, an accomplishment that few modern American writers can challenge.

Chapter 1 of this volume covers the major events in the life of John Cheever and brings together information from biographies, the letters, and the journals. This chapter also interweaves major critical opinions throughout the various stages of Cheever's literary career and serves, generally, as an outline for the entire volume. The chapter places special emphasis on Cheever's lifelong problem with alcohol and the effects it had on his family and his ability to work, both as a writer and as a teacher of writing.

Chapter 2 analyzes the earliest stories, from his first published story "Expelled," through many of the stories in his first volume of fiction *The Way Some People Live,* and stories written in his "new" style from *The Enormous Radio and Other Stories.* Though biographical elements regularly surface throughout his first book of stories, the stories beginning with "The Enormous Radio" are more obviously built on mythic patterns, particularly the myth of Eden and the fall, a pattern that remained constant in his work.

Chapter 3 compares and contrasts Cheever's two early novels, *The Wapshot Chronicle* and *The Wapshot Scandal,* and accounts for the radical difference in tone between them. These novels are Cheever's first extended attempts to mythologize his fictive world; that is, to create a world of his own, the meaning of the word *mythopoesis.* He created four distinct "worlds" within these novels that became uniquely Cheeveresque creations and permanently identified him as "the Ovid of Ossining," that is, an American master of mythic structures.

Chapter 4 examines the way Cheever extends and transforms another mythopoeic community, Shady Hill, into a depiction of the disintegration of America's spiritual values. Though the stories in *Some People, Places, and Things That Will Not Appear In My Next Novel* are not geographically centered in one fictive community, a number of the stories in this volume are as richly conceived and technically accomplished as anything he ever wrote.

Chapter 5 points out similarities and differences between the collection *The Brigadier and the Golf Widow* and *The Wapshot Scandal,* even though both of them document a darkening of Cheever's vision, particularly in regard to women. His masterpiece, "The Swimmer," is given the longest and most detailed analysis to date.

Chapter 6 proposes *Bullet Park* as Cheever's most existential novel, since it treats the source of America's moral and spiritual dislocations and bitterly satirizes helpless lives overwhelmed by Cheever's peculiar presentations of chance and fate. The chapter contrasts the quasi-surrealism of *Bullet Park* with stories in *The World of Apples,* which attempt to restore order and wholeness to the fractured spiritual lives of their characters.

Chapter 7 accounts for Cheever's new hopefulness embodied in the first novel he wrote in sobriety, *Falconer,* a work in which he confronts his agonizing struggles with addiction, homosexuality, guilt, and the possibilities of freedom. The chapter closely counterpoints information from the journals, the biography, and *Falconer* to explore the methods Cheever used to create his unique world. This chapter also contains the first extended analysis of the movement of Cheever's imagination toward ecological concerns in *Oh What a Paradise It Seems* and away from the consuming solipsism of his fictions up to and including *Bullet Park.*

Chapter 8 is the first in-depth analysis of *The Journals of John Cheever* in either book or essay form. The chapter excerpts relevant passages from the journals that document his battles with alcohol, loneliness, sexual desperation, especially his troubling homosexual impulses, family conflicts, and, most importantly, his heroic sobering-up process. Through a close reading of the journals, this chapter charts the way Cheever's emerging spiritual health became a subtext in *Falconer*.

This volume reexamines and analyzes Cheever's work as it comes out of the haunted New England world of Nathaniel Hawthorne and its Calvinist-Puritan heritage of sin, guilt, and hatred of the body. The book shows how Cheever resorts to the celebratory paganism of Greek and Roman myth to reengage the energizing ecstasies of love, passion, and the body in saving modern man from the life-denying demons of technological mechanization that William Blake called the "dark Satanic mills." It also points out the way Cheever used mythic and biblical patterns and allusions to ground his characters in less self-destructive sacred traditions and illuminates the nature of the sexual conflicts that surface throughout his work. The volume also examines the enormous role alcohol plays in the lives of his characters in light of Cheever's own debilitating alcoholism, which he finally overcame in the last seven years of his life.

As important as the connections between biographical conflicts and fictive ones is the clear progress Cheever made in refining one of modern American literature's most elegant prose styles. The dramatic change from the naturalistic prose of his earliest stories in *The Way Some People Live* to the sophistication of the stories in *The Enormous Radio and Other Stories* is analyzed in light of his journal keeping and the way those exercises expanded his writing, making it more reflective, meditative, and compelling.

Though the prose style changes and develops, Cheever's subject matter and themes remain the same for forty years: love, loneliness, the fall of families into ruin, alcoholic obsessiveness, sexual desperation, financial crisis, and the necessity of illusion. His work constitutes a profoundly existential exploration of the demythologized condition of America as it descends into the maelstrom of self-destructive mechanization and technology. The equally consistent thematic pattern running throughout his writings is his never-ending attempt to regenerate an Edenic condition of innocence and paradisiacal happiness, attainable only within the individual souls of his suffering, but hopeful, characters.

Acknowledgments

I wish to thank the administrators at the State University of New York, College at Oneonta, for their consistent support and assistance throughout the writing of this book. I am especially grateful for a reduced teaching load during the fall 1992 semester and the spring semester of 1993. My thanks go to professors Paul Lilly and Norman Wesley, chairmen of the English Department, for allowing me the course reductions, and to deans Douglas Shrader and James Mullen and vice-presidents Walter vom Saal and Joseph Nicolette for their approval of course reductions. I am especially indebted to Dr. Alan Donovan, president of the State University of New York, College at Oneonta, for his thoughtful encouragement during the writing of this book.

I also wish to thank the librarians of the Reference Department, especially Christine Bulson, Janet Potter, Mary Lynn Bensen, and Kathryn Franco for their generous and patient support in locating crucial scholarly materials without which this book could not have been completed. Many thanks also go to staff members of the Inter-Library Loan Office, especially to Andrea Gerberg and Veronica Diver for their prompt delivery of books and articles that were difficult to locate and that substantially enriched the content of the volume. Last but not least, I owe a major debt of gratitude to Candace Sweet, whose attention to detail, superb editing skills, and quick wit made the revisions of the book seem simple. I am particularly indebted to the keenly perceptive editing of Frank Day, Mark Zadrozny, and especially India Koopman.

Chronology

1946–1950   Moves to East 59th Street and continues work on a novel without success.

1947   Publishes "The Enormous Radio" and "Torch Song" in the *New Yorker,* a major breakthrough in his "new" style, in which he modified his naturalistic prose with a more elaborate and mythically resonant one.

1948   Benjamin, first son, born 4 May. Short-lived play, *Town House,* based on some of Cheever's stories, opens and closes in September.

1951   Awarded a Guggenheim fellowship and moves to Scarborough, New York, in Westchester County, which becomes the basis for the many suburban communities he creates in his fiction.

1953   *The Enormous Radio and Other Stories,* second short-story collection, published by Funk and Wagnalls in February.

1954–1956   Teaches creative writing at Barnard College and continues work on first novel, *The Wapshot Chronicle.*

1955   Receives Benjamin Franklin Award for "The Five-Forty-Eight."

1956   Is given the O. Henry Award for "The Country Husband." Takes his family to Italy for an extended holiday.

1957   Second son, Federico, born 9 March in Italy. *The Wapshot Chronicle* published by Harper and Row. Cheever is elected to the National Institute of Arts and Letters.

1958   *The Wapshot Chronicle* wins the National Book Award. Third collection of short stories, *The Housebreaker of Shady Hill,* published by Harper and Row in September. Joins the Century Club.

1960   Awarded second Guggenheim fellowship to work on another novel.

1961   Moves to Cedar Lane in Ossining, New York. Fourth short-story collection, *Some People, Places, and Things That Will Not Appear in My Next Novel,* published by Harper and Row in April.

1964   Second novel, *The Wapshot Scandal,* and fifth short-story collection, *The Brigadier and the Golf Widow,* published by Harper and Row. Travels to Russia with John Updike and begins a lifelong friendship with him. Appears on the cover of *Time* in March.

1965   *The Wapshot Scandal* wins the Howells Medal of the American Academy of Arts and Letters.

1968   Film version of "The Swimmer" appears.

1969   *Bullet Park* published by Alfred A. Knopf in April.

1971–1972   Teaches creative writing at Sing Sing in Ossining.

1973   *The World of Apples* published by Alfred A. Knopf in May. Teaches at the University of Iowa Writing Workshop. Excessive drinking begins taking a serious toll on health. Is elected to the American Academy of Arts and Letters.

1974   Attempts teaching at Boston University, but alcoholism leads to physical and psychological collapse.

1975   Enters Smithers Alcohol Rehabilitation Center and emerges a sober man. Continues working on a novel concerning prison life and addiction.

1977   *Falconer* published by Alfred A. Knopf in March to excellent reviews. Cheever appears on the cover of *Newsweek* 14 March.

1978   *The Stories of John Cheever* published by Alfred A. Knopf in November. Cheever awarded an honorary Doctor of Letters degree by Harvard in June.

1979   Wins Pulitzer Prize and National Book Critics Circle Award for *The Stories of John Cheever.* Given MacDowell Award in the summer.

1980   Suffers two neurological seizures in the autumn.

1981   Receives American Book Award for paperback version of *The Stories of John Cheever* and an honorary doctorate from Skidmore College. Cancer is discovered during a kidney operation in July.

1982   Novella, *Oh What a Paradise It Seems* is published by Knopf in March. Cheever receives the National Medal for Literature in April. Dies in Ossining 18 June and is buried in Norwell, Massachusetts.

1988   *The Letters of John Cheever,* edited by son Benjamin, published by Simon and Schuster.

1991   *The Journals of John Cheever,* edited by Robert Gottlieb, published by Knopf.

1994   *Thirteen Uncollected Stories* published in March by Academy Chicago Publishers after settlement of legal tussle with Cheever's family beginning in 1988.

Chapter One

"Fiction Is Never Crypto-autobiography": The Life of John Cheever

Few modern American writers have mapped out their recurrent subject matter and themes as consistently or as lucidly as John Cheever. From the beginning, indeed from his first published story, "Expelled," he concerned himself with the fall from a condition of Edenic happiness and childlike innocence into the chaos and pain of adult knowledge. Most of his novels and stories share this theme of the fall in various degrees or are variations on it. This recurrent concern is so ingrained in Cheever's work that he can be considered, along with William Faulkner and John Updike, a mythopoeic writer; that is, a writer who, over a period of time, managed to create a mythic world of his own. Faulkner's Yoknapatawpha County and Updike's Rabbit's world are instantaneously recognizable; and so, too, is Cheever's early St. Botolphs and his later Westchester equivalents of Shady Hill, Proxmire Manor, and Bullet Park.

Though Cheever always asserted that fiction was "never crypto-autobiography," a reader even slightly familiar with his work notices early on clear correspondences that begin to form themselves into unmistakable patterns. And once a reader delves into the letters, the recently published journals, the many interviews, and Scott Donaldson's definitive biography, Cheever's assertion takes on a new dimension. There is certainly no doubt that much of Cheever's fiction comes directly out of his own life experience and is autobiographical, but autobiographical in the patterns of those experiences rather than in a literal presentation or echo of actual events. Most important, Cheever's fictions or fictive treatments of these events create rather than record or document what those experiences meant to him. But what strikes the reader of Cheever most is the unique way in which he transforms the commonplace events of daily life into some of the wittiest and most profoundly moving narratives in modern American literature.

Cheever's Family Background

John Cheever was born into a middle-class New England family on 27 May 1912, in the seaside community of Quincy, Massachusetts, a few miles south of Boston. His mother was an English-born woman named Mary Devereaux Liley who was ten years younger than her husband, John's father, Frederick Lincoln Cheever. Both his mother's and father's figures surface regularly throughout his fiction but are never identified as such. Rather, they appear as types—the hard-drinking, charming story-teller, older father figure in dramatic conflict with the emotionally reserved, class-conscious, workaholic mother or grandmother figure. They are frequently involved in the fall of a rich and respected family from a socially prominent position owing to the father's irresponsible behavior in financial, sexual, or family matters. The mother figure is never the cause of the family's disintegration. Indeed, she is usually the agent of recovery—very much like Mary Cheever, who kept the family together by creating her own businesses after her husband lost his job and then the family home during mid-to-late 1920s.

John Cheever's talent for mythologizing or romanticizing his family's background became a standard part of his storytelling reputation throughout his life. He told friends in conversation and many interviewers that his father had owned a shoe factory in Lynn, Massachusetts, but no one has been able to find any record of such a company. His father had been, though, a successful traveling shoe salesman throughout New England and was so listed in the Quincy city directory for many years, and then as a shoe manufacturer after 1922.[1] Cheever, however, was not content to romanticize only his immediate family background. He accepted the family legend handed down to him by his father and elaborated on it with his best storyteller's voice. He rarely altered the facts of his family background, but did choose a very remote branch of the Cheever family and decided to make himself its direct heir.

He claimed that he was descended from a famous Cheever named Ezekiel, a schoolmaster at the renowned Boston Latin School. Cotton Mather, a former student of Ezekiel, preached his funeral sermon, calling him "Master Socrates." The real founder of the American branch of the family was Daniel Cheever, not a schoolmaster at Boston Latin but a prison keeper in Cambridge, Massachusetts, as was his son Israel. Daniel was a cousin of the legendary Ezekiel, which made Ezekiel a cousin of John Cheever's great-great-great-great-great-great-grandfather. John Cheever claimed to have seen the genealogical papers his father had collected, but said that they had been inadvertently thrown away (Donaldson 1988, 4). One of the recurring patterns throughout John Cheever's life was his increasing inability or unwillingness to adhere to historical facts if alluring fictive embellishments contributed to a more compelling story. And, in fact, Cheever used Ezekiel Cheever as the obvious prototype of Ezekiel Wapshot, the founding father of the Wapshot dynasty in *The Wapshot Chronicle.* Indeed, the opening chapter of the novel lists the genealogical information as it appears in the Cheever family history. The main character of Cheever's final novel, *Falconer,* is also named Ezekiel Farragut and echoes certain characteristics of his ancient ancestor.

Cheever's mother, Mary Devereaux Liley, had emigrated from England when she was six. Though Cheever came to resent his excessively strong-willed mother, there is little doubt that her family, especially her mother, Sarah Liley, was responsible for fostering John's artistic propensities. One of his fondest memories is that of his maternal grandmother reading volumes of Robert Louis Stevenson, Jack London, and Charles Dickens to him even before he attended Wollaston Grammar School. And it's difficult to overlook the obvious Dickensian wit and gift for storytelling in much of Cheever's work. Indeed, the young Cheever gained his first notoriety as one of the best storytellers at his grammar school. Some of his teachers used that gift wisely; good behavior from the class would be rewarded with a story from John. Some of the stories became serials because, Cheever later admitted, he had no definite idea of where his narratives were heading and was forced to follow his innate feel for how effectively the story was holding the attention of his classmates.

Cheever's daughter, Susan, herself a novelist, recalls her father telling her about those early storytelling adventures: "With luck, and increasing skill, he could spin the story out over two or three periods so that the teacher and his classmates forgot all about arithmetic and geography and social studies. He told them stories about ship captains and eccentric old ladies and orphan boys, gallant men and dazzling women in a world where the potent forces of evil and darkness were confounded and good triumphed in the end. He peopled his tales with his own family and friends and neighbors."[2] There is little question that the subject matter and themes of his first novel, *The Wapshot Chronicle,* and a number of his early short stories, were clearly foreshadowed in some of those grammar-school narratives. Certainly Captain Leander Wapshot and Honora Wapshot come to mind as later embodiments of the young Cheever's early fictions.

Though there are few orphans as such in Cheever's fiction, there are numerous examples of boys and young men who feel orphaned by their loveless childhoods and who are unable to express their feelings because of a kind of New England reserve built into their characters. This orphaned condition surfaces in what Scott Donaldson calls the "unwanted-child motif" that can be found in many typical Cheever narratives. It has its origin in information given to him by his own father, after a few strong drinks, concerning the circumstances under which John was conceived (Donaldson 1988, 19). It was a story that Frederick Lincoln Cheever told him repeatedly to emphasize the fact that the only child his mother and father truly wanted was his older brother, Fred. Had it not been for his father's drinking two manhattans one afternoon, so the story goes, John would not have been conceived. His parents had not wanted any more children after Fred and had even invited an abortionist to dinner one evening. So deeply did that knowledge wound John Cheever that he simply transcribed the imagined scene of the abortionist's dinner into both *The Wapshot Chronicle* and *Falconer*. He stated in 1977: "The greatest and most bitter mystery of my life was my father" (Donaldson 1988, 33).

The Beginning of the Brother Conflict

Intimately tied into the recurring "unwanted-child motif" and taking center stage throughout the rest of Cheever's fiction is his relationship with his only brother, Fred. As Cheever himself acknowledged to his daughter Susan: "It was the strongest love in my life" (S. Cheever, 8). The brothers were inseparable during their childhood and well into their twenties. The brother-motif appears as a principal theme in all of Cheever's novels. Cheever himself insisted that "Goodbye, My Brother" appear first in the chronologically arranged *The Stories of John Cheever* (1978), even though it postdated a number of stories in that collection. The brothers Moses and Coverly Wapshot are principal characters in both *The Wapshot Chronicle* and *The Wapshot Scandal*. And the murder of his brother Eben by Ezekiel Farragut becomes the cause of Ezekiel's imprisonment in *Falconer*.

The relationship between John and Fred became, after a while, simply too close. They shared an apartment in Boston for two years and took a walking tour of Germany in 1931. They had even planned to buy a house together in Boxford, Massachusetts, in the mid-1930s. But John later stated that their relationship had become "morbidly close," actually suggesting that the relationship possessed incestuous elements that evoked disturbingly equivocal love/hate feelings. These ambivalent impulses, combined with the brothers' mutually strong penchant for heavy drinking, could have become lethal. The "brother theme" is the single most important theme in all of Cheever's fiction.

Family relationships, then, form the major backdrop for much of Cheever's fiction. And even though Cheever himself repeatedly asserted that fiction "is never crypto-autobiography," his own life experiences supplied the major content of his writing insofar as his mother, father, and brother became important prototypes for many of the mothers, fathers, and brothers that appeared in his stories.

Though the young John Cheever became a grammar-school story-telling celebrity, he was never more than an average student at best, and failed important subjects like algebra and French in his middle-school and high-school years at the prestigious Thayer Academy. In fact, his grades were so poor at Thayer that he dropped out and attended Quincy High School during 1928–29, returning to Thayer in the fall of 1929 as a probationary student. His grades did not improve, and he was expelled in 1929. Cheever had additional explanations for his expulsion: he was caught smoking; he seduced the son of one of the faculty members. As Scott Donaldson cautions, however, "it was not unusual for [Cheever] to supply alternative accounts of events in his own life" (Donaldson 1988, 39). The sooner students of Cheever begin to understand that facts are of the least importance in his fictional world, the better will those students appreciate the creative significance of his work. Cheever's ability to entertain the fictive possibilities of a given situation and his ability to modify those possibilities to reveal the truth of a character's personality are much more important to his genius as a writer than so-called "facts."

Unquestionably, the most important failure of young Cheever's life— his expulsion from the highly respected Thayer Academy—became the genesis of his first published short story, appropriately titled "Expelled." Cheever's ability to transform failure into success by the alchemical power of his imagination established a pattern that he repeated throughout his life. Writing honestly and openly about his own academic failure, changing only a few details here and there, he composed a story and boldly sent it to one of the reigning literary editors at that time, Malcolm Cowley at the *New Republic.* To Cowley's credit, Cheever's story appeared in the 1 October 1929 issue. Cheever and Cowley remained close personal friends and professional colleagues for the rest of their

lives. Indeed, Cheever often went to Cowley for advice and counsel, particularly when he was having trouble getting published. More often than
not Cowley's advice, if Cheever followed it, was correct.

The publication of "Expelled" and the continuing fall of Cheever's
family into financial ruin—the bank foreclosed on the family home in
1932—were landmark experiences for young Cheever. Being a typically
reticent New England family, Cheever's mother and father did not dis-
cuss the family's obvious financial difficulty, and John's father retreated
into a fantasy world with the help of alcohol. His mother's solution was
to become a successful businesswoman, opening a gift shop in Quincy.
Rather than showing gratitude for his wife's hard work, Frederick resent-
ed her success and saw it as a form of humiliation. And in later years,
John Cheever also regarded his mother's "unfeminine" behavior as an
embarrassment. Old feelings of hostility were rekindled when he
remembered himself as a neglected child who had to make his own
meals and take care of household chores. His father's life receded into
heavier drinking as his mother's business acumen and hard work made
her a proudly independent woman. As Frederick's life slipped into deeper alcoholic despair, Mary involved herself in endless charitable, civic,
and social organizations. Young John vividly recalls the obvious lack of
affection between his parents, and later in life seemed appalled at his
mother's icy indifference toward her husband and children. Sarah
Wapshot shares many of his mother's personality traits. With the fall of
the family into both financial and emotional chaos, Cheever decided to
move out of the house and into Boston with his brother, Fred.

He left his boyhood home once he realized that his family had fallen
on hard times and ceased any formal education after his expulsion from
Thayer Academy; he continued to read voraciously on his own and
spoke, in later years, of how certain classic writers helped formulate his
youthful imagination. He cites Flaubert's *Madame Bovary* as the book
that most impressed and influenced him and claimed to have read it over
twenty-five times. He called it his "Yale College and his Harvard"
(Donaldson 1988, 25) He read Dostoyevsky and Tolstoy, Marcel Proust's
Swann's Way, and poets John Donne, T. S. Eliot, W. B. Yeats, and the
English Romantics, Keats, Byron, and Shelley. He held Keats in great
esteem and had Coverly Wapshot, in *The Wapshot Scandal,* feed all of
Keats's poetry into a computer to discover significant linguistic patterns.
In the four years that John lived with and was supported by his brother,
who was in the advertising business, he met some important members of
the literary set in Cambridge and on Cape Cod; his most important

introduction was to E. E. Cummings, with whom he struck up an immediate friendship and ran into later on in New York City. He met these people in several Bohemian bars in Boston that were favored by radical fringe intellectuals. Two older scholars became, for a short time, patrons of Cheever, and helped support him. The first was Harry Dana, a pacifist drama professor and son of the novelist Richard Henry Dana; the other was Hazel Hawthorne Werner, a fiction writer. Through these influential figures, he was introduced to the editors of both *Pagany* and *Hound & Horn,* two now-defunct avant-garde literary magazines, in which he published two early stories based on family conflicts resembling his own.

It was also during these years in Boston that Cheever began to keep a journal, which eventually reached more than 4 million words. The appearance of his story "Bock Beer and Bermuda Onions" in *Hound & Horn,* edited by Lincoln Kirstein, further promoted his burgeoning career; T. S. Eliot, Marianne Moore, Wallace Stevens, and E. E. Cummings frequently appeared in its pages. It was Cummings, however, who warned Cheever that if he had serious designs on a literary future, Boston was not the place to establish such a career. He told him quite bluntly in 1932: "Get out of Boston . . . It's a city without springboards for people who can't dive" (Donaldson 1988, 49). It took him four years to take Cummings's advice seriously, during which time he tried to get his stories published and worked in department stores and as a reporter on a Quincy newspaper. But he continued to live off his brother and several charitable patrons.

Leaving Boston for New York

Malcolm Cowley, considering Cheever's financial difficulties, suggested that he apply to Yaddo, the well-known artists' colony in Saratoga Springs, New York. This would give him the time to write and the opportunity to meet an array of writers, artists, and musicians. Elizabeth Ames, Yaddo's manager, rejected his first application, but accepted his next, in 1934, initiating a relationship with Ames that would last for nearly fifty years. He also made valuable and enduring contacts at Yaddo with novelists James T. Farrell and Josephine Herbst, with poet Muriel Rukeyser, with composer Ned Rorem, and with many other young emerging artists. After a successful summer at Yaddo, Cheever moved to Greenwich Village in New York City, where, even though he sometimes went hungry, he managed to continue writing stories. To pay the bills, he contributed some book reviews for the *New Republic,* where Cowley was still literary editor, and wrote synopses of novels for MGM at $5 apiece. Hazel Hawthorne Werner had also moved to Manhattan and offered him a sofa in her Waverly Place flat. Through her and Cowley, Cheever met the most important writers in the city. He renewed his acquaintance with Cummings and became friendly with John Dos Passos, whom he met his first night there. He also met novelists Sherwood Anderson and James Agee, critic Edmund Wilson, painter Milton Avery, sculptor Gaston Lachaise, and photographer Walker Evans. Cheever steadfastly worked on his short stories and a novel he called *Empty Bed Blues*. Most of his stories were rejected, and he again sought the counsel of Malcolm Cowley. He told Cheever his stories were not getting published because—at six or seven thousand words—they were too long. "Why don't you write a story a day for the next four days," Cowley suggested, "none of them longer than a thousand words" (Donaldson 1988, 61). The advice changed the direction of Cheever's literary career. Cheever took it literally and showed up a week later at Cowley's office with four stories. Cowley decided to publish one in the *New Republic* and sent two to the *New Yorker*, both of which the magazine accepted; the remaining story was published in a little magazine the next year. "Brooklyn Rooming House" became the first of 121 Cheever stories that the *New Yorker* printed during a period of more than forty years. From 1935 on, the *New Yorker* and John Cheever's literary career were inextricably connected. With the exception of John O'Hara, Cheever published more stories in that magazine than any other writer in its history.

Early Publishing Success and True Love

By 1937, Cheever's literary career was quickly rising as he published stories in the *New Yorker*, *Collier's*, the *New Republic*, the *Yale Review*, and *Story*. In 1938, he also landed a writing job with the Federal Writers' Project at $50 a week and moved to Washington, D.C., for about six months. He worked as a junior editor on one of Franklin D. Roosevelt's Works Progress Administration projects, in which thousands of unemployed teachers and writers wrote travel guides—which remained the standard for years after—for all forty-eight states and a few large cities.

By 1939, Cheever, at age twenty-seven, felt a deep longing for some sort of permanent relationship, and as he put it, "didn't want to sleep alone anymore" (Donaldson 1988, 77). Though not actively searching for a wife, he was emotionally ready to settle down and raise a family. As he was on his way to see his agent in Manhattan, he met Mary Winternitz, who by chance was taking the same elevator up to her job with Cheever's agent. He was struck by her beauty and grace and asked his agent, Maxim Lieber, to introduce them. Lieber did so and, as they were immediately attracted to each other, they began dating. Mary Winternitz came from a distinguished academic and medical family; both her parents were physicians. Her mother, Helen Watson, was one of the first women in America to earn a medical degree. Mary's father, Milton Winternitz, became a respected pathologist and eventually rose to the position of dean of the Yale University Medical School. Mary had been educated at Sarah Lawrence, was intensely interested in literature, and was herself a talented poet. After dating for three years and actually living together, a practice frowned upon by her family, John and Mary were married on 22 March 1941. Living with his beloved obviously agreed with John Cheever, at least when it came to creativity, because he published, in 1940 alone, fifteen stories—eleven in the *New Yorker,* two in *Harper's Bazaar,* one in *Mademoiselle,* and one in *Collier's.* All of those magazines paid well, and the *New Yorker* paid within a week of a story's publication.

World War II Interrupts a Burgeoning Career

Cheever's reputation was quickly growing but just as his writer's dream was becoming a reality, World War II broke out and Cheever immediately enlisted in the army. He spent four years at a number of dull jobs during his military career and hoped to become an officer, but his weakness in mathematics and his repeated failure of that part of the officer candidate's examination precluded that possibility. His letters to his wife from military training camps in South Carolina and Georgia indicate that Cheever was relatively naive when it came to seeing how working-class and poor people managed to live their lives. Although he was able to keep up with the rugged physical training, he was not an athletic person. And he was, at thirty, a bit younger than most of the recruits at boot camp. His letters to friends and his young wife demonstrated a pattern that lasted throughout Cheever's writing career, and that was his talent for using everyday characters and occurrences around him for literary purposes. A dozen of his better early stories came out of his military training, the most notable a piercing psychological study of a sadistic basic-training sergeant, entitled "Sergeant Limeburner."

As Cheever's unit was preparing to confront the German field mar-
shal Rommel's troops in the North African desert, Cheever got word
that Random House wanted to publish a collection of stories. He confessed years later that his lunch with Random House publisher Bennett
Cerf to celebrate his first book was the happiest day of his life. He called
the collection *The Way Some People Live* (1943), a title that embodies
Cheever's continual amazement at what people can endure. Many of the
stories address the change in the lives of common people brought on by
World War II, though none of them involve actual combat. Rather they
tell of the homesickness of young men away from their families for the
first time, the emotional and financial hardships of young wives, and the
general starkness of barracks life. The other stories deal with victims of
the Depression, particularly those who had lost jobs and homes because
of it. The collection received mixed reviews. Struthers Burt predicted
that Cheever, if he avoided certain stylistic affectations, would undoubtedly become "one of the most distinguished writers."[3] The critic from
the *New Republic,* Weldon Kees, warned that the sameness in the stories'
tone and situation made them almost generic *New Yorker* stories.[4] In
short, Cheever was running the risk of falling into formulaic writing.

More important, however, are first appearances of unmistakable autobiographical subtexts that underlay many of Cheever's fictions throughout his career. The appearance of character types such as the wanderer,
the exile, the alienated lover, and the themes of loneliness and isolation
are evident throughout *The Way Some People Live.* Most important is the
search for wholeness or, in mythic terms, the attempt to regenerate an
Edenic happiness that many of these victims had lost in their fall from
ignorance to knowledge.

Cheever's literary reputation began to thrive and to create advantages
for him, even as a private first class. Because several of his superior offi-
cers saw copies of his book in local book stores and were impressed with
the national attention he was receiving, they decided to reassign him to
Astoria, Queens, to work with other writers in the Signal Corps
Photographic Center. Had Cheever remained with his original infantry
unit, there was the distinct possibility that he would have been one of
many casualties his unit suffered. According to Scott Donaldson, four
out of five enlisted men were wounded and half were killed by the end of
the war (Donaldson 1988, 102).

As a result of his first published book, Cheever was able to work with
other literary celebrities in a casual atmosphere. Hollywood director
Stanley Kramer was the administrative head of the unit that boasted

writers such as William Saroyan and Irwin Shaw, who, along with Cheever, worked on scripts for antifascist propaganda films. Because of the contacts he made through his fellow writers, he attended parties with celebrities like Frederic March, Abe Burrows, Moss Hart, and other Broadway stars. Cheever also became renowned for his obsessive devotion to writing and the time and energy that he poured into his projects. Leonard Spigelgass, the head writer for the project, claimed that Cheever always finished his tasks before anyone else and found himself with too much time on his hands. He called Cheever "a writing machine" (Donaldson 1988, 103). But it was this very discipline that enabled Cheever to produce a huge body of work over many years in spite of such time-consuming distractions as heavy drinking and extramarital affairs.

Because of the general informality of his work with the Signal Corps, he was able to live off base in a lovely townhouse on East Ninety-second Street. The townhouse was too expensive for one family, and the Cheevers shared the five floors with two other couples and their babies. Mary Cheever had given birth to their first child, Susan, in May 1943, just before their move to East Ninety-second Street. Their life in their new home became comically complicated, and, though they lived there less than a year, Cheever was able to use some of the incidents that took place there for six stories he published in the *New Yorker* in 1945 and 1946. They came to be known as the "Town House" stories and attest to Cheever's ability to transform seemingly insignificant domestic problems into memorable art. So popular were these stories that one of Broadway's most influential directors and producers, George S. Kaufman, actually produced a play out of them called *Town House* on Broadway in fall 1948; it lasted only twelve performances. Cheever made a little more that $50 on the play, but its production was an indication that his name was becoming increasingly well known, not only in the relatively small world of the short story but in the larger and potentially more rewarding spotlight of Broadway.

After a military writing assignment sent Cheever to Guam and the Philippines, he returned to New York just in time to be honorably discharged from the army shortly after atomic bombs had been dropped on Hiroshima and Nagasaki. The family moved to a smaller apartment not far from their former Upper East Side townhouse, where Cheever immediately began a work routine that he would repeat throughout his life. He would arise early in the morning, dress in a business suit and hat, and ride the elevator with the other businessmen. They would get off on

the first floor and Cheever would take the elevator down to the base-
ment, where he would enter a storage room, remove his clothes down to
his shorts, and work till suppertime. He took a short break for lunch. He
felt that writing was as responsible and demanding a vocation as any
other and treated it with complete professional respect. By keeping his
writing separate from his domestic life, he was able to objectify his goals
and devote the proper amount of time and effort to accomplish them.
While he was a consistently disciplined writer, his vocation as a family
man and the energies he devoted to household responsibilities and pleasures were vitally important in keeping him emotionally and psychologically centered in a daily routine. In this devotion to the quotidian, he
resembles Wallace Stevens and William Carlos Williams, whose professional duties as a lawyer and doctor, respectively, kept them from being
overwhelmed by the chaos of the world.

Cheever began working on a novel with the help of a hefty advance
from Random House. The outline of this proposed novel chronicled the
disintegration of a respected New England family named Field, whose
mother, father, and two sons bore a striking resemblance to the Cheever
family when they lost their home during the Depression. It was this situation that was to become one of the principal conflicts of his first novel,
The Wapshot Chronicle. More important, however, were several stories that
signaled a major change in Cheever's style, fictive voice, and tone. He
moved away from the short stories Malcolm Cowley had urged him to
write in the mid-1930s and moved into much longer, more psychologically sophisticated stories, such as "The Enormous Radio" and "Torch
Song." These two stories, published in 1947, eventually came to be considered two of his greatest and most popular works, not only for his new,
highly developed lyrical style and brilliant character portraiture but also
for his ability to evoke deep mythic resonance within the most mundane
circumstances. Few of Cheever's female characters are as outwardly normal as Joan Harris of "Torch Song," but no other Cheever figure takes on
so ominously or subtly the obvious vampiric characteristics of the fatal
woman as she. Cheever's ability to evoke deep mythic resonance in both
stories heralded a new depth and range in his fiction. From 1947 on,
there is a deeper and richer texturing taking place in his stories, principally because he was permitting archetypal figures—like Joan Harris—
to enter his fiction. Common, everyday occurrences took on a deeper
significance, so that his best stories from these years frequently operate
on two levels simultaneously: the mythic and the everyday. At age thirty-five, Cheever's stories took on new dimensions that allowed them to

function not only as entertaining and probing psychological studies but also as archetypal resonances; in the case of "Torch Song," revealing Joan Harris as a modern-day Hecate.

The Move to the Suburbs

From the small Upper East Side flat near Sutton Place, the Cheevers eventually moved to a comfortable apartment at 400 East Fifty-ninth Street, where they lived until 1951. Cheever had by then lived in Manhattan for seventeen years, but it simply became too expensive and distracting for him to live and continue producing as resourcefully as he had before. A new child, Benjamin, had been born in May 1948, and the Cheevers decided they needed more room and less chaos, and chose to move to Scarborough, an upscale Westchester suburb some thirty miles from New York City. The house they moved into was actually a large garage that had been converted into servants' quarters on the vast estate of National City Bank founder Frank A. Vanderlip. The surrounding estate was pastoral in that it had sheep grazing in a pasture with lovely brooks, fields, and wooded areas. And adjoining the Cheever house, which was called "Beechtwig," was a large Italian garden and a rose arbor. There was also a pool, which Cheever used frequently, since swimming was his favorite athletic recreation. True to Cheever's penchant for using his immediate surrounding as settings for his stories, he began a series of narratives about the joys and sorrows of suburban life, which were published seven years later under the title *The Housebreaker of Shady Hill.* He did some of his writing in a vacant room in the house but also rented a room at the train station in downtown Scarborough. Cheever never needed the rarified library atmosphere that many writers work in. Rather, he moved his portable typewriter to any quiet place, accompanied always by his coffee and cigarettes. The closer he was to the actual pulse of everyday life—but not so close as to be distracting—the more productive he became. The financial troubles that had plagued the family in Manhattan were relieved somewhat by their move to Scarborough and also by a generous Guggenheim fellowship in 1951.

Cheever himself entered fully into the various social practices of upper-middle-class suburban males, which included heavy drinking, especially gin. Exhausted husbands emerged from their commuter trains after 6 P.M. and then went home to relax with martinis, a favorite with Cheever and many of his protagonists. He also joined the local volunteer fire department, where heavy drinking habitually accompanied drills. He became a member of the local school board and attended dances at the country club. In short, he performed all the social rituals that young, ambitious, successful businessmen pursued in the 1950s and 1960s.

In 1953, his next collection of short stories was published under the title of *The Enormous Radio and Other Stories,* which contains some of his finest stories, including the title story, "Goodbye, My Brother," "The Pot of Gold," "O City of Broken Dreams," and "Torch Song." Amazingly enough, Cheever had great difficulty finding a publisher for the collection, which many critics would later designate his greatest. These are the stories by which Cheever became renowned; they embody the unique style and tone that characterized his writing for the rest of career. Random House rejected them, even though he had received an O. Henry Award in 1951 for "The Pot of Gold." Eventually Funk and Wagnalls published the collection to mostly negative reviews. Because most of Cheever's work was published in the *New Yorker,* his name had become identified with the magazine. And as a result of that identification, his work was tarred with the same brush as some other *New Yorker* writers.

Many book reviewers were members of the New York intellectual elite, university professors in eastern schools whose attitudes were unapologetically socialist or leftist. These brilliant first-generation college-educated scholars, who had escaped the poverty of the Lower East Side or other depressed areas in the Bronx, Brooklyn, or Chicago, tended to favor fiction that demonstrated a more socially relevant, sometimes proletarian point of view closer to their childhood and adolescent experiences. These critics also considered the *New Yorker* kind of story an elitist indulgence that chronicled the shallow manners and morals of the upper-middle class. One reviewer objected to Cheever's stories in *The Enormous Radio and Other Stories* because many of their characteristics were identical to the "white collar people who subscribe to the *New Yorker*" (Donaldson 1988, 137). Other critics accused his work of being overly pessimistic and depressing because many of the stories deal with shabby lives mired in urban hopelessness. In short, Cheever's second collection of short fiction, containing stories that virtually defined what eventually became known as Cheeveresque, met with very mixed reviews.

At this point in Cheever's career, he decided to pursue his novel in earnest and try to earn some much-needed money for his expanding family responsibilities. He accepted a position at Barnard College to teach creative writing in fall 1954. He was, by most accounts, a superb and encouraging teacher. One of his former students reported that he was most concerned with transforming dull and lifeless sentences into highly effective rhetorical structures whose balance would impress and move readers. He also insisted that they write about their own lives— much as he himself did—and that they could "mythologize the commonplace"—again, a consistent and major part of his own writing patterns (Donaldson 1988, 144). It was also at about this time that he began to feel the deleterious effects of his hard-drinking life-style. He consulted a psychiatrist about both his drinking and his homosexual predilections, which, as his journals reveal, became more agonizing as he got older. On a lighter note, though, Harper and Brothers offered to buy out Cheever's contract with Random House and gave him a substantial advance on his novel-in-progress and five years in which to finish it. He had reached the point where he had titled it *The Wapshot Chronicle*.

In spite of the academic critics' hostility, Cheever began receiving literary prizes for his outstanding work in the short-story form. In 1955, he won the Benjamin Franklin Magazine Award for his brilliant portrait of suburban living in "The Five-Forty-Eight," and in January 1956 he won the even more prestigious O. Henry Award for what some consider his best story, "The Country Husband." Two sad events, however, took place within the same week in February 1956: the death of his mother at the age of eighty-two (the same age at which his father died) and of his editor at the *New Yorker,* Gus Lobrano. Lobrano, who edited Cheever's early stories, had also become a close friend by teaching Cheever how to fish. After these emotional blows, Cheever returned to Yaddo and worked nonstop on *The Wapshot Chronicle.* Still under some financial pressure, he sold off four major portions to the *New Yorker* and sent the entire manuscript to Harper and Brothers on 21 June 1956.

Other financial rewards began arriving, the first of which was $40,000 from the head of MGM, Dore Schary, for the film rights to a recently published *New Yorker* story called "The Housebreaker of Shady Hill" (which was to become the title story for his next collection). Shortly before getting the cash from Schary, he had been elected to the board of directors at Yaddo, a refuge where he had spent twenty years, off and on, under the loving care of Elizabeth Ames and where he wrote some of his best work. With the money from the film rights, the Cheevers decided to spend a year in Italy, a vacation they had been planning for many years. The Cheevers were encouraged by their friends, novelist and short-fiction writer Robert Penn Warren and his wife,

Eleanor Clark, who had maintained a second home in Rome for a number of years.

The Beginning of a Love Affair with Italy

After an uneventful trip by ocean liner, the *Conte Biancamano,* during which Cheever gathered details for a number of stories that involved the extramarital affairs that such trips can engender, the family arrived in Rome in November 1956. Cheever's story "The Country Husband" was aired on the television drama series *Playhouse 90* the day the family arrived in Rome, an event that showed that his work had reached the highest levels of the commercial literary world. With the help of Eleanor Clark, they settled into a huge apartment in the Palazzo Doria, where they spent the year. With occasional trips to Roman ruins outside the city walls and to seaside resorts such as Port'Ercole, a place Cheever later claimed was the single most beautiful place he had ever visited, the family decided to rent a ruined castle there called La Rocca during the summer of 1957.

The most important event, however, was the birth of another son, Federico, on 9 March 1957. Almost as significant was the entrance into the family of a maid named Iole Felici, who not only cleaned, cooked, and cared for her American charges but also took over the management of the entire Cheever household. So successful was her experience with the Cheever family that they brought her back to the United States, where she remained with the family for the next twenty-five years. Though Cheever got very little actual writing done during his year in Rome, he enjoyed Italian architecture, culture, and customs immensely and studied Italian with several teachers. Over the next several years he produced a number of stories depicting Americans confronting Italian culture. Though most critics would not include them as part of his best work, stories such as "The Bella Lingua," "The Duchess," "The Golden Age," and "Boy in Rome" would certainly rank as some of his most entertaining and witty stories because of the ironic way Cheever uses Graeco-Roman myths and creates satiric Italian names for many of his Italian characters. It is also evident that the mellifluous Italian language greatly appealed to Cheever's sensibilities; he loved the musical sounds of Italian and its potential for endless modulations.

Along with the birth of his son, Federico, Cheever saw the publication of his first novel, *The Wapshot Chronicle,* by Harper and Brothers in March 1957, a novel he had agonized over for twenty years. The critics were divided over its merits. Again, a number of academic critics faulted its episodic structure; it appeared not to follow a neat, orderly Aristotelian plot. Some were also put off by its overall tonal darkness. Joan Didion praised it for all the right reasons and intelligently placed it within a novelistic tradition: "*The Wapshot Chronicle* surprised some, troubled others, seemed not even a novel to those brought up on twentieth century fiction. What it was not was a sentimental novel; what it was not was a novel of manners. It was a novel more like *Tom Jones* than *Madame Bovary,* more like *Tristram Shandy* than *Pride and Prejudice.* (And more like any one of them than the novels commonly written by *New Yorker* writers.)"[5] The most influential literary critics agreed with Didion and awarded it the National Book Award in 1958; Cheever had been elected to the National Institute of Arts and Letters in 1957.

The novel's principal themes are those of many of his earlier stories: love in its various guises, specifically between brothers, among families, and between men and women. The Wapshot family saga bears an uncanny resemblance to the history of the Cheevers, with unmistakable appearances by family ancestors. Leander Wapshot is modeled after Ezekiel Cheever, and Wapshot's two sons, Moses and Coverly, resemble John and his brother, Fred. Sarah Wapshot, Leander's wife, also possesses many of the character traits that John Cheever's mother, Mary Liley Cheever, exhibited, so much so that Cheever would permit publication only after her death. Most important, however, is that the fall of the Wapshot family—like the fall of the Cheever family—from a prominent position in the community dictates the structure of the novel. The novel is not built on a linear structure, a framework that academic critics prefer. It is obviously cyclic—certainly a more appropriate form to chronicle the rise and fall of a distinguished New England family. The novel concludes where it began, and family history repeats itself, especially in *The Wapshot Scandal,* which followed seven years later. Happily for Cheever's financial condition, the Book-of-the-Month Club selected it, thus ensuring Cheever hefty royalties.

With the publication of his first novel in 1957, John Cheever's career began a steady ascent. The financial success, the honors he was garnering, and the laudatory critical reception made him more productive. Between the years 1957 and the mid-1960s he managed to publish five new books: three short-story collections and two novels. His financial situation improved to such an extent that he was able to buy a large old house in one of the more affluent neighborhoods of Ossining, New York. He also was awarded a second Guggenheim fellowship in 1960 to write

another novel. *The Housebreaker of Shady Hill and Other Stories,* a short-
story collection published in 1958, was not only one of his most highly
praised collections, containing such masterpieces as "The Sorrows of
Gin," "The Country Husband," and "The Five-Forty-Eight," but it also
established him, once and for all, as the bard of suburban angst and
ennui. Though much of his earlier work detailed middle-class lives on
the Upper East Side of Manhattan, *Housebreaker* became what readers to
this day consider archetypal Cheever stories, earning him the title "Ovid
in Ossining" from *Time* magazine a few years later.

Again, the academic critics found Westchester cocktail parties shallow
and decadent. They also suggested that Cheever lacked the moral
courage to condemn these life-styles of the rich and bored. Cheever
merely presented those lives and left ethical judgments to the readers
themselves, a virtue that later readers and critics came to respect. Part of
Cheever's reputation for being large-souled and nonjudgmental results
from his consistent effort to be objective toward his characters. What
many critics overlooked was the obvious mythical subtexts that Cheever
subtly delineated and explored in suburbia. Shady Hill is both Eden and
Hades, paradoxes that Cheever's inhabitants are perpetually torn
between. Using what T. S. Eliot called "the mythical method"—that is,
a continual paralleling of the present with the past—Cheever obliges his
readers to make their own moral judgments because he was uncomfort-
able creating ethical texts that uphold one philosophical belief and condemn another. And it is to his credit that he trusted his readers, with the
aid of mythic allusions, to participate in the spiritual dilemmas that his
characters sometimes undergo. Indeed, he came to view important parts
of his own life as mythic events, such as the hostility with which he came
to regard his wife's father, Dr. Milton Winternitz. His wife, Mary, spent
a large part of her time with her family even after her marriage, and
Cheever viewed her absence in unmistakably mythic terms: "I have come
to think of Winter [Milton Winternitz] as the king of a Hades where M
[Mary Cheever] must spend perhaps half her time," alluding to his
father-in-law as one who became "a source of darkness" in their life
(Donaldson 1988, 176). There is also no question that buying a large
house in Ossining gave Cheever what he most needed to be productive,
a solid familial base he could call his own, located in the middle of a for-
est-like area. He loved dogs and enjoyed taking them on long daily hikes
through the woods. Though he did not have a pool, he was free to use
his next-door neighbor's. His love of nature always serves as a backdrop
to the stories and the novels in which nature's perfection is the pristine

Edenic condition by which his characters measure their lives. Indeed, all of his recurrent themes of brotherly love and conflict, family strife, sexual celebration and failure, and existential musings are grounded in a natural context that becomes a metaphor for paradise. Some of his characters occasionally experience a sense of oneness with this natural paradise if they open themselves up to its restorative powers.

By 1961, firmly established in his lovely home on Cedar Lane, Cheever published his fourth collection, *Some People, Places and Things That Will Not Appear in My Next Novel.* Most critics were not pleased with the stylistic quality of its stories. Only "The Death of Justina" and possibly "Boy in Rome" can be favorably compared with the earlier accomplishments of "The Country Husband" or "The Sorrows of Gin." The tone of most of these stories is bitter, and a disturbing air of apocalyptic collapse pervades the collection. The critic in the *New Times Book Review* called Cheever "a Gothic writer whose mind is poised at the edge of terror" (Donaldson 1988, 193). It became clear that Cheever's long history of heavy drinking was for the first time showing its deleterious effects in the dramatic change of tone and attitude in a bitterly sardonic reassessment of standard themes and character types, which he catalogued in *Some People*'s final story, "A Miscellany of Characters That Will Not Appear." In this uncharacteristically postmodern story, Cheever promises to omit from any future stories such topics as "The pretty girl at the Princeton-Dartmouth game . . . All parts for Marlon Brando . . . All scornful descriptions of American landscapes [that is, *Wasteland* details such as ruined tenements, polluted rivers, etc.] . . . All lushes . . . all those homosexuals who have taken such a dominating position in recent fiction."[6] Ironically, a number of later stories include these very topics. His hostile response to homosexual fiction and his life-long abhorrence of homosexuals in general contrast with his frank confessions of homosexual experience throughout his journals. Cheever finally came to accept his homosexuality during his later years of sobriety.

A Darkening of Cheever's Vision

It was during the years 1959 to 1964 that Cheever worked on his second novel, *The Wapshot Scandal,* but it was also during these years that he confesses in his journals that his excessive drinking was creating severe problems in his family and in his writing. Cheever had always prided himself on his ability to drink vast amounts of alcohol—hard liquor— and not let it interfere with his writing. He usually rose early even after a night of heavy drinking and put in five or six hours of writing, stopping for lunch at noon. But it was becoming increasingly difficult for him to delay his first drink of the day until noon, often moving it up till eleven o'clock so that he would be able to stop shaking. His drinking also began to cause concern among friends, who noticed that after a number of drinks, Cheever, who had always been a cheerful and celebratory drinker, had become fractious and hypersensitive. He was known to ruin dinner parties with embarrassing drunken scenes.

Mary Cheever became exhausted by staying home and nursing her husband through his hangovers; she took a job teaching English at nearby Briarcliffe College, a move she later admitted saved her sanity. John was adamantly against the idea of his wife teaching and said so in no uncertain terms. It was also about this time that his brother, Fred, almost died of his own alcoholism. Cheever rushed to his bedside at Yale University hospital, where Mary's brother, Dr. William Winternitz, took him on as a patient. In spite of his own troubles with alcohol and his difficulty accepting his wife's independence, Cheever continued to work on the The Wapshot Scandal, a dark book that chronicles the complete collapse of the family. He also continued to publish short stories in the New Yorker, managing to produce, in spite of his troubles, some genuine masterpieces, such as "The Swimmer," "The Music Teacher," and "The Angel of the Bridge."

Cheever also published six sections of The Wapshot Scandal in the New Yorker from 1959 to 1964, so close observers of Cheever's work should not have been overly disturbed at the darkening vision of the bleakest book he ever wrote when Harper and Row published it in January 1964. He confessed during the writing of this novel that he had been depressed, and that writing it further depressed him to the point where he seriously contemplated suicide. His drinking was out of control; his phobias were debilitating him.

The critical response to The Wapshot Scandal was generally positive, even though the tone of the novel differed greatly from that of The Wapshot Chronicle. George Garrett best described the major distinctions between the two novels: "The sins of Chronicle are original sin. Scandal moves inexorably toward the end of the world."[7] Garrett detected a notable lack of sensuousness, particularly of smells; Cheever's prose was famous for its sensuous celebration. He also pointed out that love had given way to lust; the sensuous had become the sensual. Malcolm Cowley's letters to Cheever confessed alarm at Cheever's anger and characterized his world as one of "emotional squalor and incongruity" (quoted in Donaldson 1988, 204). Though *The Wapshot Chronicle* details the decline of an old, respected New England family in the mythical St. Botolphs, *Scandal* shows the remainder of the family, especially the brothers Moses and Coverly, attempting to find new suburban Edenic structures to replace the sacred center of St. Botolphs. Conflicts with editors at the *New Yorker* increased to such an extent that Cheever engaged, almost on a whim, a new agent who immediately acquired a lucrative promise from the *Saturday Evening Post* of $24,000 for four stories a year. Cheever published only six more stories with the *New Yorker* from 1963 till he died in 1982.

Though his family life was on the verge of collapse and his drinking out of control, *Time* magazine chose him for a cover story after the great success of *The Wapshot Scandal* in March 1964. And because he had become a world-renowned writer, he was selling his stories to the highest-paying magazines, such as *Esquire, Playboy,* and the *Saturday Evening Post.* Not only did he publish one of his best-selling novels in 1964, but he also published one of his finest short-story collections, *The Brigadier and the Golf Widow,* which contains some of his most compelling stories. Though some critics would disagree, the title story, "The Swimmer," "The Music Teacher," and "The Seaside Houses" certainly qualify as some of Cheever's best work. And "The Swimmer" catapulted him into the world of Hollywood and high living, which he enjoyed immensely. As soon as "The Swimmer" appeared in the *New Yorker,* he was contacted by film director Frank Perry, who promptly proposed a film version. Eventually, Burt Lancaster starred in the moderately successful film, which earned Cheever a small fortune. But it was also during time spent in Hollywood that he met and fell in love with film actress Hope Lange, a liaison that continued over a number of years. The adulterous affair with Lange was but one of many he conducted throughout his lifetime; he also became less guarded about affairs he was having with several young men.

In 1964, Cheever traveled to Russia as a participant in a cultural exchange program and formed lifelong friendships with Tanya Litvinov, who became the translator of his short fiction, and novelist John Updike. Though Updike was nearly twenty years younger than Cheever, the older author strongly recommended Updike for membership in the National Institute of Arts and Letters and also helped him win the National Book Award for *The Centaur,* a book whose mythic structures would certainly have appealed to Cheever's deeply archetypal sensibilities. It was also in 1965 that the American Academy of Arts and Letters awarded Cheever its William Dean Howells' Medal for *The Wapshot Scandal,* thus rewarding him for the best piece of fiction during a five-year period. Cheever was deeply honored to be placed in the company of earlier recipients, including Willa Cather, William Faulkner, and Eudora Welty.

Though he seemed to be operating at the top of his creative powers, recognized and honored with major literary prizes and awards, his drinking became an increasingly crucial issue for his family, friends, and himself. He admitted to close friends that his drinking problem was worsening. He did seek help in the summer of 1965 and transferred his addiction to tranquilizers, thanks to an unenlightened physician. He also consulted a psychiatrist and underwent some psychotherapy, during which he examined some of his early childhood traumas but did not connect them to his suicidal drinking habits.

Scott Donaldson accurately analyzed the increasingly bifurcated condition that Cheever was falling into as his drinking further divided an already dangerously damaged psyche (Donaldson 1988, v). His life had moved into a typical alcoholic paradox: he could tolerate neither isolation nor company for any prolonged period of time. Yet much of the despair and the strange mixture of self-pity and self-loathing would not come out until the publication of segments of his journals in the *New Yorker* in the early 1990s. Many serious admirers of his work would be astonished at the interminable rationalizations and the shameless manipulations of family and friends that he blatantly recorded in his journals.

Wracked by drink and guilt, he somehow made progress on his new novel, *Bullet Park.* He had also had a serious falling out with his longtime *New Yorker* editor, William Maxwell, over the effect his drinking was having on the quality of his stories. After acquiring one of the New York literary scene's most powerful agents, Candida Donadio, who was able to arrange a highly lucrative contract for *Bullet Park* with Alfred A. Knopf, he severed his long association with Harper and Row, a company that had published three story collections and two novels over an eleven-year period.

True to the evolving pattern in Cheever's fiction, in which he mirrored his spiritual conflicts in the work at hand, *Bullet Park* is his most sharply divided novel. Critic Samuel Coale characterized the conflicts throughout the novel as "distinctly Manichean."[8] Nowhere in his earlier work is there such a clear division between the light and the dark, good and evil. The mythic *Bullet Park* is a minefield of conflicted families and characters. Cheever most assuredly wants the reader to detect the Christian cross as the backdrop upon which the story is played out by "comically" giving the two principal families the names Hammer and Nailles. The reviews were mixed, and some critics confessed to being confused over the theme of the novel. Though John Leonard gave it a highly favorable review, Benjamin DeMott suggested that Cheever possessed an irksome talent for unnecessarily stretching a short story into a novel, thus weakening an already flawed novelistic structure.[9]

In the aftermath of the mixed critical reception, Cheever's drinking increased, as did the problems that it spawned. Though he consulted a psychiatrist throughout 1969 and openly admitted his alcoholic dependency, he did little to modify his destructive behavior and continued to suffer deep guilt over his drinking. His confusion over his bisexual impulses continued. His public drunkenness and insensitive behavior began to alarm his friends; and he was arrested for driving while intoxicated in 1969. His drinking was also affecting his literary output. Normally, he published five short stories a year; he published only one in 1970, none in 1971, two in 1972, and one in 1973—a drastic reduction for a writer known for the volume of his literary production. It was clear to most of his friends that he was on the verge of losing everything: his family, his reputation, and his capacity for work.

Oddly enough, since Cheever had no ideas for future novels, he decided to teach a creative writing class at Sing Sing Prison, or what was officially called the Ossining Correctional Facility. He had overheard at a Westchester cocktail party that the two thousand prisoners there had only six teachers. According to Donald Lang, a prisoner who became a close friend of Cheever, Cheever gained the prisoners' respect when he courageously showed up to teach his class immediately following the riots at Attica Prison in which thirty inmates had been killed and more than two hundred injured. Consciously or unconsciously, however, Cheever began to record with great accuracy details of prison life that would eventually surface in what many critics would call his greatest novel, *Falconer*. Cheever taught at Sing Sing till the spring of 1973, but his drinking continued unabated and did not allow him to produce any significant material for publication.

He enjoyed his teaching experience at Sing Sing and, after a particularly successful reading at the University of Iowa, was invited by Jack Leggett, the director of the Iowa Writing Program, to teach there during the fall semester of 1973. He had hoped for a geographical cure of some kind, since his marriage was collapsing and his drinking prevented any serious literary output; he casually discussed suicide. His physical health had deteriorated to such an extent that he thought he had a heart attack in May 1973 and ended up in Phelps Memorial Hospital in Tarrytown. In reality, it was a condition common to alcoholics called cardiomyopathy, with symptoms of shortness of breath and erratic heartbeat. His doctor had made the mistake of prescribing Seconal, a strong sleeping medication, which Cheever had mixed with alcohol. What occurred was pulmonary edema caused by alcohol. Because he could not drink in the hospital, he began to hallucinate and had to be put in a straitjacket. Both his family and his doctor suggested Alcoholics Anonymous, which he flatly rejected. He was pleased by both the positive critical reception given his latest collection of short stories, *A World of Apples,* and his nomination for membership to the prestigious American Academy of Arts and Letters.

In spite of his precarious physical condition and his blatant denial of his "drinking problems," Cheever traveled to the University of Iowa, where he charmed both teachers and students alike. He immediately became close friends with fellow instructors John Irving and Raymond Carver, with whom he spent much time drinking and mixing with the student population. He also met some students who later became prominent writers, namely, Allan Gurganus and T. Coraghessan Boyle, both of whom acknowledge a great debt to Cheever for helping them publish their early work and for making practical suggestions to improve their writing. Though he did collapse once during his stay in Iowa, he was able to finish the semester and return to Ossining, where his wife announced that she could no longer live with his drunken behavior; he was drinking in the morning and nothing she could do would stop him.

An Admission of Alcoholism

Cheever accepted a teaching position at Boston University for the fall of 1974, even though his drinking had rendered him emotionally and spiritually impotent. Financially, he was bringing in only half of what he needed to operate his household. He was simply not able to function as a teacher at Boston University and was barely able to finish his teaching duties before his brother, Fred, whom John had once helped sober up, took him for detoxification at Phelps Hospital in Tarrytown, New York. Cheever again suffered through the delirium tremens and, with the strong insistence of his doctor, his wife, and his children, admitted himself to one of New York City's most famous drying-out facilities, the Smithers Alcohol Rehabilitation Center on the Upper East Side of

Manhattan, the locale of many of his earliest and most successful short stories. After initial negative feelings about having to be in close contact with "common folks"—an uncharacteristic response from Cheever, who loved to mix with all kinds of people, and a measure of how radically his alcoholism had transformed him—he settled into the routine of the institute and emerged from the program a sober, shaken but hopeful person.

Though at first hostile to the notion of attending meetings of Alcoholics Anonymous, he relented and went to them on the average of three times a week and became an eloquent participant in discussions and a popular speaker. His wife noted that he acted like a prisoner who had been released from bondage, an observation that may explain why John Cheever was attracted to teaching at Sing Sing. He realized that his alcoholic addiction was as enslaving as being in an actual prison. His renewed emotional and physical response to life quickly resulted in major transformations in his daily routine. He threw out the medication his doctors had prescribed. He stopped taking sleeping pills such as Seconal, no more Valium to "relieve stress," and never touched a drop of alcohol again. Instead he drank huge quantities of iced tea and, though he continued to smoke heavily, was able to break that addiction five years later.

Once Cheever stopped his suicidal drinking, he was able to resume work on a novel about prison life. In May 1975, just a month after his release from Smithers, he began *Falconer* in earnest. Scott Donaldson states that he was able to complete about seven pages a day in that many hours, a production rate matched only in his earliest work (Donaldson 1988, 293). Cheever's attitude changed completely, and he gratefully resumed many of the recreational activities he loved, especially hiking, skating, swimming (in three different neighborhood pools). He took up new hobbies, such as cross-country skiing and bicycling. He was also able to become more open about his homosexual feelings and affairs, and had learned through regular attendance at A.A. meetings that honesty about every aspect of his life was necessary for him to maintain a firmly grounded sense of serenity and sobriety.

Cheever finished *Falconer* in less than a year, and it was published to mostly favorable reviews by such literary stars as Joan Didion and John Gardner, both finding not only new subject matter but a new attitude toward life's possibilities. Joyce Carol Oates, though, was not pleased by *Falconer* and saw its victories as glib and too easily won (quoted in Donaldson 1988, 311). But the novel also serves as an allegory of the writer's life, with particular resonance to forms of enslavement Cheever had suffered: his self-entombing alcoholism, his agonizing bisexuality, his divided feelings about his parents, and, most dramatically, his pathological love-hate relationship with his older brother, Fred. *Falconer* addressed what Donaldson called Cheever's bifurcated life and the painful issues caused by those struggles within himself (Donaldson 1988, v).

From 1977 until his death in June 1982, John Cheever's reputation grew enormously as he garnered many awards and prizes. The success of *Falconer* brought him renewed fame when he appeared on the cover of *Newsweek* in March 1977 and on the *Dick Cavett Show,* where he spoke with great candor about his self-destructive drinking, his troubled marriage, and his complex relationship with his brother. The publicity contributed to hefty sales of *Falconer* as well as his other work; he found himself a wealthy man in his midsixties. Paramount Pictures bought the movie rights to *Falconer* for $40,000 but decided not to make the picture; Cheever was delighted.

In 1978 he was awarded an honorary doctorate from Harvard University, and in 1979 received the Pulitzer Prize and the National Book Critics Circle award for *The Stories of John Cheever,* which Alfred A. Knopf had published the year before. *The Stories* intensified renewed interest in Cheever's writings on a huge scale, primarily because both readers and critics had never seen so many of his stories, sixty-one of them, together in one volume and had not realized how strong and varied they were. The reviews were extraordinarily good, with John Leonard calling the book "not merely the publishing event of the 'season' but a grand occasion in English literature" (Donaldson 1988, 321). As a result of the generally ecstatic critical reception, his agent was able to negotiate a $500,000 advance from Knopf for Cheever's next two books.

Unfortunately, Cheever would write only one more novel, *Oh What a Paradise It Seems,* a work closer to a novella that he had intended to be much longer. While on a visit to his beloved Yaddo in the fall of 1980 he suffered a grand mal seizure. Then, during urological surgery for a cancerous kidney, his doctors discovered the cancer had spread to the bone. Though he had further surgery for cancerous tumors on his bladder, by early December 1981 his doctor told his family that he had six months to live. Even though he was weak and quite obviously ill, he managed to attend a Carnegie Hall ceremony at which he was given the National Medal for Literature (and also $15,000) in late April 1982.

His last days were serene, and he was surrounded by family and friends. He died quietly on 18 June 1982. His funeral was held in

Norwell, Massachusetts, where he was buried in the Cheever family plot. Though Cheever struggled with alcohol, a loveless childhood, and his homosexual feelings, he considered himself a lucky man. He had faced his self-destructive impulses directly when he quit drinking and joined Alcoholics Anonymous. He had also faced the nature of his feelings for other men, unashamedly maintaining a long-term relationship with a younger man till the day he died. He never lost the ability to change creative direction and boldly moved away from the content of his earliest work; that is, from the fall of New England families into the shabbiness of the modern world to the alienation and despair of prison life in his last great novel, *Falconer.*

Chapter Two

"A Writing Machine": *The Way Some People Live* and *The Enormous Radio and Other Stories*

Critics are divided on the literary quality of John Cheever's early stories, particularly those in his first collection, *The Way Some People Live* (1943). Most would agree with Cheever's own estimate of their worth: "naive, provincial . . . sometimes obtuse, almost always clumsy" (*SJC,* vii). Cheever felt so strongly about their weaknesses that he refused to include any of them in his Pulitzer-Prize-winning *The Stories of John Cheever* in 1978, calling them in an interview "embarrassingly immature."[1]

Attempts to publish Cheever's early stories after his death have been met with resistance from his family, the most notable example being Academy Chicago Publishers' intention in the late 1980s to release a collection of sixty-eight stories, most of which had been published before World War II. After years of legal struggles between the publisher and Cheever's family, a small selection of stories was agreed upon, resulting in the 1994 publication of *Thirteen Uncollected Stories of John Cheever.*[2]

The relative merits of these early stories notwithstanding, there is little doubt that Cheever's literary promise expressed itself very early. Few American writers have begun their careers at the age of seventeen with a story like "Expelled," which combines the clumsiness of a youthful first effort with a remarkable maturity of vision. Published in the *New Republic* in 1930, "Expelled" established an autobiographical pattern of composition that Cheever adhered to throughout his life. The letters, the journals, and Scott Donaldson's definitive biography demonstrate beyond any doubt that virtually all of Cheever's work comes directly out of his own personal experiences. Cheever, like Henry James, whose work he revered, was a writer on whom nothing was lost; he had a keen sense of observation and retained most everything he observed.

While it is true that most modern writers use their lives as a basis for their fiction, Cheever's work stands out for its capacity to transform the most common, everyday situation into a permanent part of the modern condition. At their best, Cheever's stories move into the realm of myth and thus transcend time and place. By the time of the publication of his second collection, *The Enormous Radio and Other Stories* (1953), Cheever had laid the groundwork for what only the greatest writers attain: mythopoesis—that is, the establishment of a repertoire of characters, conflicts, and themes that recur so regularly that they evolve into a world of their own. The term *Cheeveresque* is common in critical vocabulary because his world is instantly recognizable.

"Expelled"

"Expelled" marks the first appearance of the Cheever outcast or the exile, a character type that surfaces throughout his fiction. Indeed, the outcast-as-criminal is the "hero" of what some critics consider his greatest novel, *Falconer.* The seeds of *Falconer* can be gleaned from the sometimes awkward but occasionally brilliant observations of a young boy who is expelled from a prestigious preparatory school closely modeled on Thayer Academy, the school from which the seventeen-year-old Cheever was, he claimed, expelled in the spring term of 1930.

Even more important, "Expelled" became the first example of the single most important thematic pattern in all of Cheever's fiction: the fall. In a certain sense, most of Cheever's short stories and all of his novels are variations on this persistent theme; his work is obsessed with Edenic crises in every conceivable form. Many of the novels are concerned with the fall of a house—that is, a once prosperous family that has fallen on hard times and whose major project is to regenerate an Edenic condition of innocent happiness; in short, to recreate a permanent paradise. The title of Cheever's last novel pinpoints precisely the movement of the entire body of his work: *Oh What a Paradise It Seems* (1982).

The term *expelled* is used to describe the fall of Adam and Eve from their preternatural condition of immortality into the experience of time, suffering, and death. But Cheever's modifies the traditional lesson of the story by making young Charles into one of modern literature's first antiheroes. Cheever transforms the expulsion into a "felix culpa," a "happy fall" that saves the young protagonist from the life-denying ambience of educational institutions, which actually damage genuine creativity. The young Cheever knew that a liberal journal such as the *New Republic* would be interested in a story exposing the hypocritical deadness of respected prep schools such as Thayer Academy.

What attracted its editor, Malcolm Cowley, to the story was not only the discerning insight of a teenage boy attempting to uncover the empty formalism of American education but also the young Cheever's stylistic restraint. The narrative voice is never strident. The protagonist, Charles, calmly explains that he is blaming neither teachers nor administrators: "It is not the fault of the school at all. It was the fault of the system—the non-educational system, the college-preparatory system . . . That was what made the school so useless. As a college preparatory school it was a fine school. In five years they could make raw material look like college material. They could clothe it and breed it and make it say the right things when the colleges ask it to talk. That was its duty. They weren't prepared to educate anybody. They were members of a college-preparatory system. No one around there wanted to be educated. No sir."[3]

Not only does "Expelled" adumbrate the major mythic conflict of the fall that runs throughout Cheever's fiction for the next fifty years, it also contains certain stylistic practices that he used so often and to such an extent that they became Cheeveresque conventions. Cowley noted from "Expelled" onward that Cheever knew how to immediately engage the reader; he knew how to begin. The opening line in "Expelled"—"It didn't come all at once . . ."—begins the story in the classic tradition of in medias res—in the middle of things—and not at the literal beginning of the narrative; there is no chronological beginning. The voice is so intimate and open that a reader is seduced into the story and feels immediately comfortable. In the second paragraph, Cheever uses the most specific details to create a vivid image of the headmaster's office: "with the carved chairs arranged in a semicircle and the brocade curtains resting against the vacant windows. All about him were pictures of people who had gotten scholarships to Harvard" (32). But even more important than the clean, Hemingway-like description of the office is his depiction of the natural landscape that lay beyond the window, an image that promises freedom shortly, a redemptive reprieve from the stultifying confines of the system: "It was very nice outside his room. He had his window pushed open halfway and one could see the lawns pulling down to the road behind the trees and the bushes." Time after time throughout Cheever's fiction, and especially when a character is undergoing severe stress, he looks out a window, takes a walk down a street or through the woods, and is momentarily granted entrance into a natural realm of grace that mysteriously refreshes him and spiritually removes him from the painful constraints of time and duty. One could be reading Emerson, Thoreau, or Whitman, their romantic stance so closely resembles Cheever's at these moments. Cheever is a genuine American romantic in his attitude toward nature and its ameliorative role in human affairs.

Nature and its cyclic structures often mirror the movement of Cheever's fictions and do so in "Expelled." There is no clearly delineated plot; it does not even move episodically. Once the expulsion seems completed (Cheever never really states it bluntly), the story moves along with a series of painterly portraits of compelling figures in the boy's education at the school. Each stands out as a light in the prevailing academic darkness. The young Charles recalls these figures not only because they talked about their ideals and convictions but because they embodied them and suffered accordingly. The Colonel, whose grief over the senseless deaths of young soldiers causes him to break down during a patriotic convocation, embarrasses the school authorities and students. Margaret Courtwright and Laura Driscoll, the last teachers Charles mentions, are educators in the most etymologically accurate sense of the word. *Educere,* the Latin root from which the English word originates, means "to draw out, lead out," and not to "impose" information on students. Both women engaged the emotions of their students by telling them the truth about history and permitting them to discover their feelings about their subject matter. Charles was deeply moved by Laura Driscoll's penchant for ecstatic presentations of historical facts. Margaret Courtwright's generosity of spirit led her to listen to Charles read his play to her for more than two hours and to respond to it on a genuinely emotional level: "Really it just swept me right along" (33). All of these exemplary figures stirred the young Charles because they exhibit natural emotion—their humanity touches their students.

At the conclusion of the story, Charles's precociousness enables him to make distinctions expected only of mature adults. Although he is leaving involuntarily, he confesses: "I was not sorry that I had left school. I was sorry that I left for the reasons that I did." And after indicting the pragmatic American value system for the blind arrogance of its self-canonization ("We have larger apples and better cotton and faster and more beautiful machines. This makes us the greatest country in the world"), he admits he is lost in the world, but says, "I am not sorry. And I am not at all glad."

At the story's emotionally ambiguous conclusion, Charles paints himself as an exile but identifies with the inevitability of natural cyclicity:

"And now it is August. The orchards are stinking ripe. The tea-colored brooks run beneath the rocks. There is sediment on the stone and no wind in the willows" (36). Because Cheever's imagination is grounded in the processes of nature, renewal and hope are always possible if a character is willing to enter that fearful flow and wait it out; change is always imminent. The concluding paragraph, though short, adumbrates some of the greatest codas in modern American literature: "Soon it will be time for the snow and the symphonies. It will be time for Brahms and the great dry winds." Though only seventeen, Cheever demonstrates in the conclusion his ability to interweave in the most sophisticated, poetic ways the abstract with the specific, to fashion metaphysical conceits that open up Charles's world to infinite possibility.

The story is certainly an example of a rite of passage, a painful fall, but one that enables him to move from childhood into maturity. In stating that there is no "wind in the willows," Cheever displays the first of many techniques he uses to demythologize the ignorance and innocence of childhood, as Charles realizes that life is not a children's story. Malcolm Cowley might have noted that the young Cheever knew not only how to start a story but how to conclude one.

This first story foreshadows many of the themes and techniques Cheever continued to employ: the engaging openings and unforgettable conclusions; the use of the fall; a philosophical stance toward life; the use of nature as an indicator of time, not as closure but as a measure of possibility and change; and the refusal to compose stories that conform to the conventional beginning, middle, and end of realistic fictions up to 1930. In the middle of the most hopeless situations, Cheever's characters, and Charles is his first, casually look out of a window and experience what George Steiner calls a sense of "radical astonishment" at the mere fact of being alive. They enter, but only through nature, a temporary visionary consciousness that permits them a serene sense of oneness with the natural world.

"Expelled" is also a "Cheever" story in that it came out of his own life experience. Whether he was expelled for getting poor grades, as the story asserts, or for smoking cigarettes or for engaging in homosexual behavior, as Cheever himself later claimed (see chapter 1), the official file at Thayer offers the most interesting explanation: "John Cheever, ex '31, was not expelled, but in the interest of drama considered himself to be" (Donaldson 1988, 39). Cheever might have written this statement himself. In his life, Cheever's capacity for self-dramatization was one of his most perplexing habits; in his work it enabled him to transform fact into incomparable fictions.

The Way Some People Live

Though Cheever thought little of *The Way Some People Live,* his first collection, several of the stories in it are masterpieces. Evaluating them from a distance of fifty years, there is little doubt that the best of minimalism has finally caught up with the early John Cheever. The prevailing style of these stories is lean, tight, and vivid. Though some would see Hemingway's influence in the imagistic precision and emphasis on presenting rather than describing, other critics might detect Sherwood Anderson's semibiblical evocations of impending doom in the army stories that conclude the book. Some of the stories are very short and could be called vignettes; in today's jargon, examples of "sudden fiction," "flash fiction," or "short shorts." All of them are recognizable as Cheever's because of his engaging voice, which seduces by way of the senses, especially the sense of touch and smell. The first story in the collection, "Summer Theater," begins: "It was hot. Now and then a breath of wind from the northeast would come in across the fields, heavy with the mixed smell of hay, heat, grease paint, and camphor from the rented costumes in the wardrobe shed."[4] This opening is as riveting as that of a Hitchcock film. Cheever is unerringly specific, particularly regarding geographical directions; the wind comes from a specific direction—northeast in this case—or he usually doesn't mention it. "Summer," a recurring motif in much of his fiction, especially the short stories, is immediately established here. And the story's concluding scene—a woman emerging refreshed from the ocean waves, whereas everyone thinks she has drowned—is an early foreshadowing of Cheever's many swimmers, culminating in Neddy Merrill of Cheever's most famous story, "The Swimmer" (1963). The scene also foretells the mythic presentation of the women emerging from the sea at the conclusion of "Goodbye, My Brother" (1947).

All of Cheever's major and minor themes appear in this first collection and can be used as measures of how refined and sophisticated his literary techniques became over the years. The falls of houses or families caused by the awful effects of the Depression occur throughout the volume. Alcoholic excess also fragments families and relationships. Few modern American writers were so obsessed with drinking or treated its effects with such brutal honesty as Cheever. Other recurring topics in the collection are loneliness and its effects on characters who cannot find human contact and love. Sexual repression and self-destructive behavior often combine to push their victim into temporary derangement, as in the case of Ellen Goodrich in the ironically titled "The Pleasures of Solitude." The brutal effects of the Depression separate the younger generation from their traumatized parents or grandparents, and the first of many unwanted or neglected children surfaces in stories such as "The Edge of the World" and "Happy Birthday, Enid." Autobiographical bits and pieces abound from the use of his mother's maiden name, Devereaux, in two stories, to almost straight autobiographical record—with the names changed—in the strongest story in the collection, "The Brothers." The most persistent theme is the "brother conflict," which is the main subject of "The Brothers," "When Grandmother Goes," "The New World," and "These Tragic Years." It is a buried subtext in Cheever's first and most accomplished early love story, "Of Love: A Testimony." Several brilliant, obsessive monologues first appear in this collection: "Goodbye, Broadway—Hello, Hello" and "The Peril in the Streets."

Desperate acts make up much of the action of *The Way Some People Live,* but they are desperate because of poverty, sexual repression, alcoholic loss of control, and, most of all, loneliness. The range of technical developments is as rich and various as the thematic concerns. As these stories emerge, one can clearly observe Cheever refining his technical apparatus as new developments appear in every third or fourth story. These stylistic changes accumulate into the bedrock of Cheever's early style.

The masterful "The Pleasures of Solitude," whose title belies its ironic tone, further expands the theme of the necessity of illusion in an earlier story, "Forever Hold Your Peace," into a considerably more intricate study of the way sexual repression produces a paradoxical mixture of control and generosity in the lonely Ellen Goodrich, who is neither good nor rich, but is dimly aware of her painful isolation. She is a female version, with similar unrealized yearnings, of Thomas Mann's tortured Gustave Von Aschenbach of *Death in Venice.* Ellen takes pride in her orderly life and admits that she has transformed her isolation into something bearable: "It had always been difficult for her to find friends. During the ten years she had lived in New York she had suffered a great deal from loneliness, but this suffering was forgotten now because of the care with which she arranged her solitude" (*WSPL,* 26–27). For a moment dropping her defenses, she allows two adolescent boys to take advantage of her generosity and rob her. Her loneliness, like Aschenbach's, has created a desperation so intense that any truly human contact becomes lethal and self-destructive. She also suffers great guilt over her mistaking friendship for exploitation, yet also dreams about these poor slum boys who are simultaneously pitiful, threatening, and desirable. This story is Cheever's first successful attempt to probe psychologically the complex agony of one of the first of his many alienated solitaries. Cheever masterfully interweaves the various emotional strands that make up Ellen Goodrich's character, which is tormented by sexual repression, desperate loneliness, and violence. The story also illustrates the first of many characters who find themselves trapped in self-created prisons and subtly delineates the complex ways in which people unconsciously enmesh themselves in their own treacherous traps that prohibit human contact.

If "The Pleasures of Solitude" is a story about a woman who becomes increasingly entrapped in her so-called Edenic isolation, "Cat" is a love story in which a couple discover themselves to be imprisoned in a relationship only after their cat disappears. Jack and Hannah Bannister are preparing to move to another Manhattan apartment and have lost their black cat, Steven. Both blame themselves for not paying attention to Steven. More important, though, is the notion that the lost cat has become an agent of revelation that has jarred them into realizing the true condition of their marriage. They see what they have inadvertently become: another complacent, distracted, bored couple trapped in urban paralysis. Without the intermediary, they will have to face themselves and each other and confront all the lost aspirations and hopes of finding an idealized happiness that they had previously built their lives upon. John realizes that the cat has been a substitute for the child that they really wanted. He resolves to quit drinking and: "Maybe we can get a place out in Westchester. You can have a garden. We won't live like this any more. We'll live like human beings" (*WSPL*, 38). Again, Cheever offers ways of escape out of imprisoning life styles and John and Hannah momentarily recover their dreams as actual possibilities. Paradise can be pursued only if recognized, and their renewed vision offers some hope. Cheever's style in this story is clearly influenced by Hemingway's story "Cat in the Rain," as well as by Hemingway's clean, simple style. "Cat" also foreshadows one of Cheever's landmark stories, "The Enormous Radio," in which a radio, rather than a cat, becomes an agent of revelation.

"Love: A Testimony" is Cheever's first lengthy love story. Struthers
Burt called it "one of the best love stories I have ever read" (24). It is the
length of a novella, and the opening paragraph, with its unexplained
allusion to a woman confessing to murdering her husband by hitting
him over the back of the head with a sand-filled ginger ale bottle, foreshadows an attempted fratricide ten years later in "Goodbye, My
Brother." The confessional echoes also suggest that the word *testimony,*
while primarily referring to the agonizing love relationship recorded in
the story, also implies testimony at a murder trial. More important,
though, is the fact that Joe Morgan, the main voice in the story, is the
first of Cheever's existential characters to struggle with his lack of identity. Only his working-class roots and college education give him some
sense of himself and his place in the world. But his awareness of his social
place makes him cynical: "Much of the cynicism sprang from a consciousness of his life's insignificance and lack of precedent. He often felt
the necessity of identifying himself with something more than a faded
shirt, a peculiar walk" (*WSPL,* 44). He often stares out the window at
night, a habit of "questioning the darkness" that Cheever's alienated figures practice throughout his work (*WSPL,* 44–45). Besides the falls that
enter into virtually all of his fictions, this alternating pattern of light and
dark reappears incessantly.

The restrictions of social class are responsible for the failure of Joe's
love relationship with the upper-middle-class Julia Deveraux, a graduate
of Mount Holyoke. Sears, her former lover, is a tutor at Harvard. After
her highly passionate affair with Joe Morgan, she returns to a sexually
"normal" life with the intellectual Sears, who seems to have temporarily
gotten his drinking under control. Julia breaks off her sexually fulfilling
relationship with Joe because its fervid passion frightens her: "I was
afraid . . . It seemed as if we had too much, too much . . . One night last
week, maybe you remember the night, it seemed like too much" (*WSPL,*
61). Joe's sexual prowess threatens Julia's delicate, Puritanical sensibilities. Although she sees herself as a liberated woman, she prefers to read
about sexual freedom rather than experience it. Joe's robust boyishness
later haunts Julia, as she stares out of a window in Quebec City at a
stranger who resembles Joe standing under a lamp; her memories of Joe
rekindle her desire.

Joe Morgan, too, recognizes that he has experienced the transforming
scars of true love, through which he was able to experience a variety of
personae: "I met Julia Deveraux on a windy afternoon on Boylston
Street. I fell in love with her. On a lot of nights, coming out of her house

in May and June, I felt like an anarchist, a criminal, an emperor." Most important, Cheever delineates the way love, even heart-breaking love, changed Joe Morgan's life: "Tradition led him to expect that encounters like those would each come to a final end like a step climbed or a text memorized. As we grow older we read an end into each situation and out of these we build our values and form our expectations" (*WSPL*, 63). He does not turn into a drunk, like Sears, but understands how painful, crucial experiences form his values and expectations; that is, the way he lives his life.

"Love: A Testimony" is, along with "The Brothers," one of the two most important stories in this collection as it testifies to his ability to delve deeply into the psychological complexities of love-hate relationships and demonstrates his skill in entertaining multiple points of view.

"Publick House" is probably the most blatantly autobiographical story in the entire volume, and is certainly its bitterest. The financial fall of the Briggs family in this story is a blueprint of the fall of the Wapshot family, the major theme in both Wapshot novels. Cheever presents that story, in miniature, by juxtaposing the crass reality of the Briggs family to quotations from Historical Society volumes relating the romantic adventures of settlers in Maine in the early 1800s. A young college student, Lincoln Briggs, is on a holiday visiting his mother, Agnes, at what had previously been the Briggs's summer house, now converted into a tourist inn and antique shop because the family needs the extra income. The story is a thinly veiled version of exactly what happened to John Cheever's family as his mother, after the family home was lost during the Depression, opened the profitable "Mary Cheever Gift Shop" in Quincy, Massachusetts, in 1926. His mother also opened a dress shop and two restaurants during the next ten years. Her aggressive business practices embarrassed the family, however, because they called attention to the financial difficulties the family had fallen into and made John's father, Frederick Lincoln Cheever, look like a failure.

Cheever's evolving literary technique is evident in his subtle use of irony in the treatment of the mother. Though the grandfather and the young man, Lincoln, are clearly frustrated at the mother's incessant entrepreneurial schemes, Cheever presents her as a strong-willed victim of the Depression doing what she must do to save the family from financial disaster. The title, "Publick House," symbolizes the transformation of a once-private family home to a public, commercialized place of business. What had been the young man's summer Eden is lost to economic necessity. Agnes Briggs, like Cheever's mother, fills the Inn with her "enthusiasms" as she energetically takes on the look and sound of a tourist guide. What Lincoln witnesses, of course, is that under certain circumstances, anything and everything is for sale and has its price. Cheever's juxtaposition of the romantic flavor of the old history books that Lincoln peruses with the stark realism of financial failure further dramatizes the poignance of the past glories of the family. It is a technique Cheever came to use more and more frequently, especially in *The Wapshot Chronicle*.

The most pathetic figure in this poignant story is Agnes Briggs's father, who laments the depths to which the family has fallen. He is so hungry he can't even stand up and has obviously been neglected by his daughter, as she attends to business. He declaims for all to hear the sordid theme of the story: "And I don't care if they can hear me. I'll tell them something. You've sold all my things. You've sold my mother's china. You sold the rugs. You sold the portraits. You made a business out of it—selling the past. What kind of business is that—selling the past? I was a young man here. I said goodbye to my father in this hallway when he went to sea. He was standing right there. He was a tall man. He—" (*WSPL,* 183). And the grandfather then breaks down, unable to further articulate his grief and rage. In this story, Cheever clearly identifies the fall from innocence of a young man into the knowledge that even the most sacred center, the family, is not inured to the devastating effects of financial ruin. What saves the story from becoming a mere condemnation of an overly aggressive, cold woman is the ironic concluding scene, which becomes one of Cheever's earliest examples of his gift for turning a predictable story into something chillingly epiphanic. As she tries to eat a sandwich and talk to her son, she is so exhausted that she falls into the automatic litany of her tourist palaver. Lincoln suddenly sees his mother in a new light: "He wondered why she was telling him these things until he saw she was mocking her own talk . . . She let her arms drop to her sides and her mouth fell open and she began to cry" (*WSPL,* 184). What seemed an ostensibly straightforward account of a woman enjoying her newfound managerial freedom becomes, in the last paragraph, a deeply probing psychological analysis of a strong but still vulnerable woman who seems to have no other choice but to use what she has to support her family.

Perhaps the most sophisticated story in the entire collection, at least in terms of innovations that today could be viewed as postmodernist or metafictional techniques, is "Problem No. 4." Though it is one of the seven military stories in the collection, all of them coming out of

Cheever's military experience, "Problem No. 4" brings together a number of literary devices that he had been using throughout this book and adds a few additional ones to make this story, in terms of method, the most intriguing one of the collection. What plot there is revolves around a military training exercise as recorded by a recruit named Robert. But Robert is also trying to write a letter home to his wife during the few breaks their training officer gives them. As a unit they are pretending to be in an alien country, even though Robert sees the distant church steeple in the town where he goes for a few drinks on nights off.

The story explores Robert's consciousness continuously creating new contexts as he moves through the exercise. He keeps noting the names and addresses of earlier recruits, some already dead, which they had carved onto every conceivable object—"the rifle-range pits, latrines, the web, equipment." But in the middle of his depressing survey of the names of soldiers he'll never know, Robert runs across a connecting thread and tells his wife: "Yesterday I saw on a target marker the name and address of a man from Bridgewater, New Hampshire, which is where we went to the barn dance last summer. Remember?" (*WSPL*, 234). Just as he is "carving his identity" in a letter to his wife and simultaneously inscribing his identity in a story he is writing, a point of recognition connects all of these seemingly discrete realms, creating a human context that then gives his actions some temporary significance even amid the anonymous war machine in which he is trapped. The story is a fictive variation on perhaps the most common and mysterious line of graffiti throughout World War II: "Kilroy was here."

This story brilliantly entertains a number of seemingly disconnected contexts that mirror the disorder of a soldier's life until the artist's eye recognizes a point that creates significance where previously there was none. Robert observes fellow soldiers also carving their names and addresses on the woodwork of an old house that the army has been using for years in their exercises. Though the story is ostensibly about war games, it becomes a parable about how people make meaning, how they carve their identity and, indeed, document their existence in a time of great fear and isolation and, in a very existential way, humanize the void.

The most important single thematic concern of the collection, and the one that develops most dramatically, is what critics have called "the brother conflict." Even more important than the relationship of husband and wife or parents and children, the relationship with brothers takes precedence. Cheever himself stated on numerous occasions that his relationship with his brother, Fred, was "the strongest love" of his

life. Of the many stories about brothers in Cheever's fiction, most are
undoubtedly autobiographical. Scott Donaldson devotes an entire chapter of his biography to the relationship between John and Fred.
Cheever's relationship with Fred was characterized by a classic fraternal
love-hate dichotomy, and it was grounded in the love and attention that
Fred was able to give him in a family that allowed no physical affection
or genuine emotional support. Their mother was cold and self-con-
cerned, though she spent much of her life working to support the family after her husband lost his job and the family home. The boys' father
was alcoholic, descending into heavier drinking and developing more
complex resentments as he grew older. The boys, then, were left to support each other emotionally during their childhood and well into their
twenties.

"The Brothers," which was the fourth story Cheever published, is certainly, along with "Of Love: A Testimony," the most artfully rendered
story in *The Way Some People Live*. And it is clearly autobiographical. It is
the story of Kenneth and Tom, three years younger than Kenneth, who
have been living together for four years. They are going on a weekend
visit to one of their favorite vacation spots, a farm where a woman
named Amy lives with her daughter, Jane, to escape the grinding city
life of Boston. As the story unfolds, the reader discovers through Amy's
eyes that the brothers' intense closeness has come out of the mutual
recognition that their mother's hatred for their father left no room in her
life for loving them. Her bitterness has worn the brothers out and left
them emotionally homeless. Their father had been forced out of the
house, and he died a few years later, alone in a hotel room. The bitterness of the divorce and the deepening hatred of their parents for each
other tinged their brotherly love with desperation.

Jane, a woman in her twenties, begins to take more than a passing
interest in Kenneth and tries, without success, to get him to pay attention to her. Kenneth is entirely unaware of how completely absorbed he
is in his younger brother, Tom, and his indifference begins to anger Jane.
Tom, however, sees from the beginning how exclusive their relationship
has become and how Kenneth seems constitutionally incapable of treat-
ing anybody, particularly Jane, with any seriousness. Jane, in frustration,
decides to try a direct approach:

"Want to go for a walk with me, Kenneth?"
      He looked up vaguely, unaware, it seemed, of the painful importance
she attached to the question. "I don't know," he said. He turned involun-

tarily to his brother as he had turned to him for years. "Want to go for a walk, Tom?" he asked.

"No, I don't think so," Tom said quickly. He knew what her question had meant.

"I don't think I want to go," Kenneth said (*WSPL,* 171).

In that instant, Tom fully comprehends his older brother's incapacity to perceive the pathological nature of their relationship. Tom realizes that he must go away. The story's concluding paragraph is Cheever's first great revelation, an expanded version of the brilliant conclusion of "Expelled." Kenneth, who comes down to Amy's farm after his brother's departure, begins to understand why Tom has left him. Cheever interweaves autumnal details in such a way that they become a metaphor for the psychological "fall" that Kenneth is beginning to experience: "It was one of the first great nights of autumn, and the wind tasted of winter and of the season's end and moved in the trees with the noise of a conflagration. He made a mechanical clutching gesture with his hands as if something were slipping through them . . . Now he felt the pain that Tom had brought down on both of them without any indignation; they had tried to give their lives some meaning and order, and for love of the same world that had driven them together, they had had to separate. He walked through the fields clutching involuntarily at the air, as if something were slipping from his grasp, and swearing and looking around him like a stranger at the new, strange, vivid world" (*WSPL,* 174–75). Kenneth is clearly shaken by his brother's departure; but he is now becoming increasingly conscious of his estrangement from the world, an estrangement he is unable to deny. Cheever concludes the story paradoxically; the imagery suggests not only the pain of separation but also the potential for a new revelation—that is, his perceptions resemble those of a newborn apprehending the world in its strange, vivid freshness. Though the story documents the fall of a fraternal Edenic world that Tom and Kenneth had successfully regenerated, it also tenuously suggests the possibility of redemption—that the vividness of the world Kenneth is experiencing for the first time may, eventually, enable him to live in the present moment free of past encumbrances.

The Enormous Radio and Other Stories

Cheever's next volume of short stories, *The Enormous Radio and Other Stories,* represents one of the most dramatic shifts in stylistic practices in modern American literature. Though the subject matter and themes remain essentially the same—love, the falls of families, brothers, alcoholic obsessiveness, loneliness and desperation, money problems, and the necessity of illusion—there is a deepening and enrichment of Cheever's rhetoric and a refinement of craft that make the stories in *The Enormous Radio,* according to some critics, his best.

There have been no convincing explanations as to what precipitated the radical change in Cheever's stylistic treatment of essentially the same material. With the publication of *The Journals of John Cheever* (1991), however, certain facts seem obvious. Robert Gottlieb, the editor of Cheever's last five books at Knopf, was also the editor of the journals; with the exception of family members and Malcolm Cowley, he knew Cheever better than anyone. The four-hundred-page edition of the published journals makes up only a twentieth of the complete journals, which run to between 3 million and 4 million words.[5] Gottlieb's intention in selecting and editing entries was "to follow the line of Cheever's inner life as he wrote it down day after day, year after year; to reflect, in proportion, the conflicts and the satisfactions of the thirty-five or so years that these journals represent; and to reveal something of how he worked" (*J,* 397). Though Cheever kept "some scanty passages" from before the World War II, Gottlieb opened the Cheever journals with entries from 1948 onward. The late 1940s and early 1950s were the years when Cheever was writing and publishing the stories eventually collected in *The Enormous Radio.*

A cursory comparison of these stories with the ruminations of the journals leads to the unmistakable conclusion that Cheever's journal keeping directly influenced his fiction. He moved from the straightforward naturalistic prose style of *The Way Some People Live* into the deeper, more reflective, and psychologically complex style of *The Enormous Radio* as a direct result of his meditative journal entries. The journals do, as Gottlieb hoped, "reveal something of how he worked." But they do more than that. They not only reveal, with stunning insight, the personal pain and confusion of Cheever's moral and spiritual dilemmas but also document the growth and development of his powers as a writer. The highly personal meditative content of the journals enabled Cheever to transform his earlier naturalistic style into what became uniquely Cheeveresque in his work from *The Enormous Radio* till the end of his career. The journals, then, can be read as a gloss on Cheever's life and work and as a text interacting with his fiction. They constitute an autobiographical and spiritual record but, as importantly, become a formulating factor in his burgeoning creative processes.

The effect of Cheever's new, more expansive and reflective style on three stories alone among the fourteen in the collection would have secured for him a permanent place in the pantheon of American short-story writers: "Goodbye, My Brother," "Torch Song," and "The Enormous Radio." A close analysis of "Goodbye, My Brother" reveals that Cheever had mastered longer and more complex narrative structures, structures that allowed him to include history (both genealogical and national), geography, myth, and religion, as well as a more sophisticated use of proper names (persons and places), as active agents involved in developing the story. All of these narrative components take on more than their surface appearance and substantially expand a story of family conflict into mythic dimensions. "Goodbye, My Brother" is a much deeper exploration of the love/hate dilemma than is Cheever's "The Brothers." It shows that Cheever had developed into a significantly more sophisticated writer.

"Goodbye, My Brother" is so richly textured that it could serve as Cheever's earliest model of a story that can be discussed and analyzed in terms of recurring mythic patterns, historical allusions and parallels, geographical significance, and brilliant fluctuations of light and dark that eventually evolve into a Manichean battleground. His use of proper names of characters and places enriches the interpretative possibilities and adds a quiet but distinct comic subtext to an already vivid array of characters and plot twists.

Cheever encourages biblical resonances of the Cain/Abel myth when it is obvious that "Goodbye, My Brother" is about an attempted fratricide—the unnamed narrator literally tries to inflict great harm, if not death, on his impossibly Puritanical brother, Lawrence, at the story's dramatic conclusion. But it is crucial that the reader understand that the story is also about the life-denying Puritanical nay-sayers versus the life-affirming yea-sayers. The narrator states that Lawrence reminds him of a Puritan cleric (*SJC,* 6), alluding to a family connection with Cotton Mather himself, America's earliest and most dour Calvinist. Even more important, the summer house, or Eden, of the Pommeroy family is called Laud's Head, a name which, if one knows some English religious history, undoubtedly refers to one of the most famous Anglican Archbishops, William Laud, who was beheaded by the Puritans in 1645 for attempting to bring back into the Episcopal Church music, ritual, the

Communion table, and the sacramental system the Puritans had banned. The humorous pun on "Head" and its reappearance on the other side of the Atlantic involved in the same basic conflict demonstrates not only the depth of Cheever's knowledge of English history but his wry sense of humor. And Lawrence is also "all head" and no heart—litigious and icy and a bore. The family name, Pommeroy, means in French "king of the apples"—apples being the single most important metaphor in Cheever's entire literary vocabulary because they evoke an Edenic innocence and childlike happiness that these Pommeroys are trying to regenerate during their summer vacation. One of Cheever's earliest stories is the first of what will become *The World of Apples* in 1973, his sixth short-story collection.

Lawrence Pommeroy is consistently associated with the dark, the sinister, and the east. Cheever is using the east not in its usual association as the source of light and life, the sun, however, but in connection with the encroachment of the Puritanical darkness of the bleak, dogmatic severity of Lawrence's and, by extension, the Puritans' joyless lives. Lawrence is, after all, a lawyer, and his name symbolizes his fractious rigidity. The narrator calls him a "dark figure" as he leaves the family at the story's conclusion. Earlier in the story, the narrator describes Lawrence's effect on the family's attempts to enjoy themselves: "He looked at us all bleakly. The wind and the sea had risen, and I thought that if he heard the waves, he must hear them only as a dark answer to all his dark questions" (*SJC*, 13). Lawrence is also associated with "the east wind—the dark wind, as Lawrence would have said" (*SJC*, 15). The narrator suggests a kind of mystical collusion when he states that "the easterly fog seemed to play into my misanthropic brother's hands" (*SJC*, 16).

Chaddy Pommeroy, the third brother, and Chucky Ewing, the organizer of the country-club dance and the party games, which Lawrence refuses to participate in, both have names that are cognates of Charles and, of course, Archbishop Laud supported and was supported by Charles I, who also lost his head to the Puritans under the chief Roundhead, Oliver Cromwell, because the king had tried to oust the Puritans from political power. Lawrence is also against drinking, accuses his mother of being an alcoholic, refuses to play cards, abhors dancing, and eschews all activities that Puritans considered sinful. Most important, however, he considers all of these activities "a waste of time," the major reason Lawrence gives for prematurely leaving the family after his brother tries to "crown" him. And since the Puritans were obsessed with time and apocalypse, their vision of the world was essentially eschatological, which is why Lawrence's life has become a litany of gloomy good-byes. Indeed, toward the end of the story, Lawrence reveals to his family that his primary purpose in returning to their summer home was to say goodbye; he wants to sell his equity in the house to Chaddy. (Mother Pommeroy's winter home is Philadelphia, an ironic detail since it is the City of Brotherly Love, and this story is about the opposite.) Cheever brilliantly lists the thirteen "goodbyes" that have traced the map of Lawrence Pommeroy's life, one of which, in keeping with the seven-teenth-century Puritan conflicts, is his "saying goodbye to the Protestant Episcopal Church" (*SJC*, 18).

Cheever counterbalances the dark, Calvinist gloom of Lawrence and his biblically subservient wife Ruth and their two sad and fearful chil-dren with the sensually alluring Helen, Diana, and Odette (an allusion to Proust's seductive Odette de Crécy from *Swann's Way*). The mythic resonances of the goddess of the hunt, Diana, Helen of Troy, and the "promiscuous" Odette are impossible to ignore. This fecund trinity of Dionysians and their celebration of the physical body are Cheever's response to the dark denial and shame of the Puritan ethos that his story clearly condemns. Lawrence is deeply agitated when he hears his moth-er, on three occasions, invite the family into the "fabulous" pleasures of summer. And he is infuriated when he hears the narrator repeat three times: "It's only a summer day." Cheever articulated as clearly as he ever did his stance as a late American romantic, firmly grounded in the tradi-tion of Ralph Waldo Emerson, Henry David Thoreau, and especially Walt Whitman in "Goodbye, My Brother." In a scene in which he wel-comes the transforming powers of the activity of swimming as members of his family unconsciously try to shed some of "Lawrence's rebukes," he celebrates the "mythology of the Atlantic" and "the curative powers of the sea" (*SJC*, 16). And later in the story, in contemplating the grim life of Ruth, Lawrence's wife, he juxtaposes the mystically regenerative power of nature with Ruth's "expiatory passion" and "penitential fervor" (*SJC*, 19).

Once Lawrence and his sad family are gone, the landscape lights up and their Eden is vividly regenerated: "I got up and went to the window and what a morning that was! The wind was northerly. The air was clear. In the early heat, the roses in the garden smelled like strawberry jam." He bestows the light with a quasi-sacramental aura, calling it "the grace of the light" that unifies the sea with the sun, an image that has become one of Cheever's most profoundly visionary epiphanies, but not before detailing Lawrence's crimes against nature: "Oh, what can you do with

a man like that? What can you do? . . . How can you teach him to
respond to the inestimable greatness of the race, the harsh surface beau-
ties of life? . . . The sea that morning was iridescent and dark. My wife
and my sister were swimming—and I saw their uncovered heads, black
and gold in the dark water. I saw them come out and I saw that they
were naked, unshy, beautiful, and full of grace, and I watched the naked
women walk out of the sea" (*SJC,* 21). In essence, Cheever has recreated
the primordial birth of life and the imagination in nature by reconstitut-
ing these modern goddesses in their preternatural innocence. He extends
the concept of grace beyond a limited Christian application to include
the world of classical mythology that was always grounded in natural
cycles.

In story after story and novel after novel, Cheever repostulates in
modern terms a romantic version of Nathaniel Hawthorne's conflicts
with the Puritans' rejection and fear of the body and their insistent
demonization of the powers of nature. Samuel Coale suggests that a
comparison of Cheever with Hawthorne, especially Hawthorne's "symbolic approach . . . is precisely where a reassessment of Cheever's work
should begin" (Coale 1982, 193). And even further, in speaking of the
two authors' striking affinities, states: "The themes, form, style, and
vision of John Cheever's fiction reflects Hawthorne's. The Manichean
pattern and theme can be seen in Cheever's use of two brothers as alternate visions of reality in his short stories and in all of his novels" (Coale
1982, 194). Though Hawthorne employed allegorical characters and
themes in his romances, Cheever relied more on "mythic allusions,
Christian symbols, and Biblical references" (Coale 1982, 195). And,
finally, Coale claims that the brother conflict is so important to Cheever's
work that his "use of two apparently different brothers in his fiction to
express opposite visions of reality can be explored in biographical, psychological, thematic, and structural terms." And, equally important, in
mythical terms.

"Goodbye, My Brother" becomes the first of many of Cheever's early
New York stories that deal with the necessity of exorcising an Edenic
place, situation, even mental states, of a corrupting influence. The happiness, innocence—usually in the form of benign ignorance—or the pristine condition of the protagonists' "garden" is about to be sullied, turned
upside-down or destroyed by some external force, character, or new
information. His early New York stories, such as "The Enormous Radio,"
"The Summer Farmer," "Clancy in the Tower of Babel," "The Common

Day," and "The Superintendent" follow this pattern with unerring consistency.

The first group that make up the "Edenic" questers in *The Enormous Radio and Other Stories* are at the opposite ends of the social and economic spectrum. There are the dispossessed or the "fallen ones" who are either trying to regenerate another Edenic condition, one that will endure, or make tolerable their present intolerable condition. Many of them are members of the working class and appear in "The Sutton Place Story," "Clancy and the Tower of Babel," "The Superintendent," and "Christmas Is a Sad Season for the Poor." The characters are nannies, servants, elevator operators, or superintendents, all of whom are aware in varying degrees, of their dispossessed or marginalized condition.

Mrs. Harley of "The Sutton Place Story" is an ignorant but sensitive woman who had lived "a hearty and comfortable life until her husband's death, but he had left her with no money and she had been reduced to working as a nursemaid" (*SJC,* 66). James Clancy, a grateful immigrant from Ireland, finds a job as an elevator operator, after having had a serious fall in an earlier better-paying factory job. His work in an affluent Upper East Side apartment building in New York City exposes him to the diversity of life in the big city and leaves him shocked by encounters with homosexuals, alcoholics, and desperate loneliness in what he thought was an idyllic existence. The building becomes for him the agent of the loss of innocence, exposing the sorrows of the world he was simply not ready to acknowledge.

The same fall from an ignorant or innocent vision of the world takes place in "The Superintendent," where the kindly superintendent, Chester Coolidge, valiantly tries to make sense out of having to watch some of the old, long-time residents of his building being forced to leave one social and economic class and descend into a lower one. What had been the Bestwicks' security and home, their paradise for many years, was no longer affordable. A comic example of marginalization is another elevator operator, Charlie, in "Christmas Is a Sad Season for the Poor," whose self-pity gets the better of him and who, though he lives poorly in a run-down boardinghouse, fabricates outlandish lies about his hard and sorrowful life. The lies work and he is overwhelmed with Christmas food and gifts, so much so that he shares his riches with those even poorer than he: his attempt to recreate, temporarily, a sense of communal security and happiness works. His selflessness also redeems him from the suffocating sense of victimization that had made him such a bore.

The other group of Edenic questers are the more affluent inhabitants of these expensive, East Side New York apartment buildings. They are those financially secure enough to have summer places or to afford extended vacations in New England. Frederick Karl labels the lure of these places "the promise of the pastoral," and finds Cheever firmly rooted in an American literary tradition that includes writers such as Emerson, Thoreau, Hawthorne, Whitman, and Melville.[6] The American impulse toward the pastoral, or the need to flee the city and find physical and spiritual sustenance in nature, is ostensibly the principal concern of "The Common Day," "The Summer Farmer," and "The Hartleys."

Rarely has Cheever achieved so subtly the emerging sense of discontent, which finally overtakes the narrator's feelings of happiness, that opens "The Common Day." Jim and Ellen Brown and eight other characters people this richly textured story, a pastoral United Nations. There is Emma, the French housemaid; Agnes Shay, the Irish servant who takes care of the Browns' little daughter, Carlotta; Nils, the Swedish gardener; Greta, the cook, who is also Nils's wife; Mrs. Garrison, Ellen Brown's mother and owner of the lovely New Hampshire farm; and several others. As the day wears on, what becomes increasingly obvious is that this lovely place is anything but Edenic and the promised pastoral is, in reality, a human wasteland of dislocation and alienation. The events and fractured relationships belie the title and make it ironic. Jim and Ellen Brown are looking around the area, intending to buy a farm of their own, but cannot agree on anything. In fact, they discover that they view the world in very different ways. Their daughter, Carlotta, enjoys brutalizing Agnes, whose Irish-Catholic guilt seems to welcome the abuse. Both the Swedish cook, Greta, and Agnes feel dislocated in the idyllic New Hampshire scenery and privately wish to return to their home country to bid remaining relatives a final goodbye. In retrospect, they view their homeland as paradise. Agnes complains: "These little mountains! Ireland is like a garden" (*SJC,* 29). At the story's conclusion, the characters separate into their own private worlds and find the dream of community to be only an illusion. Instead of being ennobled by their pastoral experience, they are sullied by it.

"The Summer Farmer" is a variation on the same theme, but Paul and Virginia Hollis, prosperous Manhattanites, own a farm in New Hampshire, which Paul had inherited from his father. They are older, more experienced, and less idealistic about the ameliorative effects of living in nature. And Paul welcomes the weekends he is able to spend there and enjoys his farming duties. As usual, a dark presence enters the story, here in the form of a Russian immigrant named Kasiak, a bitter, miserly man whom Paul hires to help him with chores. Kasiak is an authentic Russian peasant with scars, both physical and emotional, to document the brutality of pre-Revolutionary Russia. He is also a Communist. They meet on their first day working together in Paul's favorite area of the farm, a pasture Paul's father labeled Elysian, a name that evokes one of ancient Greece's principal Edens, the archetypal pastoral setting where the inhabitants rest in utter contentment. Cheever's depiction of Kasiak as the invading, corrupting agent is subtle but unmistakable. When the baby rabbits Paul has acquired for his two children are found poisoned, Paul immediately accuses Kasiak, who, in true peasant fashion, refuses to respond to the charges. As it turns out, the previous summer Virginia had put the poison in an old farm building where they had housed the rabbits; their death was an accident.

As the story ends, Paul leaves the idyllic farm, shaken and guilt-laden by the memory that he threatened to kill Kasiak for something he had not done, an event Paul will probably never forget. The story also juxtaposes the temporary pastoral promise of Paul Hollis to Kasiak's Marxist Eden emerging out of the bloody turmoil of class struggle. "The Summer Farmer" is a deeper and more structured analysis of the illusions involved in idyllic projects, both personal and political, that both West and East share. Paul and Virginia Hollis and Jim and Ellen Brown are the middle-class and upper-middle-class Edenic questers who want a pastoral respite from their frenetic city lives but who keep running into the same sense of disillusion and dislocation as their working class counterparts—the servants, nannies, and elevator boys of Cheever's other stories.

Another story that concerns the need for pastoral peace and tranquility is "The Hartleys," one of Cheever's most brutally sad stories. Mr. and Mrs. Hartley and their daughter, Anne, arrive at a lovely New England inn called the Pemaquoddy. They inform the proprietor, Mrs. Butterick, that they have returned after an eight-year hiatus, the year before Anne was born. As the story unfolds, it becomes clear that Anne holds their marriage together; and their relationship with her, especially her father's, is so intense that it borders on the hysterical. She sobs for hours when they leave her and ski during the day. Beneath Anne's desperate dependence on her parents, though, is a pattern of obsessive searching that her parents have been pursuing for years. Once Mrs. Hartley begins to drink, she reveals the driven nature of their journeys. Her half-drunk monologue articulates Cheever's earliest and clearest expression of the most important theme running throughout *The Enormous Radio:* "Why

do we have to come back? Why do we have to make these trips back to
the places where we thought we were happy? What good is it going to
do? What good has it ever done? . . . We go back to the restaurants, the
mountains, we go back to the houses, even the neighborhoods, we walk
in the slums, thinking that this will make us happy, and it never does"
(*SJC,* 63). The Hartleys' cyclic search for a renewed paradise in their
prelapsarian past has never worked, though they continue to believe that
their dream might, somehow, become real. It is obvious that Anne, their
beloved only child, may well have been brought into the world in a desperate attempt to keep them together. When Anne is suddenly killed in
the gears of the towing wheel, the Hartleys' cyclic search for a reality
becomes their worst nightmare. "The Hartleys" is Cheever's most bitterly ironic story in the collection. The family's trip north to renew old pastoral satisfactions turns into the ultimate journey south; their heaven
becomes their hell.

Geography and its mythical significance play important roles in many
Cheever stories, especially the early ones. The movement of families in
"The Common Day," "The Summer Farmer," and "The Hartleys" is to
the north; in Dantean terms, it is a movement away from the chaos and
threat of the south. For Cheever, the north is usually associated with
heaven, Apollo, balance, control, peace, and stillness in the sense of dis-
engagement from the restless wheel of nature and cyclic recurrence. The
"unearthly stillness" of the Elysian pasture in "The Summer Farmer"
clearly shows Cheever's adherence to the traditional associations of geographical directions to ancient mythic and spiritual metaphors.
Particularly in American literature, east and west take on more significance than mere directions on a map. Cheever uses the idea of north
ironically in these three stories, because the peace, stillness, and rest the
city dwellers seek there eludes them at best and destroys them at worst.

Three stories in *The Enormous Radio and Other Stories* are about midwestern innocents—and innocence—moving east to find their paradise
or the fulfillment of their dreams. And, geomythically, they are going
the wrong way. Moving east, particularly in American literature, is a
movement "back east" instead of "out west," and becomes a quasi-
unnatural project because east means origin and retreat. The west symbolizes possibility, progress, newness, renewal, restoration, mystery,
hope, but also sometimes death, because the sun sets in the west. In
"The Pot of Gold," "Torch Song," and "O City of Broken Dreams,"
Cheever shows two families and a couple from the Midwest attempting
to realize the dreams that New York City offers them.

"O City of Broken Dreams" is one of Cheever's cruelest, yet funniest, parables depicting the naive Evarts and Alice Malloy, and their pathetic little daughter, Mildred-Rose, and their systematic brutalization by the most decadent Broadway agents in modern literature. Evarts Malloy has written a play about an oddball in his hometown of Wentworth, Indiana, a Mama Finelli who operates a gas station and a snake farm. Again, Cheever's basic unit of happiness resides in family love. The Malloys descend into an eastern decadence that they have never suspected. The story ends when the Malloys realize that the play that brought them so close to the realization of their midwestern dream of eastern big-city success has turned into grounds for at least three law suits, including one from the subject of Evarts' play, Mama Finelli herself. Their dream of ultimate success is transformed, within a week, into a hell on earth. The agents of their fall from midwestern innocence into the corruption of eastern decadence are, ironically, the Broadway "agents" who duped them. The Malloys are so traumatized by their broken dream that they flirt with the possibility of bypassing their Indiana home and going directly to California, where, of course, they would undoubtedly meet Pacific Coast versions of their eastern "agents" of corruption.

In "The Pot of Gold," Laura and Ralph Whittemore, former midwestern innocents, are happily living in New York City; Laura had originally come from Wisconsin and Ralph from Illinois. They had met two years after arriving in the city and become "incorrigible treasure hunters." Cheever plays with their name, which should more appropriately be Whitte*less*. City life had, in a sense, corrupted them with its promise of financial success: "They were always at the threshold of fortune; they always seemed to have something on the fire" (*SJC*, 103). Though the story moves along on various get-rich-quick schemes that always fail and that lead, finally, to the total disillusionment of the couple, the magnificent revelation at the conclusion is one of Cheever's clearest expressions of the mythical traditions he increasingly used in his stories. As Laura comments on the failure of their greatest financial scheme: "It did look like the treasure . . ." And at that very moment, Ralph is able to contextualize, for the first time, his life-long hunt for the treasure with "the chimera, the pot of gold, the fleece, the treasure buried . . . the bean pot full of doubloons and bullion" (*SJC*, 116). The instant he realizes that his dream of paradise has always been an illusion, he discovers his "real" treasure, his wife, Laura, a woman worn out with their endlessly exhausting schemes, stretching out her arms to him.

Cheever transforms their awful moment of truth into one of his most moving lyrical conclusions: "Desire for her delighted and confused him. Here it was, here it all was, and the shine of the gold seemed to him then to be all around her arms" (*SJC,* 117). Ever the romantic, Cheever transforms their illusion of the pot of gold into a visionary reconstruction of their love as the illusion that becomes real and, therefore, their greatest treasure.

Not only has Cheever refined his craft in terms of an expanded use of mythic allusions as parallels to modern dilemmas, but he is now able to use them ironically, as in "The Pot of Gold" and "O City of Broken Dreams." He uses satire, a most delicate task, very effectively in "O City of Broken Dreams," but by maintaining sympathy with such abused victims as the Malloys demonstrates his increasing sophistication as a highly literary artist. But with the publication of "The Enormous Radio" and "Torch Song," two stories that critic James O'Hara calls "landmark stories," Cheever proved that his work merited comparison with the very greatest short-story writers in modern American literature, such as Fitzgerald, Hemingway, Faulkner, and Sherwood Anderson. O'Hara also states that "The Enormous Radio" is "perhaps the most imaginative story Cheever ever wrote."[7]

It is the first story in which Cheever breaks through his earlier realistic-naturalistic narrative habits to combine elements of realism and fantasy, a combination that expands both the comic and tragic possibilities of his storytelling powers. "The Enormous Radio" is also his earliest and most brilliant version of the "fall" from innocence into experience, from blissful ignorance into the horror of self knowledge, and from a comforting life of illusion into unbearable reality. Cheever has also made setting more than mere location for dramatizing marital conflicts. The apartment building in Manhattan is very much an active agent in the progress of the story. The building, initially their Edenic protection against the evils of the outside world, is transformed into a Dantean Inferno.

Unlike the midwestern pastoral questers or the "fallen" working-class servants and elevator boys in the other stories in this volume, the Westcotts are comfortably swathed in their pastoral dream. Their name comically suggests that they are fully ensconced or housed (as in where one lays one's cot) in the "West"—that is, the location of treasure, the cup of gold, the serenity that awaits them in the Western Isles—the Hebrides and so on. And, content though they seem, they also wish, someday, to move to Westchester. Jim and Irene Westcott's greatest pleasure is listening to classical music on the radio, and when it breaks down in the middle of a Schubert quartet, they must acquire a new one. Jim buys a very large and expensive new radio, and once it's attached, it not only begins to bring in Mozart quintets but also becomes a conduit to the lives in the other apartments in the building. At first, Jim and Irene enjoy the unique position the radio places them in. Privy to many of the private lives in their apartment, they become virtually omniscient—and view themselves as having attained a semi-divine status. At first they revel in their new power, but their arrogance begins to give way to feelings of guilt because they know they are violating the privacy and, therefore, the truth of their neighbors' lives.

The Westcotts' voyeurism not only exposes their neighbors' private vulnerabilities but brings about the major calamity of the story. Concurrent with their discovery of the desperate unhappiness of their neighbors, they fall into catastrophic self-knowledge. Their innocence had consisted in believing that they really lived in an urban Eden. Their fallen condition causes them to doubt everything they had ever believed. Irene discovers that her life is no different from many of her neighbors' lives: "Life is too terrible, too sordid and awful. But we've never been like that, have we darling? . . . We are happy, aren't we?" And at the very moment that they see themselves as being just like everyone else, a moment that would comfort "normal" well-adjusted people, their new knowledge totally isolates them, because they see themselves for the first time. Their innocent arrogance had positioned them, they presumed, above the rest of the vulgar crowd, beyond the malady of the quotidian. The fictive scaffolding of their lives now lies fully exposed and, like Adam and Eve, they feel ashamed and turn on each other. Now they must face their financial problems, their entrance into rueful middle age and, most painfully, dreadful memories from their past that they thought they had laid to rest. They cover their vulnerability—their nakedness—by blaming one another for their newly discovered plight. They have discovered the fictiveness of their fictions.

In a sense, "The Enormous Radio" can be considered Cheever's first truly "modern" story, if one uses the term *modern* to refer to narratives no longer concerned primarily with moral dilemmas or issues of right or wrong, good and evil. True modernity, as in one of Cheever's favorite writers, Flaubert, consists of a profound questioning of the very terms of reality and, thus, of how characters "perceive" their experience or, even more disturbing, how they unconsciously "create" realities that protect them from the brutality of time, senseless suffering, and meaningless death. Wallace Stevens defined one of the functions of the imagination as "a violence from within that protects us from a violence without"—that is, without the "violent" power of the imagination within the human psyche serving as a protective shield from brute reality, human consciousness would be overwhelmed and unable to function on a daily basis. Emma Bovery *must* commit suicide once she discovers that life is not a romance novel.

Cheever's craft showed greater narrative and philosophical refinement not only in his ability to create existential quasi-fantasies closer to the "fictions" of Latin-American writers such as Jorge Luis Borges and Julio Cortázar but, just as important, in his willingness to utilize more daring metaphors, such as the radio and the apartment house of the Westcotts. Cheever also uses the metaphor of the "house" as a Jungian symbol of the psyche as the repository of the unconscious. Once the corrupting, serpentine "radio" enters the Westcotts' garden and corrupts their pastoral contentment, they are exposed not only to the heartbreaking contents of their apartment building but, concurrently, to the contents of their "house"—that is, their unconscious psyche unprotected by their "fictions."

Additional evidence of Cheever's developing skill in using all the elements of his craft is the way he employs musical allusions throughout "The Enormous Radio." Cheever's knowledge of classical music is obvious; some of the allusions in the story are to rather esoteric pieces by Schubert and Mozart. The average reader, even of the *New Yorker,* would probably not be familiar with Schubert quartets and even less so with Mozart quintets. Schubert is normally thought of as a composer who celebrates nature, beauty, and youthfulness. But his darker and more brooding statements are to be found in his quartets, especially his later ones, such as Quartet No. 14 in D Minor, known as "Death and the Maiden." And although he wrote an early celebratory quintet called "The Trout," his very late Quintet in C Major is considered one of his darkest and most moving pieces. The fact that Cheever uses Schubert is significant; Schubert's life was a miserable one because he was poor and, in his last years, quite sickly. But his music rarely revealed his true emotional or spiritual condition and listeners would never guess at the misery beneath the lyric beauty unless they were acquainted with his life. So, too, with Mozart, especially in regard to his string quintets, all of which were written during the last five years of his increasingly painful and frustrated life. And the quintets, full of yearning and loss, are considered his greatest chamber works. Though these are some of Mozart's darker works, casual listeners would be unaware of the biographical sub-texts. Also, one of the pieces that Irene listens to just before she and her husband begin their traumatic journey into reality is Beethoven's Ninth Symphony, "including Schiller's 'Ode to Joy'" (*SJC,* 40). The irony of the position of that musical allusion need not be pointed out. And a lovely little musical foreshadowing just before they hear their neighbors' voices over the radio for the first time is a prelude of Chopin, another compos-er whose life was sad and unfulfilled. And the life of Beethoven, especial-ly during the composition of his Ninth Symphony, was anything but joyous.

Though musical allusions in "The Enormous Radio" are a minor con-sideration compared with the story's structural breakthroughs, they show an increasingly sophisticated literary imagination at work regard-ing even minor details. All of them are functional. They deepen and enrich, however modestly, the theme and tone of the story. They are also quietly witty.

"Torch Song" is, along with "The Enormous Radio," another land-mark story in Cheever's fiction. And, oddly enough, a thorough analysis seems to have eluded many of Cheever's critics. Though some agree that Joan Harris is a "fatal woman," few will go much beyond examining her as a type. But she is an intelligent, attractive woman, helplessly attract-ed to older men, especially ones who are dying. There is no question that her character has a vampiric quality, but what makes her the frightening figure she becomes as the story unfolds is that she seems totally unaware of her mythical identity or her necromantic powers. For the most fruitful examination of what her character means, one must look to sources in mythology. As Cheever himself confessed in a 1976 interview with Annette Grant when asked about the obvious biblical and mythic reso-nances that run through much of his work: "It's explained by the fact that I was brought up in Southern Massachusetts where it was thought that mythology was a subject that we should all grasp. It was very much a part of my education. The easiest way to parse the world is through mythology."[8] And mythology is also the easiest way to parse "Torch Song," one of Cheever's more hermetic parables.

For one thing, Joan Harris is always dressed in black and always asso-ciated with a series of men who are ill and dying, a pattern that protag-onist Jack Lorey takes an inordinate amount of time detecting. Once he sees himself as one of those men, he forces her to leave his apartment in a manner that resembles an exorcism. Joan Harris is also, in a manner of speaking, "carrying a torch" for the many men she has affairs with and, subsequently, accompanies to their grave. The most obvious Greek mythical figure whose job was to carry torches to light the way into Hades is Hecate. And Joan Harris's last name begins with the same letter and contains the same number of letters, a technique that many authors, particularly James Joyce and Henry James, employed throughout their careers. Zeus also made Hecate a nurse to the young. And she is always associated with crossroads since she has no home. Joan Harris adheres to all three of these characteristics: she "carries torches" for the many men she associates with; Jack Lorey meets her at Penn Station, or on crosstown buses, as he is going somewhere else; and she is a "nurse," ironically, to the many men whom she conducts to their death. In some stories from Greek mythology, Hecate actually kills people with her torch, which she uses not only to light up the descent into Hades but as a weapon. In the great epiphany at the story's conclusion, "she lighted a cigarette and put it between his lips," a gesture so revelatory that Jack Lorey makes her leave his apartment. Hecate was also known as one of the most notorious witches or sorceresses of the ancient world.

It is significant, given Cheever's sensitive use of patterns of light and dark, that the only time Joan Harris communicates intimately with Jack Lorey is in the dark, during an air-raid drill whose insistent sirens signal lights out. Joan is, of course, another kind of siren, a siren who draws men to their doom. One of the few occupations that Joan Harris was successful at when she first arrived in New York from Ohio (oddly enough the same city that Jack Lorey is from) was as a hostess, greeting people and leading them to their tables. Again, she, like Hecate, functions as a threshold guardian at a "crossroads" in a nightclub. Cheever may also be playing with the name Joan, if one associates it with the most famous Joan in Western history, Joan of Arc, who was burned at the stake as a witch or sorceress. Though Hecate is not mentioned in Homer, her figure first came into prominence in a hymn from Hesiod's *Theogony,* in which she is associated with the ghost world. There is also a consistent pattern of travel in which Jack Lorey, after she asks him for financial help, must travel "downtown" to her various semipermanent residences in Greenwich Village.

Most significant, however, is the concluding scene in which Jack Lorey realizes who Joan Harris is, not as an individual but as a mythic or archetypal figure: "Does it make you feel young to watch the dying? . . . Is that the lewdness that keeps you young? . . . My life isn't ending. My life's beginning. There are many wonderful years ahead of me . . . and when they're over . . . I'll call you and give you whatever dirty pleasure you take in watching the dying, but until then, you and your ugly and misshapen forms will leave me alone" (SJC, 102). Cheever's use of the word "forms" clearly raises her to mythical status as a recurring figure who has many embodiments and names: the fatal woman, the threshold guardian, the sorceress, the siren, the dark figure, the goddess of the night, and so on. None of Jack Lorey's angry, semihysterical accusations have the slightest effect on Joan, who calmly responds: "I'll see you later. I'll come back tonight. You'll feel better then, you poor darling" (*SJC,* 102).

Jack comprehends her oracular and necromantic identity and quickly prepares his escape. He realizes that it was the first time she had ever come to see him and that she had sought him out sensing from afar that his drinking and dissolute life were taking their toll: "He was trembling and crying with sickness and fear . . . He emptied the ashtray containing his nail pairings and cigarette butts into the toilet, and swept the floor with a shirt, so that there would be no trace of his life, of his body, when that lewd and searching shape of death came there to find him in the evening." And, as Hecate, she will accompany him and light the way with her torch into Hades, a possibility that drives Jack from his apartment for good. As Cheever clearly indicates, Joan Harris is a "form" and a "shape" and, therefore, more than human. She is also a precursor to a similar figure in "The Music Teacher," the mysterious Miss Deming.

Conclusion

Cheever's literary development between the years 1943 and 1953 was astounding. Although he later came to denigrate the early stories of *The Way Some People Live* and considered them apprenticeship works, he mapped out the basic thematic directions that remained for with him the next forty years. The dramatic growth of his mastery of larger and more complex narratives and a deepening expansion of the elements of story came out of his persistent journal-keeping. By the late 1940s, there is evidence that his journals allowed him to exercise his emotional and spiritual faculties more confidently. As a result of the establishment of an authentic dialogue between his soul and his self, the stories in *The Enormous Radio* are longer, more reflective, and psychologically more probing and complex than his earlier naturalistic stories in *The Way Some People Live.* His often painful and guilt-laden journals, which show his penchant for bitter self-laceration, ironically worked to refine, deepen, and expand his prose style into one of the most lyrically elegant voices in modern American literature.

Chapter Three

"Mythologizing
the Commonplace":
The Wapshot Novels

The Wapshot Chronicle

John Cheever's first novel, *The Wapshot Chronicle* (1957), propelled him
into literary prominence, a position his short stories were unable to
secure for him. Critics grumbled about the novel's seeming lack of a
coherent narrative structure—that it was composed of a series of related
episodes rather than an easily accessible linear plot with a beginning, a
middle, and an end. Scott Donaldson mentions that some critics accused
Cheever of sentimentalizing the past, while others could not detect "any
underlying seriousness of purpose" (Donaldson 1988, 158). John
Cheever had spent almost twenty years trying to write a novel and had
rejected a number of versions before deciding on the format for *The
Wapshot Chronicle.*

The most obvious accomplishment of this work is that it is Cheever's
first extensive and clearly mythopoeic novel, one that inaugurated a variety of mythopoeic procedures he continued to expand and refine not
only in his next two novels, *The Wapshot Scandal* (1964) and *Bullet Park*
(1969), but throughout his literary career. He also developed, concurrent
with the community of St. Botolphs, a Westchester Edenic equivalent
that he called Shady Hill, the setting of his stories in *The Housebreaker of
Shady Hill,* published in 1958, the year after *The Wapshot Chronicle.* What
The Wapshot Chronicle established most clearly is a blueprint for all of the
mythopoeic communities, major and minor, that he had created earlier,
in *The Enormous Radio and Other Stories,* and later, including Bullet Park,
Proxmire Hill, Maple Dell, Remsen Park, and, most important, St.
Botolphs, the prototype for all his Edenic communities.

The Enormous Radio and Other Stories firmly established history and
geography as crucial to the foundation of Cheever's early stories. Time

and place became the fictive constituents of Cheever's mythical communities, which are as authentic and believable as William Faulkner's Yoknapatawpha County and Sherwood Anderson's Winesburg, Ohio. The spectacular verisimilitude that sustains *The Wapshot Chronicle* is grounded in actual history, geography, and genealogy. As Scott Donaldson observes: "St. Botolphs was based on Quincy, Newburyport, Bristol, New Hampshire, and the geography of his imagination" (Donaldson 1988, 159). And, as some studies of the novel have shown, the major characters greatly resemble his paternal grandfather, his father, his mother, his brother, the author himself, and a few aunts, uncles, and cousins. But what interests readers most is what John Cheever's imagination makes out of the chaotic mixture of history, geography, myth, fable, and family gossip and the ingenious ways he transforms them into a uniquely Cheeveresque cosmos.

For one thing, there was a historical St. Botolph, a medieval English abbot from the seventh century who, with his brother and fellow monk, St. Adulf, "established a monastery at Icanhoh, usually identified with Boston ('Botulf's stone') in Lincolnshire."[1] The Boston alluded to here is, of course, the English Boston, after which the American city was named. The English Boston on the east coast of England was also known, historically, for the place where the Pilgrims, who came to America in 1620, were jailed for trying to leave England in 1607. Not only does Cheever establish the center of the Wapshot family in one of the oldest parts of America, he also connects it to its English prototype, the "original" Boston that is etymologically derived from "Botolphs stone." St. Botolphs grounds the geography of the novel in both the English and the American Boston. It also establishes another brother motif, that of St. Adulf, who helped his brother establish a monastery that eventually became the English Boston.

Cheever's detailed genealogy of the Wapshot family and family name covers large geographical areas of England, ranging from the extreme north to the far south, from Northumberland to Dorsetshire. Cheever also goes into lengthy detail as to the origin, etymologically, of the name Wapshot. It was originally the French-Norman name *Vaincre-Chaud*—*chaud* meaning "hot or agitated" and *vaincre* meaning "victor or conqueror." And the family name's origin is certainly more than decorative; it embodies the passionate aggressiveness of all the paternal progenitors down to the major character of the novel, Leander Wapshot.

Cheever also establishes a tradition of writing in the family insofar as they were "copious journalists" who recorded everything: "They chronicled changes in the wind, the arrival and departure of ships, the price of tea and jute and the death of kings. They urged themselves to improve their minds and they reproached themselves for idleness, sloth, lewdness, stupidity, and drunkenness."[2] The journals and letters of Leander Wapshot are more than quaint, sentimental remnants of eighteenth century epistolary habits used to evoke a lovely, bygone era. Rather, he uses the journals and letters to *chronicle* the Wapshots' lives: to establish permanent evidence of their existence. Though Leander Wapshot's consciousness pervades the book, the journals and letters document the lives of the Wapshots.

It is crucial for readers to understand that Cheever is also instructing them in how to read his book when he uses the word *chronicle* in the title. That word evokes other historical uses, particularly in English history, from the *Anglo-Saxon Chronicles* of King Alfred and Venerable Bede to Holinshed's *Chronicles,* which Shakespeare and other writers made liberal use of. The literary forms of these chronicles are anything but consistent, often being collections of letters, journals, diaries, and legal documents much closer to a miscellany than neatly coherent historical documentation. Likewise, Cheever chose to organize his first novel exactly the way he wished. His love of eighteenth-century novels, especially *Tristram Shandy,* is evident in both the flavor and structure of *The Wapshot Chronicle.*[3] There is little question that the "chronicle" novel of *Tristram Shandy* is much closer to the "miscellany" of *The Wapshot Chronicle* and that Laurence Sterne's untrammeled celebration of the vividness of life embodies the spirit of Cheever's first novel.

Key to understanding and appreciating this work is that it must be read on its own terms. Its four-part structure traces a cyclic rather than a linear trajectory, as Scott Donaldson aptly points out, because the content dictates such a structure. As Charles Olson, another proud New Englander, points out in his classic statement on literary form: "Form is never more than an extension of content."[4] The novel opens and closes on the Fourth of July, Independence Day, and that is clearly a cyclic return to a temporal and spatial center. The most basic mythic journey in Western literature is that of departure and return—the necessary ingredients of a journey. The important journeys the novel chronicles are those of Leander Wapshot's two sons, Coverly and Moses, as they leave and return to their home in St. Botolphs. Their trips are classic rites of passage insofar as they return transformed. Their call to adventure is issued by Honora Wapshot, their father's Puritanical cousin, who controls the family fortune and demands that the boys search for wives and father sons. If they fail at their quests, they will lose their inheritance. The absolute authority of Honora's demands carries with it the ominous flavor of a fable, fairy tale, or riddle.

The narrative pattern of the novel is that of two sons departing from a center and returning to it, repeating a cyclic journey until they fulfill their genealogical obligations, when they are free of their ties to a center and celebrate their own Independence Day. The concept of a "center" is Cheever's most important mythopoeic ingredient because it establishes the possibilities of either maintaining or regenerating an Edenic condition that is always, in Cheever's world, posited in a geographical location.

St. Botolphs is that Edenic place in *The Wapshot Chronicle* but it is in decline as the novel opens on Independence Day, an ironic reference to one of the major themes of the novel. It is clear that Leander Wapshot, though he is the captain of his ship, *Topaze,* is anything but independent of his controlling wife, Sarah, who makes her initial appearance regally sitting atop a Women's Club float. She is to be the main speaker because she founded the club, but before she is able to approach the podium, a firecracker goes off beneath one of the chairs on the float and the horse bolts up Hill Street. Chaos interrupts her speech, order has been broken—a small but significant foreshadowing of future eruptions in the community. On the evening of this Independence Day, there is a violent car accident involving Rosalie Young and her boyfriend, Charlie, who is instantly killed. They had just had sex on the beach. Though seriously injured, she stays on at the Wapshot home, West Farm, and recovers, soothed by the healing tranquility of the Wapshot household. Rosalie— a name that is an ironic symbol of innocence, a young rose—is accidentally observed by the adolescent Moses as she bathes naked in the nearby river where he is practicing the fishing techniques his father, Leander, has just taught him.

Ironies humorously proliferate as Moses Wapshot, whose Old Testament counterpart was himself discovered on the banks of the Nile, discovers a naked woman in a river. Cheever directly evokes another biblical scene when he describes Moses' fall from an innocent childhood into the potential dangers of adolescent lust: "He watched his gleaming Susanna, shame faced, his dream of simple pleasure replaced by sadness, some heaviness that seemed to make his mouth taste of blood and his teeth ache" (*WC,* 71). The allusion is to the biblical story of the attempted rape of Susanna by the Elders, who were ultimately put to death after unjustly accusing her of adultery. Until seeing Rosalie naked in the river,

Moses had not been drawn to her because she had reminded him of his mother, Sarah, alluding to the great mother of the Jewish race, Abraham's wife. Cheever's mythic and biblical allusions create a quietly witty counterpoint. Later, Moses cannot resist Rosalie's sexual allure, and they consummate their lust in one of the family bedrooms at West Farm, as Honora accidentally overhears their animal pleasure from within a closet of the bedroom. Honora flees the house to regain her virginal equilibrium. She experiences lewd and lascivious dreams that night and decides that Moses must leave home—mythically, of course, he is expelled from the Edenic garden of his childhood.

At this point in part one of the novel, Cheever juxtaposes the sensuous, Dionysian character and life-style of Leander with the Puritan, Apollonian despiser of the body, the aptly named Honora, a sixteenth-century word used by Shakespeare in *Hamlet* meaning "virginity." Honora, then, unconsciously uses her sexual repression as a mechanism of control when she threatens to sell Leander's prize possession, the *Topaze,* unless he and Sarah agree "to let Moses go"; that is, to force Moses to leave West Farm and find his way in the world. Mythically, they are expelling him from paradise. Ironically, Rosalie Young's father, an Anglican priest, comes to retrieve his daughter from West Farm and insists that they take $30 (an echo of thirty pieces of silver) for attending her during her recovery.

With Honora's radical attempts to repair the moral integrity of the Wapshot family by engineering Moses' premature departure from West Farm, Honora becomes a figure embodying social, moral, and religious values antithetical to those of Leander, a figure who celebrates the sensuality of life as a kind of domesticated satyr. Cheever refuses, though, to identify either Leander or Honora as representative of Manichean light and dark or good and evil. Rather, he draws two vividly sympathetic characters and lets his readers bring their own moral assumptions to them. How one views and judges Honora and Leander may reveal to the reader moral positions he or she may not have been aware of. And this ability to draw out and expose readers' unconscious ethical positions accounts, in great part, for the disturbing effect his work sometimes has. His ability to engage complex moral issues through his characters and their struggles gives this book a depth and seriousness that his earlier work does not possess.

In the antithetical moral worlds of Honora and Leander, Cheever establishes two opposing conflicts or tensions that run throughout *The Wapshot Chronicle* and many of his short-story collections. The virginal

Honora represents the WASP, Calvinist moral sternness that sustained and motivated the darker, guilt-laden souls of the Pilgrims who founded America. Though Honora guiltily enjoys going to Red Sox baseball games, her sense of moral duty, her work ethic, and her cultivation of tradition make her not only a model of emotional stability but also a modern version of Dickens's Miss Havisham, in which stability disintegrates into stasis. Opposing Honora's Apollonian balance is her Dionysian counterpart, Leander Wapshot, who is committed to process and change.

He celebrates the body as only a man of the sea can and imitates, unconsciously, the romantic literary character he is named after, the Leander of Christopher Marlowe's poem "Hero and Leander." Marlowe's Leander is so passionately in love with Hero, a priestess of Venus, that he swims nightly across the Hellespont to visit; but one night, exhausted by the swim, he drowns. Hero is so brokenhearted by his death that she drowns herself rather than face life alone. Though descended from a family of sea captains, Leander has been reduced, in his fallen world, to operating an excursion launch from Travertine, the place where the Boston train lets off its passengers to Nangasakit, an amusement park across the bay. He captains his pathetic little ship the *Topaze* on its endless cycle. Mythically, Leander has become a New England Charon, a boatman-guide ferrying his passengers to Hades.

What gives the situation a comic twist is that Leander-Charon is locked in the stasis of cyclic recurrence because he carries his passengers to an Eden manqué, an amusement park that is a mere imitation of paradise, the happy isles, Avalon, the Elysian Fields, and many other commercialized versions of the heavenly city. But Leander's role is further endangered by Honora's threat to sell the *Topaze* if he doesn't force his son Moses to leave West Farm and enter the world. When the *Topaze* is wrecked in a storm and towed into port, Leander's wife, Sarah, transforms it into "The Only Floating Gift Shoppe in New England." Honora and Sarah embody the stasis that has finally triumphed, and Leander is left with the only option that his namesake offers him: drowning.

Part 2 of *The Wapshot Chronicle* details the other options, activities, and roles that Leander samples before he decides to drown himself. In many ways, part 2 is the spiritual center of the novel. Leander's journal and the early adventures of his sons take up much of the action. It is also the longest part of the novel, taking up more than a hundred pages. Though John Cheever is never thought of as a postmodernist writer or metafictionist—he did not hold such writers in high esteem—part 2 begins self-

reflexively: "Writer's epistolary style (Leander wrote) formed in tradition
of Lord Timothy Dexter, who put all punctuation marks, prepositions,
adverbs, articles, etc., at the end of communication and urged reader to
distribute same as he saw fit. West Farm. Autumn. 3 pm" (*WC,* 97). Part
of what makes this section of the novel so compelling is its departure
from standard narrative and the way the journal mode enriches the
novel's texture by creating additional levels that interweave time and
place. What emerges is the richest tapestry in the novel (the word *tapestry* comes from the Latin *textum,* meaning "a thing made" or "text").
Leander is metaphorically attempting to "tie things together," such as
his family history, by documenting in writing the paternal characteristics
of his lineage—the moral and ethical beliefs of his immediate and distant
ancestors—and interweaving all that information, hearsay, gossip, and
scandal into coherent statements about his life and the lives of his sons,
Moses and Coverly. Leander's journal also becomes an alternate text. It
can be used by the reader to compare later versions of family events, and
it demonstrates the actual process of creativity as it records and remembers and, most important, creates significance. Leander is not only keeping a journal but is showing how and why he is doing it. Without
chronicling these events, these lives, including his own, are simply
minute fractions of the millions that live and die unconsciously involved
in the destructive duration of cyclic recurrence. He keeps a journal that,
metaphorically, "keeps" the family in existence.

Cheever establishes in part 2 the genealogical, historical, and spiritual
foundation for his intricately emerging mythopoeic world, St. Botolphs
being the first of many. He was quite honest in admitting that he used
parts of his father's journal in this chapter, an admission that offers even
more interpretative possibilities.

Certain recurring motifs appear throughout Leander's journal and life
that intermittently surface in the lives of his sons. Leander had an older
brother, Hamlet, whom he detested but who was his mother's favorite.
Their father, Aaron, abandoned the family and was not heard of until
years after his death. All of these characters are, of course, right out of
Cheever's family background, which provided motifs he used over and
over throughout his writing career. Certain names counterpoint each
other. Beatrice, for instance, is the name shared by two women with
whom Leander and Moses have youthful sexual experiences; these
Beatrices are ironic versions of Dante's Beatrice, who became, next to
the Blessed Virgin Mary, the archetypal symbol of pure love.

Additionally, both father and son are subject to more than their share of blackmail threats, both stemming from involvements with women. The threats occasionally intermingle, particularly when Honora threatens to sell Leander's floating Eden, the *Topaze,* unless he forces Moses out of the house. Leander is also blackmailed by his boss J. J. Whittier, who has gotten a poor girl, Clarissa, pregnant. Whitter forces Leander into marrying her (Clarissa is Leander's first wife; Sarah his second) and giving the baby away. Yet another blackmail attempt occurs years later when the same illegitimate child, now grown, returns to confront Leander, demanding money for her silence.

Another important theme that appears in part 2 is the beginning of Leander's evolving role of paternal counselor. Leander records his development as a mythical, wise guide for his sons, particularly in their certain confrontation with the great sorrows that life will continue to inflict on them. His response to the loss of Clarissa, who drowns herself after being forced to away give her baby, was: "Have no wish to dwell on certain matters, sorrows, etc. Bestiality of grief. Times in life when we can count only on brute will to live. Forget. Forget" (*WC,* 152). As Cheever states at the end of the chapter: "This was the first chapter of Leander's autobiography, or confession, a project that kept him occupied after the *Topaze* was put up the year his sons went away" (*WC,* 102).

But Leander's journal also takes on the characteristics of earlier literary examples of a father's advice. Benjamin Franklin's *Autobiography* instructs his son in the ways of the world, and Lord Chesterfield's *Letters to His Son* (1774) offers his son advice on how to behave like a gentleman. Leander is hopeful that once his sons come to an understanding of their father's life and his relationship to his father and mother, they will be better able to understand their own lives. In short, they will know they are experiencing a life, and they will recognize their childhood and understand it in a familial context. Mythologist Joseph Campbell calls this mythic experience "father atonement" and breaks the word down into its syllabic units of "at-one-ment": Leander sees how his life is a mirror of his father's life and an adumbration of his sons' lives. Moses and Coverly will see their lives as reflections and reenactments of their father's life and will experience a sense of "at-one-ment," or oneness, with their father. The journal becomes, then, the spiritual or mythic center of their lives, a permanent record of their involvement in what Leander calls "the continuousness of things." The efficacy of the journal also transcends time and place; it will "be there" long after the Wapshots have disappeared.

One of Cheever's earliest and most perceptive critics, Samuel Coale, sees Leander as one of Cheever's clearest examples of a "romantic" hero, insofar as he embodies "the lyric celebration of nature." Lest readers are swept away in the inhuman recurrence of natural cyclicity, Leander celebrates the natural world "in the poetic catalogues of his journals . . . St. Botolphs generates that state of mind wherein the past lingers on into the present as a reminder of the continuity of all things . . . It is at such moments, when both the past and natural beauty are evoked, that 'a searing vision of some golden age' blossoms in the mind, and man's lost innocence, his sense of awe and wonder, is regained."[5] Leander wishes Moses and Coverly to "grasp that the unobserved ceremoniousness of his life was a gesture or sacrament toward the excellence and continuousness of things" (WC, 53). Cheever, as much as Emerson or Whitman, views the natural world as sacred because it is "whole," the etymological root of "holy."

By the conclusion of part 3, Coverly, who left home with Moses, finds work in New York City and marries Betsey MacCaffery. Moses travels to Washington, D.C., has a disastrous affair with Beatrice, a musician's wife, and eventually finds gainful employment.

Part 3 is a fairly straightforward narrative that details the various adventures of both Moses and Coverly. Moses falls in love with the lovely Melissa, a ward of his eccentric Cousin Justina, whom he meets at Justina's anti-sexual estate, Clear Haven, a kind of Dickensian "Satis House" from *Great Expectations*, an Eden based on monastic principles. Moses is forced to reenact Arthurian love quests if he wishes to be with his beloved Melissa, and must climb naked over the dangerous roof of Clear Haven to visit her bedroom. Though Melissa temporarily becomes a man-hating, anti-sexual version of Cousin Justina (herself a more extreme mirror of Cousin Honora), once Moses manages to get her in the greenhouse of the estate, she returns to her old, sensual self. After they discover that the priceless art treasures housed at the estate are forgeries, like the unnatural lives lived there, Clear Haven mysteriously burns to the ground and Justina moves to Athens, Greece. Moses and Melissa reunite, more deeply in love than ever.

Coverly moves with his wife, Betsey, to Remsen Park, one of Cheever's most lifeless suburbs, where Betsey experiences a malady resembling Melissa's—losing interest in erotic activity—and leaves Coverly confused, depressed, and desperate. During her absence, Coverly becomes friendly with a fellow worker who is homosexual. Although Coverly does not engage in sex with this man, he begins to doubt his heterosexual orientation. Two factors help him through his sexual crisis: a brilliantly comic letter from Leander, confessing his own mixed feelings about other men when he was young, and Moses' wife, Melissa, who sparks deep feelings of heterosexual passion in Coverly. Finally, Betsey returns home, happily transformed into her old vivacious self.

Part 4 is the shortest section of the novel, running to barely eight pages. Moses and Coverly plan to return to St. Botolphs with their sons. Cousin Honora, true to her name, grants them their benefices, and the boys want to buy their father a new boat. Before they can do that, Leander decides to return to the sea in his own fashion. After having deeply disturbing, lewd dreams in which he sees himself transformed into a desperate and dirty old man, Leander goes to Christ Church and prays. He then swims out to sea, makes the sign of the cross, and disappears into the water. Eyewitnesses are not sure if Leander actually made the sign of the cross, and no one wants to admit that it was an act of self-destruction.

The concluding half of the fourth section of the novel presents Leander's funeral. Although Sarah expects sparse attendance, the church is packed. Coverly reads the text from Shakespeare that Leander insisted be read at his gravesite, Prospero's concluding speech from *The Tempest*. The final scene in the novel unambiguously identifies Leander, the drowned hero of Christopher Marlowe's poem, with Prospero, the reigning monarch of an enchanted island; and Leander's journal has made him the reigning spirit of the Wapshot family. Coverly, returning to St. Botolphs on the following Independence Day with Betsey and their son, William, discovers a note in his father's hand inside his grandfather Aaron's copy of Shakespeare. Entitled "Advice to my sons," it instructs them in how to live their lives courageously and with honor. It is the valedictory chapter to Leander's journal, his confession, his autobiography, and the spiritual legacy he has left his sons.

The Wapshot Scandal

Though there was only a seven-year gap between the publication of *The Wapshot Chronicle* in 1957 and the *The Wapshot Scandal* in 1964, differences in tone and attitude are dramatic. Though the characters remain basically the same, there is much greater emphasis on women in the second volume, and its tone oscillates between bitter satire and tragic despair. Scott Donaldson calls the presiding spirit of this bleak novel "demonic" and offers, as a controlling metaphor for the novel, an image from one of Cheever's uncollected stories called "Homage to Shakespeare," in which a grandfather detects "gleaming through the vanity of every incident . . . the phallus and the skull."[6]

The Wapshot Chronicle's celebratory sexuality of Leander-Dionysus benignly opposing the Puritan reserve of Honora becomes in *The Wapshot Scandal* classic Freudian conflicts between Eros and Thanatos. Suicides proliferate, and those who do not or cannot kill themselves are obsessed with thoughts of suicide. Honora drinks herself to death, and Moses, at the novel's conclusion, is a helpless alcoholic. Melissa is overwhelmed by episodes of desperate sexual depravity, seducing the nineteen-year-old Emile Cranmer, a grocery boy, and moving to Rome. Rev. Applegate, rector of Christ Church in St. Botolphs, becomes a dysfunctional alcoholic. There is little doubt that *The Wapshot Scandal* chronicles the complete fall of the family and measures its depleted energies. The drowned Adam-Prospero-Leander appears as a ghost in an early chapter and, though leaving his journal and a few instructions behind, his potentially redeeming figure cannot hold back the final collapse of the family. Honora, to the horror of Moses, Coverly, and the townspeople of St. Botolphs, has never paid *any* taxes to the Internal Revenue Service. Coverly and Moses are thus deprived of their promised legacies and enables Moses to justify his self-destructive drinking. The only character to escape reasonably unscathed is Coverly, who becomes the novel's principal figure, but even his survival is tenuous at best.

Though using biographical information in literary analysis is a dubious undertaking, a serious scholar of Cheever's work cannot avoid the overwhelming evidence in the journals of his increasing dependence on alcohol, particularly during the writing of *The Wapshot Scandal*. Cheever had been a heavy drinker from his early twenties on, but his drinking never seemed to seriously affect his work or relationships with friends or family. He did not try to hide it and humorously blamed himself for the inevitable hangovers. Numerous references to the agony and guilt over his increasing drinking appear in the journals with alarming frequency especially between 1961 and 1964, the years he was writing *The Wapshot Scandal*. Cheever also suffered from guilt over the periodic homosexual affairs he engaged in as a adult as well as over the relatively innocent homosexual experimentation of his adolescence. The combination of alcohol, particularly the guilt-induced hangovers, and the lure of dangerous homosexual meeting places—such as the men's room at Grand Central Station—combine into what he called the "erotic abyss" (*J*, 140). He also loses perspective and suspects his young son Ben of homosexual activity with an "effeminate friend," projecting his own youthful desires and memories onto his son: "Are they cobbling each other as I sometimes did, in a damp toolshed, while the irrecapturable beauty of the autumn afternoon begins to fade?" (*J,* 141). Fear, jealousy, depression, and anger over aging, coupled with his drinking and his guilt, occasionally produced massive despair.

Cheever's crisis with alcohol, however, seems to provide the clearest and most obvious reason for the radical change in tone between *The Wapshot Chronicle* and *The Wapshot Scandal.* The behaviors, attitudes, and problems he vividly recorded in his journals would come as little surprise to most alcoholics and those who lived with them, although they deeply disturbed many *New Yorker* readers when they appeared there in the early 1990s. The journals are devastatingly accurate documents of the agonizing destructiveness of alcoholic behavior that has plagued so many American writers. John Cheever was the first major American author not to die from the lethal effects of alcohol, which destroyed Ernest Hemingway, William Faulkner, F. Scott Fitzgerald, Thomas Wolfe, Sinclair Lewis, and many more. Indeed, most of the principal characters in *The Wapshot Scandal* either are practicing alcoholics, such as Moses, Honora, and Melissa, or, having lived with alcoholics, are engaging in pathological masochistic behaviors that make their lives and those around them a living hell. Cheever's many phobias, such as his terror of crossing bridges and his constant feeling of being on the verge of "the abyss," are typical alcoholic indicators.

While in attitude and tone *The Wapshot Scandal* is expressive of Cheever's alcoholism, the debilitating effects of his drinking are not perceptible in his stylistic control. His style is as magnificent and, in some ways, funnier. The satire is dark, but occasionally comic. Missing from this novel is the redemptive humor of Leander, whose journal grounded everything in the central, though crumbling, mythopoeic paradise of St. Botolphs. The novel opens with West Farm empty, except for the ghostly voice of Leander, which Coverly hears in the middle of the night. Cheever's narrator, a neighbor of the Wapshots, surveys the crowd at Christ Church's Christmas Eve ceremony in the manner of Thornton Wilder's *Our Town* or Edward Arlington Robinson's *Tilbury Town.* In fact, the spirit of Robinson, a fellow alcoholic, is present throughout *The Wapshot Scandal,* especially in the cosmic despair of Robinson's "The Man Against the Sky." George Garrett, one of Cheever's most perceptive critics, pinpoints precisely the major mythic differences between the two Wapshot novels: "Things disintegrate, decay, blur out of focus, fall apart. The relationship is much like that of *The Rainbow* and *Women in Love* or, closer to home, of *The Hamlet* to *The Town*. Which is to say the two books are Cheever's old testament, written of the time of myths, the law and the prophets, and his new testament, beginning now on Christmas Eve and ending, although on Christmas, with a curious last supper to be followed shortly by the last book of the Bible—the *Apocalypse*. The sins of *Chronicle* are original sin. *Scandal* moves inexorably toward the end of the world and an apocalyptic mood pervades the novel" (Garrett, 57–58). Garrett's most telling revelation of the difference between the two novels, however, is of the absence of the sensuous—the evidence and celebration of the five senses, a characteristic habit of his: "Cheever's writing has always been marked by its representative use of the five senses. But in *The Wapshot Chronicle* it is the smell, the odors of the world, the flesh and the devil, which predominate. There are great patches and lists of good odors, rich savors. *The Wapshot Scandal* is, by contrast, practically odorless" (58). The sensuous has been replaced by the sensual; that is, a sexual obsessiveness that enchains rather than liberates. Garrett's insight also applies to what happens to the senses of alcoholics, whose capacity to taste and smell is drastically reduced by the numbing effect of alcohol. For so sensuous a writer, whose literary reputation was built on his celebration of his characters' unrestricted capacity to feel life and his readers' grateful participation in those feelings, the absence of a sensuous apprehension of the world signals a massive darkening of Cheever's vision.

The predominant imagery of *The Wapshot Scandal* is that of the wasteland: the empty house at St. Botolphs, Proxmire Manor (*proximus* in Latin meaning "next to"; *mire* meaning "a deep, slimy bog," or "to entrap or entangle"), the suburb where Moses and Melissa move. And Talifer is a missile site that Coverly and Betsey are assigned to because of a computer error. The wasteland in this novel is mechanistic, the computer, "the mechanical encrusted on the human," as Henri Bergson expressed it. Talifer (a name derived from the Norman-French *talifert*, meaning "ferocious warrior") is a missile site supervised by Dr. Cameron, who possesses the one-dimensional, static sensitivity of a camera (a "copy" of life) and whose realm, six levels underground, is an obvious allusion to Dis, the capital of hell, which is in the sixth circle of Dante's *Inferno*.

Cheever had earlier established his suburban underworld as Shady Hill in the 1958 short-story collection *The Housebreaker of Shady Hill*. The Greek version of Hades, or the underworld, was not the Christian fire-

and-brimstone pit of eternal damnation and infinitely increasing suffering but a melancholy place of shadows and shades where the inhabitants wander about sadly. Only when Coverly surveys the Elysian Fields, the cow pasture upon which the missile site is built, and fails to connect it to the natural beauty of St. Botolphs, does he realize that he is in Hades wherever he is. He is as "mired" in Talifer as Moses and Melissa are in Proxmire Manor.

Talifer, under the control of Dr. Cameron, has become the realm of what Wallace Stevens called "logical lunatics." The missile site has become more than an example of what Leo Marx characterized as "the machine in the garden" in his metaphor of the encroaching mechanization of American society. In *The Wapshot Scandal,* the garden has been replaced by the machine, which has become a permanent atomic threat to the entire planet. Gertrude Lockhart, a pathetic neighbor of Moses and Melissa in Parthenia, a suburb of Proxmire Manor, and another midwestern innocent from Indiana, loses her battle with the forces of mechanization when her domestic machinery begins to break down in a series of disasters. The toilets back up and the septic tank freezes, and no one is available in Parthenia to fix them. She takes to drink and licentiousness when a young man in tight jeans comes to fix the septic tank and attend to her newly discovered libido.

After the oil burner breaks down and, again, no one can be found to fix it, she has a complete nervous breakdown. She realizes she is incapable of technically fixing anything; she is only a wife and a mother: "It was this feeling of obsolescence that pushed her into drunkenness and promiscuity."[7] After the oil burner breaks down again and she propositions the milkman in a drunken stupor, she hangs herself in the garage. There is some humor in Cheever's rendition of the plight of this helpless woman, but it is grisly. Gertrude Lockhart's surname shows the effect of technology and mechanization on the emotional life of normal suburban citizens.

The inability to adapt to modern living takes its toll on just about everybody in the novel. Betsey, wife of Coverly, invites a large group of Coverly's fellow employees at Talifer to a cocktail party and none show up; they are obsessed with security and fearful of being friendly. Betsey becomes more alienated and irritable, taking refuge in the safe world of television. One of the strangest events in the novel occurs after Coverly's deepening depression over the coldness of Talifer's inhabitants and Betsey's emotional withdrawal. He decides to take a walk over the farmland on which the missile site rests and encounters a strange figure, a man dressed in red, a hunter who has fired an arrow at Coverly that barely misses him (he had bent down to tie his shoe). The arrow sinks into a tree instead, and Coverly interprets the event as a call to action of some sort; he must "do something illustrious" to help humanity. He decides, then, to feed all of Keats's poetry into a computer to see which words appear most often and discovers a poem beneath the poem. Most important, the rhyme scheme emerges as "fall, all, grace, face, gall." And the subjects of each line are "grief, death, love, scar, heaven." These words certainly comprise not only the principal themes of *The Wapshot Scandal* but of Cheever's other works as well. Keats's poetry, fed into a computer, has replaced the vivid humor of Leander's journal. The transmission of the computer, what it found in Keats, is an unmistakable message of suffering and death. After some surrealistic assignments from Dr. Cameron, Coverly returns to St. Botolphs to witness Honora's slow death.

Moses takes to drink and Melissa has run away—like Honora had—also to Rome, with the grocery boy, Emile Cranmer. Melissa's response to the mechanistic emptiness of her life is to become the seductress, a fatal woman. George Hunt correctly characterizes her as Circe, wielding great sexual power over the willing Emile Cranmer.[8] The name Emile, a possible allusion to the idealistically educated young boy in Rousseau's educational treatise of the same name, ironically underscores the degraded position he ends up in—as a slave to his Oedipal impulses and as a "slave" at a male beauty pageant where Melissa "buys" him. And Cranmer, whose name is a reference to the famous Archbishop of Canterbury and translator of the Bible that was Cheever's favorite, counterpoints the Christian in conflict with the Greek, or the Apollonian in conflict with the Dionysian, one of the consistent tensions throughout Cheever's fiction.

One of the most ghastly, though still comic, scenes in *The Wapshot Scandal* is Melissa's final appearance in the novel as she wonders about the Supra-Marketto Americano in Rome with her hair dyed red. Cheever directly connects her to Ophelia, with tears wetting her cheeks. She is not gathering garlands of flowers and coronets but grocery items, such as Bab-o, Kleenex, salt and pepper, and other "necessities." The final triumph of the powers of mechanization, technology, and consumerism is to be seen in Melissa's transformation into a walking-talking advertisement: "She chants, like Ophelia, snatches of old tunes. 'Winstons taste *good* like a cigarette should. Mr. Clean, Mr. *Clean*,' and when her coronet or fantastic garland seems completed she pays her bill and carries her trophies away, no less dignified a figure of grief than any other" (*WS,* 298). Though Henri Bergson saw the "mechanical encrusted on the human" as a possible comic dilemma, Melissa's transformation into a machine seems ultimately tragic.

The darkest character to come out of *The Wapshot Scandal* is certainly the Dr. Strangelove character, Dr. Cameron, who, though a convert to Roman Catholicism, can enjoy sex only with his Roman mistress, a prostitute. Cameron changed his name from Bracciani, which, appropriately, means "embers or ashes" in Italian. And there is little doubt that Dr. Cameron/Bracciani is more than willing to reduce the planet earth to ashes and embers. In a stunning admission during a Senate investigation of Talifer, he casually states that he fully believes in the inevitability of nuclear warfare. And after estimating that there would be a substantial number of survivors, he answers the following question: "'In case of reverses, Dr. Cameron, would you be in favor of destroying the planet?' 'Yes,' he said. 'Yes, I would. If we cannot survive, then we are entitled to destroy the planet'" (*WS,* 216).

This statement directly follows an impassioned plea for international harmony made by an elderly senator. His short but trenchant speech summarizes the essence of Cheever's romantic beliefs and could have been taken from Emerson or Thoreau: "We possess Promethean powers but don't we lack the awe, the humility, that primitive man brought to the sacred fire? Isn't this a time for uncommon awe, supreme humility? . . . Oh, please, please don't destroy the earth" (*WS,* 215). Again, Cheever evokes the "center" as the basis of the sacred and, therefore, as justification for a sense of awe in the presence of the sublime. The weeping senator asks that a natural piety and humility replace planetary arrogance and possible annihilation. The prevailing tone of *The Wapshot Scandal* evokes a kind of nuclear winter before the dropping of any bomb, and Cheever's stance has changed into that of a disillusioned romantic.

Cheever offered another metaphor for his growing feelings of alienation and fear during the mid-1950s: "something went terribly wrong. The most useful image I have . . . is of a man in a quagmire, looking into a tear in the sky . . . Something has gone very wrong, and I do not have the language, the imagery, or the concepts to describe my apprehensions. I come back again to the quagmire and the torn sky" (Donaldson 1979, 181). The prevailing mood of the novel shares more than a little of the pessimism of E. A. Robinson's "The Man against the Sky" insofar as both works are deeply concerned with the role of chance and fate in human affairs. Though Robinson's vision is one of the bleakest in modern literature, Cheever's vision in *The Wapshot Scandal* is bleaker, precisely because humanity has created both its own quagmire and the tear in the sky. The "blind atomic pilgrimage" described in "The Man against the Sky" takes on an infinitely greater irony when brought into the "atomic age" in which small communities such as Talifer have been created with the express purpose of destroying the world.[9] Talifer's aggressive, phallic-shaped missiles threaten the younger generation of Wapshots and the world on a daily basis. It is no wonder that all of the sexual relationships, except that of Coverly and Betsey, are masochistic, if not self-destructive.

The novel ends as it began, on Christmas Eve at Christ Church, but Coverly recognizes none of the other five attendants. The station master, Mr. Jowett, has disappeared, as has the Greek-Roman humanistic tradition of his namesake, Benjamin Jowett, translator and preserver of Plato and other classical authors. Though Honora is dead, she left a bequest in her will to continue a charitable tradition of serving a dinner for the blind of St. Botolphs. The maid, Maggie, had set the table for twelve guests, a number evoking an image of the Last Supper, since it is precisely that. Coverly broods deeply after the Christmas dinner during a lightning storm that reflects the shift of light and dark that is Cheever's single most recurring image.

Coverly has obviously failed in his quest of *The Wapshot Chronicle* to connect the present to the past: "To create or build some kind of bridge between Leander's world and that world where he sought his fortune" (*WC*, 118). In *The Wapshot Scandal*, Coverly hears "a cavernous structure of sound, a sort of abyss in the stillness of the provincial night opens along the whole length of heaven and the wooden roof under which I stand amplifies the noise of rain." He knows he will never return to St. Botolphs because there will be nothing left "but the headstones to record what has happened; there will be really nothing at all" (*WS*, 309). The echoes of the abyss that conclude the novel make it Cheever's most obviously existential. It questions, among many things, the way meaning comes into the world and suggests that, without some kind of sacred center to ground and preserve it, the world will sink into a quagmire of nothingness.

Chapter Four

"Ovid in Ossining": *The Housebreaker of Shady Hill* and *Some People, Places, and Things That Will Not Appear in My Next Novel*

Though very different kinds of story collections, *The Housebreaker of Shady Hill* (1958) and *Some People, Places, and Things That Will Not Appear in My Next Novel* (1961) are two of Cheever's most accomplished. The fictional community of Shady Hill is the first mythopoeic Eden to unite a selection of short stories that share the same families: the Bentleys, the Farquarsons, the Lawtons, the Parminters, and so on. Most significant, though, *The Housebreaker of Shady Hill*, once and for all, identified John Cheever as "Ovid in Ossining"; that is, the writer who mythologized modern American suburban life. Scott Donaldson states definitively: "With the publication of *The Housebreaker of Shady Hill and Other Stories* in September 1958, he became known, overnight and always, as a chronicler of suburban life. It did not matter that he moved on to write about Italian expatriates and prison inmates—a great many people had pinned their butterfly to the wall and would not let him free. He was John Cheever, who wrote those funny-sad stories about the suburbs for the *New Yorker*" (Donaldson 1988, 170).

Donaldson also points out that some critics were not pleased with the idea of a writer making the suburbs the subject matter of his work. Again, many of these critics were New Yorkers, some out of the working-class social strata of the Lower East Side who found little or no means of identifying with the problems of relatively comfortable, college-educated (many on the G.I. bill) business executives. The unapologetic socialist critics' worst enemies were these WASPs whom Cheever wrote so passionately about. Even worse, he wrote about them with humor, compassion, and deep understanding while simultaneously avoiding any obvious ethical or moral judgment on their life-style. Cheever had changed his subject matter from the probing psychological studies of the inhabitants of Sutton Place to those members of the Upper East Side who found city life too demanding and decided to seek their regenerated paradise in the idyllic northern suburbs of Westchester County. And with Cheever, the most obvious explanation is always geographical; he and his family had moved to Scarborough in 1951 and then Ossining in 1961. *The Housebreaker of Shady Hill* was his fictive report after seven years in Eden.

The Housebreaker of Shady Hill and Other Stories

What the New York City critics also seemed to overlook in their abhorrence of the flight to the suburbs was the obvious deepening of Cheever's ability to develop his characters and to dramatize the agonizing dilemmas they experienced. Shady Hill is another name for Hades in Cheever's world. In Greek mythology, Hades was not a place of fire and brimstone where the souls of the damned suffered eternally, as in the Christian scheme. It was the underworld, the netherworld and abode of the shades of the dead, thought to be located in the western reaches of the Greek world. It was also a melancholy place. And, of course, it was under the rule of Hades in his role as keeper of the House of the Dead and dispenser of earthly riches. It is certainly no accident that Johnny Hake, the protagonist of the title story, bears some strong resemblances to the mythical Hades, after whom he seems to be named. But in this story, Hades is not the dispenser of earthly riches; Hake, ironically, is experiencing grave financial problems and is so desperate that he actually begins to rob some of his neighbors in the middle of the night.

The name Hake means "street peddler" or "trader"—a hunched figure who carries wares on his back and "hawks" them. And Johnny Hake does start his own company after he is fired from his old job. He works in the "shady" part of Shady Hill, both morally and nocturnally. Hake is obsessed with premonitions of death—admitting he has "experienced all kinds of foolish melancholy—and with "how sad everything is" (*SJC,* 257). He also acknowledges that after his first night raid on one of his closest friends, the Warburtons (the name's Old English root means "fortress"), "the moral bottom had dropped out of my world" (*SJC,* 260). He recalls first stealing from his drunken and cruel father, a Cronus-figure whom Johnny blames for turning him into a thief. Scapegoating his father, though, does not permit him to escape from the unmistakable feelings of guilt and the fact "that the act of theft took precedence over all the other sins in the Decalogue and was a sign of moral death" (*SJC,*

261). After Johnny Hakes's wife, ironically named Christina, summarizes their life together—"It's been hell" (*SJC,* 266)—he runs into Tom Maitland, a millionaire, at the country-club swimming pool. Seeing how vulnerable and helpless Maitland is, Hake decides to rob his house that night. Ironically, the name Maitland means "master of the land," and Hake-Hades is preparing for a night battle. It is during Johnny's unsuccessful robbery attempt that he has a semivisionary experience: "The door was open, and I went in, just as excited and frightened as I had been at the Warburtons and feeling insubstantial in the dim light—a ghost" (*SJC,* 267). Hades, whose prize possession was his helmet of invisibility, is alive but not very well in his modern Shady Hill.

Hake's adventures come to an unexpected conclusion as he is on his way to rob the Pewters, who were known as Shady Hill's most famous drunks. Another, much more compelling visionary experience ensues as he contemplates his "terrible destiny." He hears a "harsh stirring in all the trees and gardens, like a draft on a bed of fire, and I wondered what it was until I felt the rain on my hands and face, and then I began to laugh" (*SJC,* 268). It was the smell of rain "flying up my nose" that became the transforming agent of his newly discovered freedom and release from the nightmarish guilt of his desperate thefts: "I was not trapped" (*SJC,* 268). And in one of Cheever's greatest romantic revelations—right out of Whitman and Wordsworth—he proclaims: "And it was no skin off my elbow how I had been given the gifts of life so long as I possessed them, and I possessed them then—the tie between the wet grass roots and the hair that grew out of my body, the thrill of my mortality that I had known on summer nights, loving the children, and looking down the front of Christina's dress" (*SJC,* 268).

He then returns the $900 he had stolen from the Warburtons, gets his job back, and reenters life a redeemed Hades, "whistling merrily in the dark." Hades-Pluto also means "the rich one," and Johnny Hake has obviously learned the preciousness of life and love during his dangerous night journeys through the darker side of Shady Hill. Hake also understands that he has a choice and is free. Cheever's brilliant use of irony, particularly his ability to turn mythic elements upside down, and his reversal of those ironies into a "happy" ending, demonstrate, again, that he was developing and enriching not only his skills but his spiritual vision as one of modern American literature's most romantic writers. Hake's epiphany takes place only when he perceives momentarily that he is joined to nature and "naturally" baptized by the rain. His response transforms a potential tragedy into redemptive comedy and functions, as all comedy does, by moving the protagonist from a condition of isolation back into the community. Order has been restored to Shady Hill.

Though "The Housebreaker of Shady Hill" portrays the fall and redemption of one misguided soul in Cheever's mythopoeic "paradise," "The Sorrows of Gin" treats only the fall from innocence of a ten-year-old girl named, ironically, Amy. Her name means "love," something she rarely receives, except from some of the servants who work in her home. Mr. Lawton, her alcoholic father, habitually responds to her by giving her orders and creating rules and regulations—laws—which she must obey. The name Lawton also means "burial mound or hill," an apt description of the emotional condition of the household. The meaning of the name also makes even more ironic Mr. Lawton's concluding sentence in the story: "How could he teach her that home sweet home was the best place of all?" Nowhere does Cheever trace with such insight and depth the dynamics of the fall into knowledge and the devastating effects it has on a child as he does in this brilliant and critically neglected story. Nor has Cheever ever captured so subtly the ambiguous cruelties of alcoholic behavior and manipulation. There is no lonelier little girl in all of Cheever's work, nor are his other victims' seemingly Edenic worlds as steeped in the deleterious effects drinking has on both the privileged class and its servants.

The alcoholic father is undoubtedly a victim of his alcoholic servants; the Lawtons fire five cooks during the year in which the story takes place. The last cook they hire, Rosemary, becomes Amy's only confidante. She is Amy's wise guide, helping her understand the tragic consequences of alcoholism for families. Rosemary tells Amy about how drink destroyed the life of her beloved sister, who was once "a lovely person, with a peaches-and-cream complexion and fair hair" (*SJC*, 199). Through Rosemary, Cheever defines and specifies the insidious ways in which alcoholic addiction ruins lives. Rosemary explains that drinking makes some people "gay—it makes them laugh and cry—but with my sister it only made her sullen and withdrawn . . . Drinking made her contrary" (*SJC*, 199). Rosemary then goes into a long and convincing description of why servants take to drink—to cheer themselves up and give themselves more energy and so on. Rosemary finds consolation only in her Bible and promises to read parts of it to Amy, who welcomes the attention and Rosemary's obvious affection. Rosemary also suggests, after noting the drinking habits of Amy's family and friends, that Amy might "empty [her father's] gin bottle into the sink now and then—the filthy stuff!" (*SJC*, 201).

Disaster strikes, however, when Rosemary appears at the Shady Hill train station so drunk that she has to be sent back home. Amy takes the next opportunity to dump her father's gin down the sink; she has intervened courageously. Amy has also learned two important but painful lessons: she can trust no one, even the sweetly religious Rosemary. But she is able to detach the lesson from the teacher and continues to pour her father's gin down the sink because she feels empowered to restore order into the chaos of her father's house.

This story shows Cheever's ability to delineate clearly the psychologically complex strands of familial relationships and the misery of alcoholic households. Amy's newfound maturity and sense of responsibility is instantaneously transformed into a nightmare of guilt when the new cook, Ruby, is unjustly fired by her father because he assumes she has been stealing his gin. At this juncture, Amy sees that her task is much more complicated than she had suspected. Cheever then proceeds to entertain, through Amy's still innocent consciousness, various notions of what constitutes the condition of intoxication and its lure. She muses over the degree of her parents' drinking behavior, that "she has never seen them hanging on to a lamppost and singing and reeling, but she has seen them fall down" (*SJC*, 205). She also relates their condition to her own experiments with self-induced "drunken" imitations when she twirls herself around so quickly that she falls down and finds "herself not unhappy at having lost for a second her ability to see the world" (*SJC*, 205).

Continuing her ruminations over drunken states, she tries to understand her parents' and their friends' obvious ontological denial when her father walked into a wall and "collapsed onto the floor and broke most of the glasses he was carrying . . . and most of them pretended that he had not fallen down at all . . . Amy had once seen Mrs. Farquarson miss the chair she was about to sit in, by a foot, and thump down onto the floor, but nobody laughed then, and they pretended that Mrs. Farquarson hadn't fallen down at all" (*SJC*, 205). Amy finds an analogy in her experience in school drama, observing that her parents and their drinking friends "seemed like actors in a play." If someone knocked something over accidentally on stage, they were to unobtrusively pick it up as if it had never happened and not destroy the illusion of order. Amy's next trauma will move her from her intelligent musings over the relationship between "pretending" and "denial" into what she finally discovers to be the chaos and madness of her father's household.

The climactic scene takes place when her father unjustly accuses the baby-sitter, Mrs. Henlein, a long-time native of Shady Hill (the name

Henlein actually means "old line") of stealing his gin. What ensues is a traumatically embarrassing scene as Mrs. Henlein loses control and begins to scream at Mr. Lawton, demanding that he take back his accusation and, along the way, bitterly suggesting that it was drunken outsiders like the Lawtons who corrupted the pristine garden of her youth. She threatens to call the police. The scene brings home to Amy with brutal force her own complicity in the ensuing melee. At that moment—and few writers have so lucidly articulated such a devastating epiphany—Amy "perceived vaguely the pitiful corruption of the adult world, how crude and frail it was, like a piece of worn burlap" (*SJC*, 208). But then she fears that the police (who are not called) will find her fingerprints on the gin bottle, and her heroic act will have caused nothing less than "the collapse, in the middle of the night, of her father's house. It was all her fault . . . she felt sunk in guilt . . . She would have to go away" (*SJC*, 208).

Amy loses her innocence and will feel responsible for years for the traumatic dismissal of the innocent Mrs. Henlein. She actually goes to the train station and buys a one-way ticket to New York, but Mr. Flanagan, the station master, calls Mr. Lawton, who intends to bring her back home. The story ends as Mr. Lawton is contemplating through the station window his daughter's figure on the bench. It is one of the most mystical scenes in all of Cheever's work, because its densely entangled mixture of past sights, smells, and songs flows through Lawton's memory so forcefully that he practically reexperiences them. He meditates on the power of Amy's figure to move him and relates it to the longing he felt one night when, "driving home late and alone, a shower of leaves on the wind crossed the beam of his highlights, liberating him for a second at the most from the literal symbols of his life—the buttonless shirts . . . the order blanks, and the empty glasses" (*SJC*, 209). The effect of these nostalgic memories is so compelling that it creates the distinct possibility that the closed-minded, narcissistic Mr. Lawton might actually learn something about himself and the hellish life his daughter is living.

What does evolve, as is so often the case with narcissistic alcoholics, are sentimental reminiscences of his lost youth that collapse into self-pitying victimization. He, not Amy, becomes the victim of all those lonely nights on the road and, with time, he muses, she just might discover what a wonderful home she lives in. Cheever brilliantly demonstrates the hopelessness of Amy's situation with Mr. Lawton's egomaniacal question in the last line of the story: "How could he teach her that home sweet home was the best place of all?" (*SJC*, 209). Mr. Lawton comes close to seeing himself for what he really is, but his arrogance (in its deadliest form of "you think *you've* suffered!") ultimately blinds him to the desperate condition of his household. With the possible exception of F. Scott Fitzgerald, no modern American writer registers a more penetrating analysis of alcoholic behavior on drinkers and their victims than Cheever does in this story. Along with Joyce Carol Oates's "Blue Skies," it is one of the most perceptive treatments of addictive denial in modern American fiction.

The stories in *The Housebreaker of Shady Hill* are some of the longest Cheever wrote, and certainly "The Country Husband" is the longest and best known in the collection. Some critics suggest it is his greatest story. None other than Vladimir Nabokov called it "a miniature novel beautifully traced" (Donaldson 1988, 141); it won the prestigious O. Henry Award for 1956. Rarely has Cheever packed so much diversity into one story: elements of myth; literary, artistic, and geographical allusions; and the old Puritan battleground between the flesh and the spirit, Dionysus versus Apollo.

Francis Weed, the country husband—that is, the ruler of his pastoral paradise of Shady Hill—is portrayed at the beginning of the story as a returning hero after an almost fatal airplane crash, but no one in his household is the least bit interested in hearing his tale of heroic escape. Francis is presented early in the story as an Apollonian character, unemotional, neither reflective nor ruminative: "Wood smoke, lilac, and other such perfumes did not stir him, and his memory was something like his appendix—a vestigial repository" (*SJC,* 330). He is not particularly conscious of being conscious, and one of the major transformations of the story is his metamorphosis into a highly conscious, Dionysian seducer, precisely because of his memory. In short, he undergoes the birth of love. The circumstances that activate his transformation and the way Cheever arranges them make this story one of his greatest creative achievements.

Again, Cheever's use of names is vital in defining his characters; here he uses most of the important names ironically. Francis Weed's first name means several things. It means "France," the memory of which is crucial in awakening Francis to love's possibilities, and it is also the place where he wishes to take his beloved Ann Murchison, the teenaged babysitter with whom he falls madly in love. Francis also means "free, open, candid, straightforward"—all the qualities that Francis lacks and that love eventually imbues him with. In fact, love so transforms him that "Francis los[es] his head" when he first comforts Ann after she begins weeping and telling him about her abusive, alcoholic father. The experience also opens his heart and frees him of his Puritanical moral restrictions. He becomes vulnerable and, therefore, human.

What critics seem to have overlooked is the significance of the incident that occurs at a cocktail party shortly before he meets Ann. Francis recognizes the maid serving drinks and realizes he had seen her in a French village just after World War II, when he was in the army. She had been charged with collaborating with the Germans and, as a punishment, had been forced to strip naked and then been beaten before a crowd. His vivid recollection of this terrible event affects Francis profoundly: "The jeering ended gradually, put down by the recognition of [the crowd's] common humanity. One woman spat on her, but some inviolable grandeur in her nakedness lasted through the ordeal." She was "the woman who had been punished at the crossroads" (*SJC,* 331). Because of the emotional impact of his memory, Francis begins to see the emptiness of the suburban Shady Hill crowd, all of whom behave as if there had never been a war, an attitude that secures them in their false Eden. The maid, Francis Weed's secret sharer, becomes an agent, not of corruption but of his recognition of the horror of the world that life in Shady Hill does not permit him to experience. Her figure awakens him to their common humanity—their suffering.

Cheever's delineation of the spiritual effect of the maid is masterful: "but the encounter left Francis feeling languid; it had opened his memory and his senses, and left them dilated" (*SJC,* 300). It is in this open, free, emotionally vulnerable condition that he meets Ann Murchison. Expecting to see his usual baby-sitter, Mrs. Henlein (the same character from "The Sorrows of Gin"), and seeing Ann instead, he says: "You're new." Ann is literally "new" because he has never seen anything like her. She was "beauty and perfection . . . and he experienced in his consciousness that moment when music breaks glass, and felt a pang of recognition as strange, deep, and wonderful as anything in his life" (*SJC,* 331).

Francis Weed is also becoming his surname, because he is now growing like a "weed," attached to nature and its life-generating processes. Cheever is a romantic, and just as Johnny Hake was liberated from his suffocating solipsistic life by redemptive rain, so Francis Weed's open sensibilities signal his attachment to the natural juices of passion. The story registers his range of choices now that he has entered what Kierkegaard called the "dizziness of freedom." His banal life in Shady Hill has been transformed into a bower of bliss; and his dreams are filled with images of recrossing the Atlantic in his old troop ship, the *Mauritania,* and "living with [Ann] in Paris." Francis has also discovered the romance of France embedded and hidden in his name. As he takes the train into the city the next morning, he sees things he has never noticed before because love has awakened him to "the miraculous physicalness of everything" (*SJC*, 333).

As he is watching, as if for the first time, the express train from Buffalo to Albany, he has a vision, an accidental voyeuristic glimpse into one of the sleeping cars passing quickly by: "Then he saw an extraordinary thing; at one of the bedroom windows sat an unclothed woman of exceptional beauty, combing her golden hair. She passed like an apparition through Shady Hill, combing and combing her hair, and Francis followed her with his eyes until she was out of sight" (*SJC*, 334). Counterpointing this vision and his meeting with the goddess Ann the night before, he encounters the goddess as crone in the significantly named Mrs. Wrightson, the social dictator of Shady Hill, a feminine Hades, and promptly insults her. The minute he realizes that his rudeness has had the desired effect, that he has violated the stasis of suburbia, his imagination begins to work in a consciously mythical manner. The previous image of the naked woman on the train becomes attached to the romance of ancient Greece: "A wonderful feeling enveloped him, as if light were being shaken about him, and he thought again of Venus combing and combing her hair as she drifted through the Bronx" (*SJC*, 334); he becomes aware of the awakened life that Ann had activated: "He was grateful to the girl for this bracing sensation of dependence . . . and the world that was spread out around him was plainly a paradise" (*SJC*, 334). The allusion to Titian's famous painting of Venus combing her hair is unmistakable, as is the direct reference to Venus and Eros in the following paragraph.

At this point in the narrative, however, the mythic allusions begin to foreshadow difficulties that may be in the offing. Francis notices, for the first time, that on the letterhead of his firm "there was a drawing of the Laocoon and the figure of the priest and his sons in the coils of the snake appeared to him to have the deepest meaning." And after buying Ann a bracelet, he experiences a strange premonition: "On Fifth Avenue, passing Atlas with his shoulders bent under the weight of the world, Francis thought of the strenuousness of containing his physicalness within the patterns he had chosen" (*SJC*, 335). He is confronting the "erotic abyss" that troubled some of Cheever's earlier frustrated males, and he remembers that the snakes constraining Laocoon were Apollo's punishment for Laocoon's marrying and having children, as he had been expressly forbidden to do. Atlas, too, was punished for defying Zeus and was condemned to support, on his back, the western part of the world. Francis sees clearly his dilemma in a moral and mythic continuum, that his unfulfilling marriage and his plan to abduct the innocent Ann could have the severest consequences within the moral constraints of Shady Hill. His "left impulses" ("left" symbolizing the sinister, the dark, and the mysterious) are now prompting his erotic desires; he had earlier confronted the opposing power of the "right"—the law-and-order world of Mrs. Wrightson at the train station. That image shows him polarized between promises of Venus and the Apollonian restrictions of Mrs. Wrightson.

Francis begins to face the terrible dilemma that his erotic desires have put him in. While he may view his love-maddened condition and erotic pursuit as a perfectly natural expression of his real feelings, his wife, Julia, would see it as a vulgar indulgence of impulse, and the law calls it "statutory rape." As he, for the first time, actually begins to write Ann a love letter, and Julia calls him to a family photographing session, he physically feels the stress: "the abyss between his fantasy and the practical world opened so wide that he felt it affected the muscles of his heart" (*SJC*, 337). More significant, "The Country Husband" is beginning to move from a slightly comic moral and social parable into the much more serious precincts of appearance and reality: what is reality and what makes it real and how does one know it is real? Cheever's story moves into phenomenological questions that finally send Francis to a psychiatrist.

One of the threshold guardians that Francis encounters in his pursuit of Ann is Clayton Thomas, who Francis accidentally discovers is Ann Murchison's fiancé, but only after he and Clayton have had a serious philosophical discussion. Though Clayton is graceless and homely, intellectually priggish, and morally pedantic, he delivers a stingingly accurate assessment of the vulgarity and shallowness of Shady Hill: "I thought a lot about it, and what seems to me to be really wrong with Shady Hill is that it doesn't have any future. So much energy is spent in perpetuating the place—in keeping out undesirables, and so forth—that the only idea of the future anyone has is just more and more commuting trains and more parties. I don't think that's healthy . . . I think people ought to be able to dream great dreams" (*SJC*, 338). Cheever, though putting those words in the mouth of one of his least attractive characters, has rarely been so forthright and open about suburbia's odious shortcomings.

After Clayton's quasi-sermon, he confesses that he wants to enter divinity school, disapproving of the drinking habits of Shady Hill after what he observed the previous Saturday night: "Mr. Granner trying to put Mrs. Minot into the trophy case. They were both drunk" (*SJC,* 338). Clayton defines his "religion" as "Unitarian, Theosophist, Transcendentalist, Humanist," and corrects Julia's attempt to connect Clayton with Emerson as a transcendentalist; Clayton snobbishly aligns himself with the English: "I mean the English transcendentalists . . . All the American transcendentalists were goops" (*SJC,* 339). He then continues to make matters worse when he reveals the depth of his Manichean moral stance by declaring that he is engaged "in writing a very long play about good and evil" at about the same time that T. S. Eliot was writing similar moralistic verse plays on English saints in English settings. In fact, Clayton's expressed desire to make "a retreat at one of the Episcopalian monasteries" has the distinct echo of Eliot's post-conversion life with Anglican monks and rectors in and around London. Clayton's desire to work for a publisher brings him even closer to the Eliot prototype since Eliot spent most of his life working for one of England's most prestigious publishers, Faber and Faber.

Francis Weed's jealousy immediately takes the form of a deep and unbending vengeance toward the bleak Clayton, as he begins his campaign to discredit him at every opportunity calling him "lazy, irresponsible, affected and smelly" (*SJC,* 339). Immediately following Francis's mean-spirited condemnation of Clayton, Julia confronts Francis with his offensive behavior toward Mrs. Wrightson. There can be little doubt that Clayton Thomas is symbolically the "son of the right," as embodied in the banal, moralistic tyrant Mrs. Wrightson, who, Julia claims, rules the social life of Shady Hill. And in that function, she is the threshold guardian who determines who enters the inner circle of Eden: "Mrs. Wrightson's the one who decides who goes to the assemblies" declares Julia to her unbelieving husband who asks: "You mean she can keep Helen [their daughter] from going to the dances?" (*SJC,* 340).

Julia proceeds to morally tongue-lash Francis for his self-indulgent behavior, spitting her words into his face, as she defends the caste system of Shady Hill. Francis, outraged that she would deny his right to express his true feelings, acts out: "He struck her full in the face" (*SJC,* 340). Julia then threatens to leave Francis, and the scene that ensues interweaves the comic with the serious, particularly in the way Julia psychoanalyzes his leaving his dirty clothes all over the place as a subconscious expression of hatred toward her. In the course of their extended argument, Francis reveals for the first time exactly what has been missing in their lives in Shady Hill: "Julia, I do love you, and I would like to be as

we were—sweet and bawdy and dark—but now there are so many people" (*SJC*, 341). These are the exact qualities that Ann embodies, which
abrogate the life-denying ordinances of Mrs. Wrightson's domain.

After the couple argues over who is more dependent on the other,
Julia decides she can't leave Francis because he would be lost without
her. With the opening of the doors of erotic perception, the Apollonian
Francis has begun to explore the ecstatic chaos and orgiastic possibilities
his new Dionysian consciousness has activated within him. Along with
his renewed passion for life and for the young and innocent Ann, Francis
had developed an acute consciousness of what he is morally capable of.
In short, he understands evil more fully and realizes he has choices.
Talking from his office over the phone to a friend, he deliberately lies
about Clayton Thomas, calling him worthless, undependable, and a
thief; he is fully conscious that he is committing a serious sin. Francis
consciously observes his moral fall and feels deep guilt as his secretary
walks out of the office, "leaving him to face alone the wickedness of what
he had done to the Thomas boy" (*SJC*, 343). His awareness of having
committed an evil act (he has been about as bad as he could be) causes a
major epiphany: "He was in trouble. He had been lost once in his life,
coming back from a trout stream in the north woods, and he had now
the same bleak realization that no amount of cheerfulness or hopefulness
or valor or perseverance could help him find, in the gathering dark, the
path that he had lost. He smelled the forest. The feeling of bleakness
was intolerable, and he saw clearly that he had reached the point where
he would have to make a choice" (*SJC*, 344). This epiphany resonates
with the opening of Dante's *Inferno*, in the dark wood where Dante
admits he is lost. And the minute Francis admits that he is lost, so lost
that he can smell the forest, the possibilities for freedom and choice open
up, much in the way alcoholics and drug addicts take the first step in
their recovery in admitting that they are "powerless" over their enslaving
addiction.

Many of the critics who ignore the importance of Francis's memory of
the French collaborator also overlook the importance of the terrifying
experience Francis has prior to lying about Clayton. As Francis rides to
work in the morning, he believes he sees Ann board the commuter train
and pursues her through a number of cars. It turns out not to be Ann
but another, older woman, wearing glasses. This experience so discon-
certs Francis that he becomes aware that he may be losing touch with
reality, a fear that blossoms into a full-fledged existential crisis. He
begins to question the very terms of reality "for if he couldn't tell one

person from another, what evidence was there that his life with Julia and the children has as much reality as his dreams of inequity in Paris or the litter, the grass smell, and the cave-shaped trees in Lovers' Lane" (*SJC*, 343). It is in this scene that John Cheever seriously confronts both epistemological and phenomenological dilemmas: what constitutes reality? whose reality is it? how does one know what is real? Only after fully experiencing the terror of the existential abyss and the horrible possibility that life could be "full of sound and fury signifying nothing," Francis consciously discovers that what he does, his actions, determine the boundaries of his reality and that he, and only he, is responsible, morally, for his actions. But it is only in his descent into the erotic abyss, that inferno, that he finds freedom. Concomitantly, he realizes that he is free to make choices among several options: he could go to a psychiatrist; he could go to church and confess his lusts; he could go to a Danish massage parlor; he could rape the girl or trust that he would be prevented from this; or he could get drunk.

The country husband's decision is to seek help from Dr. Herzog, his secretary's psychiatrist and a doctor who surfaces elsewhere in Cheever's work. *Herz* means "heart" and *zog* means "pull or tug," and it is Francis's heart-tugs, now fully acknowledged, that have caused his midlife crisis. The story concludes as a closed circle in which the cast of characters remains the same, only now Francis is working hard at his newfound hobby, or occupational therapy, woodworking. He is building a coffee table because Dr. Herzog has recommended woodwork as a specific therapy. Most significant, though, "Francis finds some true consolation in the simple arithmetic involved and in the holy smell of new wood" (*SJC*, 345). Once again, nature has saved a Cheever character from losing himself in the dark, Dantean woods and humorously presents him using wood as a means of grounding himself in "a" reality called Shady Hill. Cheever uses the phrase "the holy smell of new wood" to underscore the redemptive powers that nature possesses in its capacity to heal fragmented lives; that is, to make them whole. And "whole" and "holy" share the identical etymological roots.

Having found his place within the sullied Eden of Shady Hill, Francis Weed can grow and participate in his neighborhood's nightly operatic coda, consisting of Mr. Goslin's melancholic rendition of Beethoven's Moonlight Sonata, Mr. Nixon's Shakespearean declamations at the squirrels in his bird feeder, and the Babcocks' naked pastoral gambol in their semisecluded terrace, a perfect example of the kind of domesticated, but private, romantic activity that is acceptable in Shady Hill.

Concluding the regenerated Edenic scene is the local king of the jungle, the dog Jupiter, "who prances through the tomato vines, holding in his generous mouth the remains of an evening slipper" (*SJC,* 346). Only the unselfconscious animals are allowed to behave "naturally" because they do not "know" any better, a condition that Francis was willing to explore. What Francis and the rest of hyper-self-conscious humanity are left with is contained in the brilliant last sentence: "Then it is dark; it is a night where kings in golden suits ride elephants over the mountains" (*SJC,* 346).

Francis either realizes or will soon realize, as he creates his coffee table, that human beings can do anything they wish in the infinite realm of their own imaginations. During his existential crisis on the commuter train, he dimly understood that there is no demarcation between reality and one's imagination of reality, and the concluding sentence in the story documents the authenticity of that observation. And it is more than coincidental that Leander Wapshot (and John Cheever himself) instruct-ed his son Coverly to read Prospero's speech from *The Tempest* at his funeral: "We are such stuff that dreams are made on, and our little life is rounded with a sleep."

Another frequently anthologized story that treats some of the same themes of frustration and anxiety over aging and the inability to under-stand why life seems to be passing one by is "O Youth and Beauty!" (This story, as well as "The Sorrows of Gin," was successfully adapted for PBS in 1979, the former by A. R. Gurney, the latter by Wendy Wasserstein.) Again, Cheever opens the scene in Shady Hill at the end of a long Saturday night party in which the protagonist, Cash Bentley, is being chided by one of his friends, Trace Bearden, an old friend of Francis Weed, for his aging body and his thinning hair. The destructive-ness of time is the enemy in this story, as it was in "The Country Husband." Cheever is at his best criticizing the shallowness of a secular-ized society whose commercialism creates the kind of world that must pay homage to eternal youth and beauty. Disturbing echoes of Clayton Thomas's critique of the meaningless cyclicity of the lives of the inhabi-tants of Shady Hill resonate in the reader's memory. Clayton asserted that Shady Hill had no future because its primary purpose was simply to perpetuate itself. What he perceived was the existential emptiness of a paradise manqué, an emptiness of stark recurrence and senseless repeti-tion. It is this emptiness beneath the surface of his life that drives Cash Bentley to heavy drinking and desperate acts.

Trace Bearden cruelly reminds Cash that he is growing older, thus pressuring him to prove to both himself and his community that he is still the youthful track star, that his aging is an illusion. Louise Bentley, his wife, is practicing her own brand of denial as she excises from the pages of, ironically, *Life* magazine, any and all "scenes of mayhem, disaster, and violent death that she felt might corrupt her children" (*SJC*, 218). Each time Cash begins to feel the pressure of time, usually after a number of drinks, he rearranges the furniture in whatever house he's in, especially his own, and hurdles his way through the living and dining rooms to the applause of his fellow inebriates, who willingly share with him the illusion of timelessness and eternal youth. It is this recurring ritual that Cash needs to make himself feel young again.

One particularly drunken evening, the old track star breaks his leg at a party thrown by the Farquarsons to celebrate the Bentleys' seventeenth wedding anniversary. Cash lands in the hospital for two weeks and returns home depressed and confused over what has happened to him. His senses, especially his sense of smell, begin to pick up odors that reek of death and putrefaction, such as the spoiled meat in the refrigerator. His perceptions are riveted to morbid scenes of decay and loss, such as the sight of "an old whore standing in a doorway" on a sidestreet in Manhattan: "She was so sluttish and ugly that she looked like a cartoon of Death, but before he could appraise her . . . his lips swelled, his breathing quickened, and he experienced all the other symptoms of erotic excitement" (*SJC*, 214). He, like Keats in "Ode to a Nightingale," is more than "half in love with easeful death."

These and other obvious forebodings of death begin to accumulate as the story moves toward its inevitable conclusion, and though Cash is unable to articulate the nature of his ennui over the meaningless circle that his life moves within, the young people's party at the home of the Rogers, his next-door neighbors, plunges him into agonizing despair. The sounds of teenage voices, their laughter, and their seemingly casual existence remind Cash of everything he has lost: "There is nothing on their mind but the passing summer nights. Taxes and the elastic in underpants—all the unbeautiful facts of life that threaten to crush the breath out of Cash—have not touched a single figure in this garden. Then jealousy seizes him—such savage and bitter jealousy that he feels ill" (*SJC*, 216). Few modern writers have so vividly expressed the envy the aging feel toward the young and the beautiful as Cheever. Such open regard for these sensitive issues may remind readers familiar with classical literature of the equally devastating poems of Horace and Catullus on the same "Ubi Sunt?" (where have all those happy times gone?) theme.

What follows Cash's wave of nausea, an American version of Roquentin's darker but similar vision in Sartre's novel, is one of American literature's great meditations on mutability and the destructive effects of time: "He does not understand what separates him from these children in the garden next door. He has been a young man. He has been a hero. He has been adored and happy and full of animal spirits, and now he stands in a dark kitchen, deprived of his athletic powers, his impetuousness, his good looks—of everything that means anything to him. He feels as if the figures in the next yard are the specters from some party in the past where all his tastes and desires lie, and from which he had been cruelly removed. He feels like a ghost in the summer evening. He is sick with longing" (*SJC*, 216). T. S. Eliot's line "After such knowledge, what forgiveness?" comes to mind because Cash has nowhere spiritually to go.

While some may view Cash's confession of his body's failure to support his mind's illusion of youth as self-pitying narcissism—and a case could be made for such an interpretation—Cheever's delineation of Cash's essential emptiness points to only one cause: the materialistic, narcissistic American dream that proposes suburbia as its Edenic reward of eternal youth. The myth that Cash, so aptly named, unconsciously invested in was that he would somehow never grow old if he worked hard enough and fulfilled the requirements of WASP rugged individualism. In the Puritan-based Babbittry that embodies the unconscious subtext of the American dream, material success becomes a "sign" of divine approval and eventual salvation. Cash—who is facing the gradual loss of youth and is also struggling with financial failure—thus feels deeply guilty; somehow *he* must be responsible for his present condition.

Few stories so ingeniously probe the unconscious dynamics of self-destruction as "O Youth and Beauty"; self-destruction is the actual theme of the story, but it is the self-destruction that the illusive American dream exacts. Even after breaking his leg, Cash drunkenly insists on replaying his track star role and, though he does not break anything, the effort almost kills him. Cheever's parody of Michelangelo's "Pieta" in the penultimate scene of the story, detected by James O'Hara,[1] foreshadows Cash's inevitable demise: "His clothes were soaked with sweat and he gasped for breath. [His wife] knelt down beside him and took his head in her lap and stroked his thin hair" (*SJC*, 217).

In one of the great hangover scenes in Cheever's work ("Oh, those suburban Sunday nights, those Sunday-night blues!" [*SJC*, 217]), while

Louise is upstairs cutting out potentially corrupting scenes from *Life* magazine, Cash determines to accomplish two tasks: to test the illusion once more and prove to himself that he is still the youthful track star and, concurrently and unconsciously, to kill himself because his spiritual poverty offers him no other alternative. He has been betrayed by the American dream as embodied in Shady Hill. He calls Louise down to fire the "starting pistol"—an ironically named instrument within the context of this story. She has never fired a weapon and knows nothing about gun safety and, as he hurls himself over the sofa, "She shot him dead." By concluding the story suddenly, without analysis or explanation, Cheever leaves the reader troubled, so much so that one might be tempted to question the "accidental" nature of Cash's death. On the unconscious level nothing is accidental, and Louise's shallowness precludes any serious contact with her unconscious.

Cheever offers two typical American middle-aged protagonists, Cash Bentley and Francis Weed, for comparison. One, in essence, commits suicide; the other seeks psychological help, which enables him to live a relatively well-adjusted life, a life that millions of other American suburbanites share and understand. Cash lacks inner spiritual resources even though he attends Christ Church, an affiliation that seems to have little influence on his desperate plight. The key differences between their dilemmas is that Francis becomes consciously aware that life consists of choices that he is free to make. The disturbing memory activated by seeing the French collaborator at the cocktail party and his "happy fall" into the chaos of love-lust awakened him to a freedom of which he had been previously unaware. Cash Bentley, the "timeless" track-star hero, had never seen the world as anything other than his personal paradise, had never been tempted to pursue an adulterous affair with a teenaged girl or blatantly rebelled against the powers-that-be by insulting Mrs. Wrightson-Hades, had never been forced to understand the plight of a Nazi collaborator. Only by losing his innocence, by "falling" in love and in "sin" (his evil treatment of Clayton), does Francis discover the possibilities of redemption. And his strange empathy for the collaborator opened him up to the depths of human depravity and the possibilities of survival. Cash Bentley never loses his lethal innocence because he never grows up and becomes an adult. Indeed, the imperative to grow up and become consciously aware that he is no longer a boy is precisely what kills him.

In a sense, it is the limited linear conception of life that Cash Bentley is constitutionally incapable of envisioning that drives him to his unconsciously arranged death games. Francis Weed learns that life consists, rather, of cycles within which people are free to make choices. In short, Francis is willing to entertain the cyclic possibilities inherent in the American romantic dream as Emerson, Whitman, and Thoreau expressed them, an open-ended proposition that permits him to consciously live within the complementary contraries of the imagination, rather than the divisive polarities of a closed, linear, Calvinist either/or existence. Cash Bentley has no way of breaking into the potentially redemptive capacities of nature, and his name symbolizes that entrapment. And since his affiliation with Christ's Church is purely cosmetic, he is also left without a potentially redeeming spiritual resource. On the other hand, Francis (as in the *one* Christian saint, St. Francis of Assisi, with the ability to speak to the animals and work within nature) Weed (the commonest object in nature) is encoded from the beginning with the potential to grow into the "natural" possibilities of his name.

"The Five-Forty-Eight" is Cheever's most brilliant treatment of the theme of manipulation and victimization. The icy and detached Mr. Blake has absolutely no "natural" feeling for others, especially for pathetic, wounded souls such as Miss Dent, a name that symbolizes her damaged emotional condition. As a business executive in Manhattan, he hires a nearly unemployable Miss Dent to work in his office. She performs well and expresses her gratitude by giving him little gifts. Finally, she gives herself to him because she is lonely and feels genuine affection for Mr. Blake, who has given her work and sexual attention. He, on the other hand, uses her solely to satisfy his libidinous desires; Cheever's description of the post-love-making scene reveals the soul of a heartless machine: "When he put his clothes on again, an hour or so later, she was weeping. He felt too contented and warm and sleepy to worry much about her tears . . . The next day, he did what he felt was the only sensible thing. When she went out for lunch, he called personnel and asked them to fire her" (*SJC,* 239). She came to the office a few days later, but Blake instructed his secretary not to let her in.

As the story opens, Miss Dent is again trying to see Mr. Blake. She eventually catches up with him as he boards the "Five-Forty-Eight" on his way home to Shady Hill; she sits next to him and calmly presses a gun to his ribs. Though Mr. Blake knows that Miss Dent could easily kill him, he is so socially conscious that he cannot call out for help. And of the many Shady Hill neighbors he spots on the train, he is not close enough to any of them to feel they would be willing to come to his aid. The narrative concludes as Miss Dent takes him behind the facade of the train station of Shady Hill and forces him, under the threat of death, to grovel in the dirt before her. She apparently feels that she has had her revenge.

Though the story is about cruelty and revenge, it is essentially a character study of Mr. Blake as a soulless automaton, one of Cheever's most revolting sociopaths, with the possible exception of Dr. Cameron of *The Wapshot Scandal*. The ironic use of the name Blake adds to the story's "heart-versus-head" theme. William Blake, the great transitional poet between the Age of Reason and the Age of Romanticism in English poetry, could not be further from the bloodless rationalist in this story. And, in fact, the gift that Miss Dent brings to Mr. Blake is a rose, which he drops into a waste basket because "Mr. Blake doesn't like roses" (*SJC*, 238). Certainly one of William Blake's most famous and enigmatic poems is "The Sick Rose," an apt symbol of the corrupting powers of rationalism embodied in the dark satanic mills of British industrialism that destroyed the poor, the vulnerable, and the disenfranchised of nineteenth-century England. Of course, Miss Dent possesses all of the same qualities.

What makes Cheever's Blake so despicable is that he responds most emotionally to women who are vulnerable and easily victimized. His reasons for choosing Miss Dent were: "Her diffidence, the feeling of deprivation in her point of view, promised to protect him from any consequences. Most of the many women he had known had been picked for their lack of self-esteem" (*SJC*, 238). Cheever's Mr. Blake becomes, then, a demonic version of the visionary English poet whose primary purpose was to release people from the dehumanizing forces of mechanization. Cheever's Blake devises his own marriage of heaven and hell by transforming Miss Dent's heaven into her worst hell, while his heaven consists of brutalizing the many women in his life and making their lives a living hell. One of the ways he punishes his pathetic wife, Louise, when she doesn't have his dinner waiting for him, is to circle a date two weeks hence on the calendar when he will resume speaking to her. And though Louise weeps and protests his sadistic threat, he keeps his promise. His circling of the date and his pitiless refusal to deal with her on a human level subtly alludes to those creatures at the bottom of Dante's frozen ninth circle of the *Inferno* who are punished for the premeditated, rationalistic atrocities they committed against their defenseless victims.

Another Blakean allusion that ironically juxtaposes Mr. Blake to the poet Blake is the letter Miss Dent makes him read, which contains one of William Blake's recurring themes: "they say that human love leads us

to divine love, but is this true?" (*SJC*, 244). And one of the first statements Miss Dent makes to Mr. Blake on the train is to quote the *Book of
Job:* "'Where shall wisdom be found' it says. 'Where is the place of
understanding?'" (*SJC*, 243). Those familiar with William Blake will
recall that *The Book of Job* and Dante's *Divine Comedy* were seminal influences on his imagination, both as a poet and as an engraver. His illustra-
tions for both masterpieces attest to the deep regard he held for them.
Cheever's modern parable of heartless manipulation and the withholding
of love resonates with biblical, Dantean, and Blakean themes showing
that his stories are more than simply social criticisms of the American
cultural wasteland. Indeed, these venerable allusions reintroduce within
a demythologized context questions that have become the central existential concerns of the twentieth century: what are wisdom and understanding, human and divine love? Raymond Carver was so moved by
this story that he wrote a sequel to it, called "The Train," and dedicated
it to John Cheever.

Some People, Places, and Things That Will Not Appear in My Next Novel

Cheever's next collection of short stories, *Some People, Places, and Things
That Will Not Appear in My Next Novel,* differs markedly in tone and
organization from *The Housebreaker of Shady Hill.* Some of these stories
were written during the time Cheever was working on *The Wapshot
Scandal* and, as a result, share a dark, cynical tone. The general feeling
throughout the collection is one of discontent and disillusion. Malcolm
Cowley summarized the overall spirit of the book in a 1961 letter:
"What is becoming evident in your work is a sort of apocalyptic poetry,
as if you were carrying well-observed suburban life into some new
dimension where everything is a little cockeyed and on the point of
being exploded into a mushroom cloud" (Donaldson 1988, 193).

The principal distinction between the two collections is that *Some
People* is not a collection of stories connected by a common place like
Shady Hill and, therefore, is not an obvious mythopoeic cosmos. Though
some characters seem to come out of *The Wapshot Chronicle*—Moses in
"The Death of Justina"—a number of the stories take place in Italy;
namely, "Boy in Rome," "The Duchess," and "The Golden Age," while
"Brimmer" chronicles the seeming demise of a satyr on his way to Italy.
Cheever also begins to actively comment on the course of his literary
career, a postmodernist practice that he usually condemned in other

writers. The story "A Miscellany of Characters That Will Not Appear" shows him cleaning his literary house of exhausted character types and hackneyed, stereotypical Cheeveresque conventions. Many of these items surfaced in some of his later stories in spite of his promise to excise them.

There is little question that "The Death of Justina" is the gem of this dark collection because of its morbid humor, which borders, at times, on the lugubrious. Its satire has a scathing edge. Thematically, it extends the dehumanizing effects of mechanization that "The Five-Forty-Eight" so bitterly recorded but rehearses that theme with a carefully crafted sardonic wit. The story opens as Moses, the narrator, meditates on the nature and purpose of his art—he is a writer. But his concern is with the function of fiction and its ability to anchor meaning, since life's movement seems to centrifugally throw the artist farther and farther away from a central memory and, therefore, from the source of his creativity. His imagination appears to be the only power amid the chaos of modern life that grounds him in a meaningful context: "Fiction is art and art is the triumph over chaos (no less) and we can accomplish this only by the most vigilant exercise of choice, but in a world that changes more swiftly than we can perceive there is always the danger that our powers of selection will be mistaken and that the vision we serve will come to nothing" (*SJC,* 429). Like Wallace Stevens, Cheever is becoming a connoisseur of chaos in this story and wants to test the boundaries of reality within Proxmire Manor to see if they can be used as some sort of temporary stay against the yawning existential void.

The reaction of the community to the death of Justina becomes a metaphor for modern society's inability to deal with the reality of death. Her death also becomes the backdrop against which the narrator measures his own impending sense of morality. His wife's old cousin, Justina, dies suddenly at his home and his wife calls him at work to inform him of her death; the narrator's boss insists that he finish a commercial that a colleague of his could not. The advertisement addresses a variety of middle-age complaints. The obvious parody of the mythic "Elixir of Life," or the Holy Grail, gives Cheever an opportunity to satirize the Judeo-Christian myth of eternal life as it emerges in its decadently desacralized form on Madison Avenue. Without belief in a spiritual afterlife, the mythic search for the Grail collapses into a commercialized quest to convince consumers (formerly known as communicants) that such products supply eternal youth and happiness. The narrator's intention is to obliterate the false promises of Elixircol and to expose them for what they are—blatant denials of the terms of reality: "Are you growing old? . . . Does your face in the morning seem rucked and seamed with alcoholic and sexual excesses? . . . Have you drafted your will? Are you easily winded? . . . If this or any of this is true you need Elixircol, the true juice of youth" (*SJC*, 431–32).

Once the narrator officially exposes the illusions of a desperate society based on the myth of eternal youth, he returns to his Edenic suburb of Proxmire Manor to attempt to bury poor Justina. He immediately confronts the local powers of denial as encoded in the absurd city ordinances and as they are enforced by the dispassionate bureaucrats who can function only on a literal level. Since Justina had died in Zone B—the zone in which Moses lives—she cannot be buried there, since former zoning provisions prohibit not only funeral homes but also cemeteries and, by extension, deaths. Once Cheever mines as much humor as he can from the Faulknerian formula, he forces the Mayor's hand and succeeds in burying Justina.

The most effective part of this odd story is the penultimate scene in which Moses describes a dream he had. The dream is one of Cheever's most dramatic surrealist constructions, in which he brings together images out of the Book of Revelation, Dante's *Inferno,* and the visionary paintings of Flemish artist Hieronymus Bosch. The setting is a modern supermarket in which thousands of shoppers—"penitential and unsexed"—are pushing their carts. The shoppers are of every nation and race, but the items they purchase are a step beyond the generic: "Nothing was labeled. Nothing was identified or known. The cans and boxes were all bare" (*SJC*, 436). In spite of the utter abstraction in which they are involved, these lost souls deliberate painfully over which items to purchase. Once they approach the checkout counters, their purchases are viciously ripped open, an experience that overwhelms them with guilt. They are then kicked beyond the door into "dark water," after which Moses hears "a terrible noise of moaning and crying in the air" (*SJC*, 436). Cheever transforms the typical American supermarket into the apocalyptic Valley of Jehoshaphat and the Valley of the Shadow of Death from both the Old and New Testaments and Bunyan's *Pilgrim's Progress* in a terrifying vision of the inevitable apocalypse that a cannibalistic consumerism demands. After having his next Elixircol commercial rejected because it moved from American myths of eternal youth to dire forebodings of atomic fallout and the complete collapse of Western civilization, Moses simply copies, from memory, the words of the Twenty-third Psalm, beginning with the line: "The Lord is my shepherd . . ."

The causes that transformed Cheever's short fiction from its earlier lyrical celebrations of natural piety are exactly the same ones that produced the marked contrasts between the two Wapshot novels. As his journals clearly show, Cheever had begun drinking so much that it sullied everything in his life; anger, self-pity, and despair are clearly detectable in "The Death of Justina." The discernible entrance of surrealist dream visions bordering on the D.T.'s becomes a part of his fiction and culminates in his next novel, *Bullet Park.* More and more spoof, parody, and burlesque surface after "The Death of Justina." The artist-narrator, Moses—who at one point suffers from hallucinations after a radical attempt to give up drinking—concludes the story by falling back on the Twenty-third Psalm because there seems to be no other text available to release him from the alcoholic nightmare that his life has become.

Drinking and alcohol are the subject of another cleverly constructed and witty story called "The Scarlet Moving Van." Though there are no surrealist dream-visions or apocalyptic supermarkets, this story documents one of Cheever's most penetrating analyses of the harmful effects of alcoholic behavior. It also explores the desperate love that alcoholics can have for one another. The story opens as the Folkstones, Charlie and Martha, watch their new neighbors, Peaches and Gee-Gee, move into the house next door. The Folkstones are what their name implies, they are "the folks" and represent the solid, established social structure—the ground—the foundation of this unspecified place known as B___ .

One of the major characters in the story is Gee-Gee, which means "Greek god." Gee-Gee's wife explains that ever since he was in college, he was the golden-boy athlete—"an All-American twice . . . Everybody loved him. Now it's all gone" (*SJC,* 361). What continues to ruin Gee-Gee's life is his alcoholism. He is perfectly fine until he takes the first drink. Then he loses complete control and ends up taking off most of his clothes, breaking furniture and dishes, and saying unforgivable and insulting things to his guests or hosts. Such a scene immediately takes place at the Folkstones', but Charlie and Martha are understanding and blame his antics on exhaustion from moving. Though the story is ostensibly about the ruinous effects of pathological alcoholism on a former All-American, it is also about the dark influence that Gee-Gee has on Charlie, which exacerbates his drinking problems. As the story progresses, Cheever focuses on the changes that Charlie undergoes as he confronts, tries to help, and finally gives up on Gee-Gee and his chaotic life-style, a struggle that culminates in Charlie's descent into one of the ugly housing developments on the plains below. Charlie, in short, becomes Gee-Gee, and ends up losing his job and using the identical scarlet moving van to find other possible places to settle temporarily as he and Martha begin their own wanderings.

Mythic elements abound in "The Scarlet Moving Van," and Cheever invites readers to notice and interpret them. Most of the stories in *Some People,* now that Cheever has uprooted his characters from their comfortable suburban Shady Hills, concern characters in motion, moving away from stable centers of any kind. It's clear that Moses of "The Death of Justina" will soon lose his job and may be forced to move his family; three stories take place in Italy, and one takes place as characters move between America and Italy. All of these characters, dislocated or displaced, search for a satisfactory life that cannot be realized within the precincts of the American dream. Gee-Gee, the former Greek god, and his family are moving into their ninth home in that many years and, knowing Cheever's penchant for Dantean allusion, it seems fairly obvious that B___ will shortly become their own personalized ninth circle of the *Inferno.* It is also obvious that Gee-Gee is a combination of Dionysus, Pan, and Dionysus's favorite companion, Silenus, who was never sober and who wreaked havoc wherever he appeared. And some would view both Silenus and Gee-Gee as Dionysus gone to fat, an older, ruined version of the great god.

Silenus was also the tutor of Dionysus and many others, and in this story serves as a kind of Falstaffian corruptor of the "innocent" Charlie Folkstone. It is also quite clear that Gee-Gee, in spite of Charlie's heroic offer to help him give up drinking by giving it up himself, wins Charlie over to his side; that is, Charlie is metamorphosed into Gee-Gee in a subtle Ovidian warp. Gee-Gee/Silenus is certainly a modern-day satyr, and at the climax of the story, in which Charlie begs Gee-Gee to stop drinking, Gee-Gee makes a chilling, final statement that suggests he is somehow conscious of his mythic role of Silenus-as-tutor to the entire community. One of the incremental repetitions that accompanies Gee-Gee's drunken declarations is: "I have to teach them . . . They've got to learn" (*SJC,* 360). Gee-Gee also feels divinely guided throughout his ruinous alcoholic excesses as he repeats, almost as a mantra: "I have my guardian angel . . . I have my angel" (*SJC,* 365). Most significant, though, is the stunning revelation that Gee-Gee makes to Charlie after Charlie's heroic offer to stop drinking with him:

"Will you go on the wagon if I go on the wagon?"
"No."
"Will you go to a psychiatrist if I go with you?"
"Why? I know myself. I only have to play it out" (*SJC*, 363).

Gee-Gee admits, then, that he is aware of the destructive nature of his addiction and its predetermined consequences, an admission that so stuns Charlie that he identifies with him and sees Gee-Gee's role as a clairvoyant. He envisions Gee-Gee as a kind of drunken John the Baptist initiating Charlie into the dark mysteries that compel Gee-Gee into his self-lacerating, ecstatic celebrations. Few stories have better revealed the masochistic love that one alcoholic has for his fellow alcoholic than "The Scarlet Moving Van," and the almost sexual intimacy that suddenly evolves: "There seemed to be some tremendous validity to the drunken man. Folkstone felt an upheaval in his spirit. He felt he understood the drunken man's message; he had always sensed it. It was at the bottom of their friendship . . . He only meant for them to be prepared for the blow when the blow fell. But was it not possible to accept this truth without having him dance a jig in your living room? He spoke from some vision of the suffering in life, but was it necessary to suffer oneself in order to accept his message? It seemed so" (*SJC*, 363).

Once Charlie is able to elevate Gee-Gee's drunken chaotic life to the level of visionary experience, he has sealed his own doom and has, in essence, become Gee-Gee's initiate. For Charlie, Gee-Gee becomes a Dionysian victim of his own hyperconscious sensibilities, a wounded hero of consciousness whom no one but another suffering addict can ever understand. Both Gee-Gee and Charlie yearn to regenerate their lost youth; and Charlie finds deep poignance in remembering Martha's plea to Gee-Gee to "'Come back! Come back!' She was also calling back the youth that Charlie had never known" (*SJC*, 367). The only condition sadder than watching Gee-Gee destroy himself over his lost youth is Charlie destroying himself over a youth he never experienced. Once Charlie views himself through the Greek tragedy of Gee-Gee's fall into ruin, he himself has nowhere to go but down the same destructive path.

The motif of traveling satyrs continues in another dark story from *Some People* called "Brimmer." The narrator begins the story with a detailed discussion of satyrs and their ubiquitous presence in the Mediterranean. He notes that in ancient classical mythology, they far outnumber gods and heroes. The highly moralistic narrator, actually a priggish bore, is con-

vinced that a fellow traveler on board their ship to Naples *is* a satyr—that
they are still around but that only the initiated, like himself, can recognize them: "His eyes had a pale horizontal pupil like a goat's eye.
Laughing eyes, you might have said, although they were sometimes very
glassy . . . but the grapes could be accounted for by the fact that he
almost always had a glass in his hand. Many of the satyrs stand on one leg
with the other crossed over in front—toe down, heel up—and that's the
way he stood at the bar, his legs crossed, his head up in that look of permanent glee, and the grapes, so to speak, in his right hand" (*SJC,* 387).
And, of course, Mr. Brimmer, the satyr, is speaking to a woman named
Mme. Troyan, and even though her first name is never revealed, it may as
well be Helen because Brimmer keeps carrying her off repeatedly during
their southern journey. The righteous narrator actually feels threatened by
the open sexual coupling that goes on between Brimmer—a satyr "brim-
ming" with sexual energy—and three women on board the ship. Besides
Mme. Troyan, there is an older, dark, hard-looking South American
woman with "the eyes of a viper" and a guttural voice. Sometimes known
as the "Roman businesswoman," the Mediterranean "sorceress" is accompanied by her secretary, "a hard-faced blond woman." All three women
end up having passionate and open affairs with Brimmer. The narrator is
alternately disturbed, threatened, and disgusted by the "carnal anarchy"
that has taken over the liner. He finds refuge with a southern Christian
family and an Episcopal clergyman. But the narrator is more than merely
priggish; he is a modern version of early America's most serious religious
zealot, Jonathan Edwards, when he employs the identical metaphor that
Edwards used in his most famous sermon, "Sinners in the Hands of an
Angry God," an image of a sinner dangling over the fires of hell. After
hearing of Brimmer's terminal illness and presuming he is dead, the narrator is able to identify, at last, with a now nonthreatening Brimmer: "I
remembered the finesse of his hands, the light voice, and the cast in his
eye that made the pupil seem like a goat's; but I wondered why he had
failed, and by my lights he had failed horribly. Which one of us is not sus-
pended by a thread above carnal anarchy, and what is that thread but the
light of day?" (*SJC,* 394).

Carnal anarchy became hell for the narrator and revealed his true attitudes toward sexuality. He is revolted by the blatant sexual activity
going on in Brimmer's cabin, which is next to his, activities that threat-
en the moral structure of his world, particularly if Brimmer is not eventually punished. When he hears of Brimmer's illness and probable death,
he openly admits: "What I remember feeling was gladness" (*SJC,* 393).

The Mediterranean sexuality that keeps him awake at night goes against everything he believes about life's purpose: "It has been my experience, my observation, that the kind of personality that emerges from this kind of promiscuity embodies an especial degree of human failure. I say observation and experience because I would not want to accept the tenets of any other authority—any preconception that would diminish the feeling of life as a perilous moral adventure . . . Yet if we relax our vigilance for a moment we pay an exorbitant price" (*SJC,* 391).

The Puritanical narrator openly admits in a strange military metaphor that his knowledge of the orgiastic behavior in Brimmer's adjoining cabin has caused a serious fall into knowledge and possibly sin: "But the sounds next door served as a kind of trip wire; I seem to stumble and fall on my face, skinning and bruising myself here and there and scattering my emotional and intellectual possessions. There was no point in pretending that I had not fallen, for when we are stretched out in the dirt we must pick ourselves up and brush off our clothes" (*SJC,* 389). Cheever suggests that the narrator may have "fallen" into sin—had impure thoughts or masturbated—as a result of the orgy next door. In the 1950s, however, a writer could only delicately allude to such activities.

Much to the Calvinist narrator's surprise, while deep-sea diving with his son near Porto San Stefano, he discovers on the floor of the Mediterranean a photograph of Brimmer on the back pages of an Italian scandal sheet. The photograph depicts Brimmer marrying an Italian movie actress, looking happy and healthy as he assumes the stance of his "true" identity: "He has his left arm around her slender waist, his right foot crossed in front of his left and in his right hand the full glass. He looks no better and no worse, and I don't know if he has sold his lights and vitals to the devil or only discovered himself" (*SJC,* 395). Like most American romantic writers, Cheever uses the sea as a place of visionary experience, even for the Calvinist narrator.

The narrator forgets his gloomy guilt in the sea, and all of his grim, Christian schemes of an angry God punishing sinners for their carnal anarchy disappear in the blazing Italian sun. Cheever's parable juxtaposes the ecstatic Dionysians Pan and Silenus against the abstract, Judeo-Christian's brooding God, where the body is the primary obstacle to divine union.

Cheever became quite familiar with the Italian landscape and its relaxed way of life during the year (1956–57) he spent there with his wife and children. Of the three stories in *Some People* actually set in Italy—"The Duchess," "The Golden Age," and "Boy in Rome"—the first two offer comical contrasts of the historical reason for the "southern journey" (the trip to Italy, begun in Chaucer's time, in which the English were to absorb the ameliorating effects of classical Renaissance culture) with the modern motivation for such a trip.

In "The Duchess," Donna Carla Malvolio-Pommodori (the last name meaning "evil-intentioned" or "bad tomatoes"), an incredibly wealthy duchess, resists the ameliorating effects of her Italian heritage. She is pursued by many European suitors but, because she is half English, finally marries the family's English bookkeeper, Cecil Smith. Her mother, Winifred-Mae Bolton, had been exiled to Italy and had resisted the charms of Italian culture. She did not learn the language and had little use for Italian cuisine, preferring the old British standby, fish and chips. She pursued her gardening, using as a model English railroad station gardens, and spelled out her husband's name "in pansies" (*SJC,* 349). The humor in the story, really an extended sketch, comes from the idiosyncratic antics of quirky British stereotypes who find their English traditions much more comforting than all of Italian culture. Donna Carla and Cecil Smith have two children and name them Cecil and Jocelyn rather than Giovanni and Lucia. Donna defers to her mother and finds a more satisfying spiritual and cultural center in her less refined Anglo-Saxon roots, choosing to regenerate an English paradise in the middle of an Italian one. And to the Italians around them, they become what their name literally means, "bad tomatoes."

"The Golden Age" is another variation on basically the same theme of "The Duchess," except the American visitors, a Mr. Seton and his family, have come to Italy—that is, have undertaken their southern journey—for very different reasons. As a television writer of an immensely popular serial called "The Best Family," Seton wants to get away and soak up ancient Mediterranean culture on the western coast of Italy. He feels devoid of "culture" and needs revivifying contact with the origins of Western civilization. As an American workaholic, he savors the possibilities of the title of the story, the Golden Age and the ancient treasures that contact with it promises. Seton loves diving into the sea and bringing up shards of ancient Greek vases, objects intimating Keats's famous "Grecian Urn," Western culture's permanent symbol of ancient art. Seton also feels intense guilt because of the deference with which his Italian hosts treat him because he has told them he is a poet—"Il poeta." He feels he is a fraud and dreads the moment when they discover that he is a mere television scriptwriter for a popular weekly serial, which will be shown later that night.

Seton hopes his contact with the origins of Western culture might somehow turn him into a "real" writer, the way Goethe's years traveling through Italy, recorded in *The Italian Journey* (1816), helped him modify his German Romantic temperament into a more balanced, classical one. Byron, Keats, and Shelley and many other English poets made their obligatory Italian journey hoping for the same outcome as Seton. As the story progresses, Seton notices a Roman family behaving in frantically "American" ways and finds that he must reluctantly revise many of his preconceived notions about the vivifying culture he thought he could absorb in this quaint seaside village. The place has become Americanized. The village "hero," Mario, who dives into the sea to kill the dreaded shark, strikes Seton as all wrong when he tries to envision Mario as a medieval knight protecting the vulnerable villagers; once they see there is no shark, nobody pays any attention to Mario, who in real life is a stonemason.

What Seton learns is that he and his fellow Americans, who ostensibly travel to Italy to immerse themselves in the reviving waters of the Renaissance, have become, in reality, the agents of corruption by bringing their crass materialistic consumerism to this ancient culture. Until the last scene, Seton feels deep guilt about his unwitting role as a corruptor in this seemingly innocent paradise. He expects to be rejected and embarrassed when the villagers discover that he is not a "real" poet, only a mere television writer. But the final scene depicts a village delegation, led by the mayor and the doctor, coming to honor him and to let him know how moved they were by his American television show: "It was so beautiful, so comical, so true to life!" And as the mayor embraces him, he delivers the ironic punchline of the story: "'Oh, we thought, signore,' he said, 'that you were merely a poet'" (*SJC,* 403). The mythic invasion pattern occurs when the barbarians sweep out of the east and across the western "civilized" lands destroying their Edenic peace. But Cheever reverses that pattern and has the American western barbarians corrupting Italian innocence and vulgarizing their high culture. The Golden Age is an enduring myth, and Seton presumably discovers that such a label lost any real meaning long, long ago.

The third Italian story in *Some People* is the most accomplished of the three. "Boy in Rome" again reverses the expectations and presents an American teenager, Peter, wanting desperately to return home to the island of Nantucket, off the Massachusetts coast, the site of his most fondly remembered vacations. Even though Peter's mother inherited a fortune from Peter's dead father and is part of a thriving but bored com-

munity of American expatriates, Peter seems dislocated and lost in a for-
eign culture. He and his mother have remained in Italy because his
father is buried in the Protestant Cemetery. Cheever embeds a clever bit
of Roman Catholic humor beneath the narrative when Peter plays hooky
from the Franciscan St. Anthony of Padua School and his "homeroom"
teacher, Father Antonini, comes searching for him. Ironies multiply
because St. Anthony of Padua is the patron saint of "lost" objects and a
diminutive version of him—Antonini meaning "little Anthony"—is
engaged in trying to find the "lost" Peter and bring him back home. The
Franciscans were mendicant friars who prided themselves on *not* having
a home base and lived on the road. Cheever's use of proper names underscores the story's theme of dislocation and isolation. Of course, the name
Peter, patron saint of Rome and founder of the Roman Catholic Church
(and whose name means "rock"), takes precedence over the later and less
exalted St. Anthony: Father Antonini fails to find Peter. And to carry the
ecclesiastical humor even further, Peter, "the rock," wants to escape the
very stasis that his name embodies.

What makes this particular story stand out among his many expatriate stories is the way Cheever delineates the increasing poignance of
Peter's sense of dislocation and not belonging. As Robert Morace points
out in his essay "From Parallels to Paradise," Peter's situation parallels
the plight of other emotional foundlings, such as the lost girl, Gertrude
Flannery, in "The Country Husband," and Francis Weed's "situation as
'weed' in his suburban Garden of Eden. Similarly, the John Barth-like
intrusion near the end of 'Boy in Rome' is entirely appropriate to
Cheever's purpose in that both the homesick boy in Rome and the
author-narrator in Ossining are exiles yearning for that elusive America
of the soul where they hope to find relief from their 'incurable loneliness.'"[2] But Cheever makes even more heartfelt Peter's loneliness by
using what Morace calls "incremental repetition" of several lines interwoven throughout the story: "I thought it was my father come again
from the kingdom of the dead" and "I was never going to get all the
loving I needed, no, never." Peter tries unsuccessfully to get a young
lady named Eva to fall in love with him, ironically becoming the male
tempter and not the victim of the mythic Eve's fatal wiles. He also
becomes involved in an art-smuggling scheme that falls apart, arranged
by his mother's closest friend, the permanently bored and exhausted
fop, Tibi.

The conclusion is one of Cheever's most dramatic epiphanies brilliantly showing the painful clash of the old culture with the new. Peter wants

to go, if he can't return to Nantucket, "to a place where I would be understood"; but he is haunted by the compelling memory of an old woman in Naples "shouting across the water, 'Blessed are you, blessed are you, you will see America, you will see the New World,' and I knew that large cars and frozen foods and hot water were not what she meant" (*SJC*, 466). Peter comes to understand that what the old woman was really talking about was an escape from all the old, useless greed, the institutionalized bribery and dishonesty, the fear of war and hunger and cold. He adds, showing real maturity and deep insight into what people need to endure: "and if all she imagined was not true, it was a noble idea and that was the main thing" (*SJC*, 466). The story concludes with Peter's first feelings of connection with other victims of dislocation, as he realizes that there are conditions worse than having to live in a place where one doesn't feel completely at home.

Chapter Five

Into the Abyss of Self:
The Brigadier and the Golf Widow

The early 1960s were highly productive years for John Cheever, in spite of increasingly heavy drinking and alienation from his family, especially his wife. Though she came close on several occasions to divorcing him, she threw herself into her own writing projects and her increasingly successful teaching career. In 1960 Cheever won another Guggenheim fellowship, which enabled him to work on *The Wapshot Scandal* and to continue to publish some of his finest short stories. These stories appeared in *Some People, Places, and Things That Will Not Appear in My Next Novel* in 1961 and *The Brigadier and the Golf Widow* in October 1964. The family's move to a large, comfortable old house in an exclusive section of Ossining gave Cheever a deeper sense of familial security; he assumed the role of lord of the manor with a deep sense of satisfaction.

It was also in the early 1960s that Cheever began to attain his first genuine fame and wealth. His picture appeared on the cover of *Time* magazine on 17 March 1964, and the author of the lengthy essay, Alwyn Lee, called him "Ovid in Ossining." That title encapsulates probably better than any other designation Cheever's major attitude toward his subject matter and identifies his use of myth as the major structuring principle of his fiction. His specific use of Ovidian themes of transformation and metamorphosis becomes increasingly obvious from *The Brigadier and the Golf Widow* till the end of his career, particularly in two of his most frequently anthologized stories, "The Swimmer" and "The Music Teacher."

Accompanying the kind of fame that being on a *Time* cover brings was a check for $75,000 for the film rights to the Wapshot novels, which Alan J. Pakula and Robert Mulligan had acquired, and the beginning of a love affair with the youthful Hope Lange that lasted for many years. There was serious talk of Spencer Tracy playing the role of Leander and Katharine Hepburn as Honora with the young, relatively unknown Robert Redford to be cast as Moses Wapshot (Donaldson 1988, 208–9). The film was never made. The Cheevers also became close friends with

John Updike and his wife, Mary, during a cultural exchange trip to Russia in 1964. *The Wapshot Scandal* won the prestigious William Dean Howells Medal of the American Academy of Arts and Letters in 1965, and in 1968 Frank and Eleanor Perry filmed "The Swimmer," starring Burt Lancaster. William Peden, a leading American critic of the short-story genre, declared *The Brigadier and the Golf Widow* John Cheever's best volume of short stories.[1] Lynne Waldeland notes that this collection, along with *The Housebreaker of Shady Hill* contains "the greatest number of frequently anthologized stories, including 'The Swimmer,' 'The Angel of the Bridge,' 'Clementina,' and 'The Music Teacher.'" Waldeland also sees transformation and metamorphosis as the unifying themes of the volume and divides the collection up into the "suburban stories, expatriate stories, and vacation stories, with the suburban stories dominating the book."[2]

The title story of the collection is one of Cheever's most sophisticated satires on suburban life, especially its Edenic satisfactions. But in its obsession with the bombscares of the 1950s, it could be more accurately called an eschatological parable; that is, the entire focus of the story, its tone and theme, deals with the end of the world, the last judgment, and heaven and hell. This story takes a step beyond Cheever's frequent theme of apocalypse because the premise of the Pasterns, the protagonists, is that the apocalypse is not only unavoidable but imminent; and they are convinced that it will be a nuclear holocaust. As a result, they have built at considerable expense ($32,000) a well-stocked bombshelter. Cheever has, in short, transformed the Garden of Eden into versions of Hades, hell, the grave. The Pasterns have actually erected their shelter in the middle of their lovely garden: "It bulks under a veil of thin, new grass, like some embarrassing fact of physicalness, and I think Mrs. Pastern set out the statuary to soften its meaning. It would have been like her" (*SJC*, 498). Cheever is obviously describing a cemetery with new graves and gravestones. The irony inherent in their pride over their bombshelter borders on the grotesque, and the way Cheever plays with "who gets a key to the shelter" suggests that the Pasterns are, unconsciously, looking forward to their last days in their cozy hideaway grave.

The name Pastern is undoubtedly a parody on its etymological origins, the Latin word *pastor,* meaning "shepherd" or, in ecclesiastical jargon, "pastor." Charlie Pastern is the brigadier, or shepherd, of the Grassy Brae Golf Club lockerroom light infantry. He marches up and down the aisles of the lockerroom shouting: "Bomb Cuba! Bomb Berlin! Let's throw a little nuclear hardware at them and show them who's boss"

(*SJC*, 498). The etymological root of his name, Charlie, means "man," but his name also shares a root with a word defining Charlie's overly aggressive manhood perfectly: "churl"—that is, a rude, boorish, vulgar person. One of Cheever's favorite biblical passages was the Twenty-third Psalm, which begins with "The Lord is my shepherd" and then defines the good shepherd's loving duties. Charlie functions ironically, as the "Bad Shepherd," in his exhortation to destroy the world. On the day the story opens, Mrs. Pastern is involved in her own ancillary eschatological activities as a leading fund-raiser for infectious hepatitis. She will canvass and collect checks from eleven other women, each involved in their own pathological specialty: "Mrs. Horowitz was in charge of diseases of the nose and throat, Mrs. Templer was tuberculosis . . . Mrs. Craven was cancer . . ." (*SJC*, 499). The twelve women form a group resembling a kind of contaminated twelve apostles. As their leader, Mrs. Pastern feels she is fulfilling her vocation: "It was her destiny; it was her life" (*SJC*, 499). Both of the Pasterns shepherd groups of people according to their own morbid appetites; Charlie has become the bad shepherd as the brigadier-hero at the Golf Club (the Grassy Brae, or hill—another image of the grave) as he exhorts his charges to apocalyptic behavior in the very center of the phallic-aggressive male mysteries: the locker room. Charlie practices a form of nuclear pastoralism, while Mrs. Pastern shepherds her devotees of affliction on their ghoulish rounds, reminding decent people that horrible diseases await them if they don't contribute generously.

It is one of the rounds that Mrs. Pastern cannot make that occasions the fatal meeting between Charlie and the red-haired Mrs. Flannagan. Oddly enough, the name Flannagan means "red or ruddy." The first word Charlie shouts out to get her attention is "Infectious hepatitis!" Once Mrs. Flannagan lets Charlie know that her husband is away, they begin their illicit affair, but only after six strong drinks. When Mrs. Flannagan becomes guilt-ridden over their sinful affair, she wants to cut off the relationship but agrees to continue only on the condition that Charlie give her a key to the bomb shelter. After weighing the significance of his action, he gives in to his desire: "he took the key off its ring—a piece of metal one and a half inches long, warmed by the warmth of his hands, a genuine talisman of salvation, a defense against the end of the world—and dropped it into the neck of her dress" (*SJC*, 505).

In such a small community, word gets out by way of Mrs. Pastern's cleaning woman, Beatrice, who tells her that Charlie has given Mrs. Flannagan a key to the shelter. Though a small point, the name Beatrice is usually associated with Dante's guide through purgatory and into paradise; it means "blessed one," and it serves an ironic function in this story because she is the agent that causes both Mrs. Pastern and her husband to begin their descent into the inferno of marital betrayal and collapse. But her husband's infidelity is only part of his betrayal: "she had never imagined that he would betray her in their plans for the end of the world . . . She couldn't go back to mother. Mother didn't have a shelter . . . And then she remembered the night—the night of judgment—when they had agreed to let Aunt Ida and Uncle Ralph burn . . . when they had conspired like murderers and had decided to deny mercy even to his old mother" (*SJC,* 508). If the betrayal of their uniquely American "Liebestod" and the full exposure of their craven behavior weren't enough, Mrs. Pastern's final epiphany comes in their last scene together near the bomb shelter. What finally dawns on her with full force is the cynicism of Charlie's death wish, and the death wishes of others like him: "I began to see your plan. You *want* the world to end, don't you? Don't you, Charlie, don't you? I've known it all along, but I couldn't admit it to myself, it seemed so ruthless—but then one learns something new every day" (*SJC,* 510).

   The narrator, an unnamed next-door neighbor, returns at the end of the story to record, by means of a letter from the family that move into the Pasterns' house after they lose it, the pathetic scene as the divorced and poverty-stricken Mrs. Flannagan returns to contemplate the shelter "and just stood there looking at it. I don't know what in the world she was thinking of but the shelter looks a little like a tomb, you know, and she looked like a mourner standing there" (*SJC,* 511). Mrs. Flannagan "had lived up on the hill" and had symbolically fallen from her high position. Cheever's use of the bomb-shelter metaphor also brings home with devastating irony the story's theme of self-entombment. Mr. Pastern, the evil shepherd, is a demonic Orpheus bankrupting the family to build his eschatological tomb, where he leads his wife and where they will spend their last days contemplating the Hades they have generated. Hell has replaced Eden, but they have created it, not fallen into it, a scenario that becomes the ultimate expression of their obsessive death wish and their need to punish themselves by actualizing hell. Cheever has also created an American version of Jean-Paul Sartre's *No Exit* by creating a place in which Charlie could end his days with both his wife and his mistress.

   Though the story is dark and cynical, Cheever manages to make it humorous, especially in the way he has the local bishop come on a surprise visit to the Pasterns. Of course, as bishop, he is the authentic spiritual "pastor" of his flock in this idyllic spot. The purpose of his visit, however, is not to provide spiritual guidance but to peruse the bomb shelter and possibly to get a key—an invitation from Mrs. Pastern to be included in the select few who will escape nuclear immolation when the inevitable bomb is dropped. The bishop resembles Charlie because he does not come as a good shepherd but as one who cravenly wishes to escape pain and death and has no intention of ministering to his wounded and desperate flock when they will need him most.

Another story that contains obvious mythic patterns is one of Cheever's most frequently anthologized, "The Music Teacher." And next to "The Swimmer," it is the most ingeniously wrought story in the collection. Once again, the mythic scaffolding upon which the narrative rests reveals, if carefully examined, its central meaning. The music teacher, Miss Deming, bears some resemblance to Joan Harris of "Torch Song" primarily because both characters are based on the Greek sorceress Hecate. But Miss Deming combines and embodies the darkly magical powers of Hecate with the great fertility goddess, Demeter; identifying Miss Deming with Demeter is the key to the story. Hecate is an older version of Demeter and, as such, is the goddess as crone.

The story opens with the disintegration of the marriage of Mr. and Mrs. Seton as Jessica, the wife, is again burning the nightly meal as Seton returns from work. After ten years of marriage and three daughters, Jessica appears to be moving through her maternal duties mechanically, and it is obvious that she feels trapped in her roles as wife and mother. Oddly enough, her name comes from the Hebrew word for "confined" or "shut up." The children's names—Jocelyn, Millicent, and Phyllis—are conventional names from English Renaissance pastoral poetry depicting the Edenic lives of rustic shepherds singing to their idealized lovers. The opening scene depicts a domestic wasteland, as she burns the lamb and the children destroy the furniture with a can opener.

Jack Thompson, a close friend of Seton, advises him to take up a hobby, playing the piano, which, Jack tells him, mysteriously solved similar problems he was having with his wife. His friend's name, Jack Thompson, was one that thousands of piano students would have been very familiar with, particularly during the 1950s and 1960s, when the most popular set of piano method books was the "John Thompson" piano practice books. Though it is a minor point, Cheever rarely missed an opportunity to be humorously factual, especially regarding proper names. It turns out that Seton's other close friend, Mr. Carmignole, was also a student of Miss Deming and that his name refers to an eighteenth-century dance popular during the French Revolution; its root comes from the Latin word *carmen, carminis* meaning "song." And it so happens that the Carmignole household has recently become the center of social activity and musical soirees in the town.

Seton goes to Miss Deming's and begins taking piano lessons, but she gives him one particular piece to practice over and over again. Finally, Jessica begs him to ask Miss Deming for another practice piece because the constant repetition is driving her and the children to distraction. Jessica, meanwhile, has mysteriously stopped burning the nightly dinner and the house has become clean and tidy. Seton, relating his wife's request, asks Miss Deming if she could assign him another piece. She responds that the wives always ask this, adding, "None of the gentlemen who come here have ever complained about my methods . . . You want to bring her to her knees, don't you? Isn't that what you're here for?" (*SJC*, 420).

Seton begins to understand, vaguely, who this woman really is and what he may have gotten himself into: "The unholy woman's remarks had stunned him . . . Had he, by condoning the stuffiness of the place, committed himself to some kind of obscenity, some kind of witchcraft? Had he agreed to hold over a lovely woman the subtle threat of madness? The old crone spoke softly now, he thought, wickedly. 'Play the melody lightly, lightly, lightly,' she said. 'That's how it will do its work,'" (*SJC*, 420). When Seton had first telephoned Miss Deming he noted that "her voice was the voice of a crone." It is evident that Seton's journey is a literal and symbolic descent into darkness that begins in early autumn, moves through evenings during the fall, and concludes on the dark night Miss Deming is murdered. His journey is clearly into Hades, a passage Hecate was in charge of.

Cheever also makes clear references to Miss Deming's mythic identity and wants the reader to see her in that light when he describes at length the deeply disturbing, isolated condition that Seton finds himself in, a condition so guilt-laden that he cannot tell anybody about it: "he would not be able to put it into words. This darkness where men and women struggled pitilessly for supremacy and withered crones practiced witchcraft was not the world where he made his life. The old lady seemed to inhabit some barrier reef of consciousness, some gray moment after waking that would be demolished by the light of day" (*SJC*, 420–21). Again, the connection to Hecate is unmistakable. Even her house on Belleview Avenue, which is anything but a "beautiful view," suggests the mythic Miss Deming's Near Eastern origins—the home-

land of myths surrounding both Demeter and Hecate: "Belleview
Avenue was one of those back streets of frame houses . . . that are orna-
mented . . . with little minarets and wooden beading, like a mistaken or
at least a mysterious nod to the faraway mosques and harems of bloody
Islam. This paradox gave the place its charm" (*SJC*, 417).

The word *charm* is to be taken in its transforming capacity, since that
word defines the effect Miss Deming's teaching has on her male devotees. She raps Seton's knuckles, suggesting the domination that Hecate
demanded of her adepts. Demeter, though never married, was also a fertility goddess who, according to Robert Graves, "initiated the bride and
bridegroom into the secrets of the couch."[3] Miss Deming's secret techniques have certainly improved the marriages of her students. She also
wore her hair "braided, and pinned to her head in a sparse coronet. She
sat on an inflated cushion, with her hands folded in her lap" (*SJC*, 418).
A coronet is a crown and her throne is an inflated cushion where she is
the queen of the underworld "on the other side of town."

The climactic scene in the story takes place as Seton arrives for his
fifth lesson and finds a disturbingly transformed scene at Miss
Deming's. He immediately smells cigarette smoke—Hecate's torches—
in the hallway in spite of a no-smoking rule at her home. He sees two
young biker-types drinking beer and bantering with the proper Miss
Deming. Cheever describes them as threatening figures: "Their dark
hair gleamed with oil and was swept back in wings. They wore motor-
cycle boots and red hunting shirts, and their manners seemed developed, to a fine point, for the expression of lawless youth. 'We'll be
waiting for you, lover,' one of them said loudly" (*SJC*, 420). When
Seton asks who they are, she calls them "My boys . . . They come from
New York. They come up and spend the night sometimes. I help them
when I can, poor things. They're like sons to me" (*SJC*, 420). These
Hermes-like sexual youths ascend from the underworld, the south—
New York City—and are probably responsible for Miss Deming's death
at the story's conclusion.

When Seton arrives for his last lesson, his household has been
cleansed from all its wasteland detritus. Jessica, his wife, has surrendered; she begged him "on her knees" to find a new melody. He is
ashamed of his association with Miss Deming and "oddly self-righteous"
about the transformation of his domestic happiness—"and when he
thought of Miss Deming he thought of her with contempt and disgust.
Caught up in a whirl of palatable suppers and lovemaking, he didn't go
near the piano. He washed his hands of her method" (*SJC*, 421).

But it was her "method"—that is, her magical charm or spell—that restored the Seton family to its former happiness. Cheever very carefully contrasts the high point of Seton's emotional life, that redemptive light, to the darkest part of the narrative, in which Seton enters the realm of the goddess that disorients him to such an extent that he experiences a quasi-vision. The language used is ritualistic as he invokes her: "He called her name three times" and then thinks he sees her, even though there is no verbal response, at three different thresholds in her house: "but she seemed to be standing in the door to the kitchen, standing on the stairs, standing in the dark at the end of the hall" (*SJC*, 421).

After he returns home, the police pick him up and take him to where her body has been found in a "dead-end place, a dump . . . It was a scene for violence—bare, ugly, hidden away from any house, and with no one to hear her cries for help. She lay on the crossroads, like a witch" (*SJC*, 422). Hecate's place was always at the crossroads. When the police ask Seton if he had seen any young men around her house, he denies knowing anything because he understands the realm in which he has been involved, that of the sorceress, a witch whose powerful magic has enabled him to transform his family into a harmonious unit. Seton knows that he has somehow shared in these mysteries and, vaguely recognizing the necromantic nature of that experience, is fearful of sharing it with anyone else. But he also knows that he has been permanently changed.

"The Music Teacher" is one of Cheever's supreme achievements in its ability to evoke both humor and fear simultaneously and to re-create the myth of Demeter-Hecate, which grounds the story in the haunting power of ancient narrative.

The more complex Cheever's work becomes, the more obvious is its debt to mythic structures and patterns, configurations that add depth and significance to both his stories and his novels. Cheever uses myth not merely as a clever way of metaphorically relating the present to the past but as a means of demonstrating what James Hillman calls "the interchangeability of mythology and psychology." In his analysis of the relationship of the unconscious to dreams, *The Dream and the Underworld,* Hillman points out crucial connections between the past and the present: "Mythology is a psychology of antiquity. Psychology is a mythology of modernity. The ancients had no psychology, properly speaking, but they had myths . . . We moderns have no mythology, properly speaking, but we have psychological systems . . . called fields, instincts, drives, complexes."[4]

Cheever as Ovid in Ossining increasingly used these archetypal patterns in *The Brigadier and the Golf Widow,* not only in "The Music Teacher," a parable with Demeter-Hecate as its muse, but in what many critics consider his greatest story, "The Swimmer." No Cheever story ever projected its hero so deeply into the frightening waters of the unconscious. And because of this, it took Cheever much longer than his usual three days to finish. "The Swimmer" took him two months to complete, and he confessed that he made 150 pages of notes for the story (Donaldson 1988, 212). Even though it earned him fifty thousand dollars for the screen rights, it cost him deep psychological stress: "It was a terrible experience, writing that story. I was very unhappy. Not only I the narrator, but I John Cheever, was crushed." Cheever, not normally so forthcoming about the genesis of his work, talked quite openly about the changing evolution of a story with a blatantly mythological figure: "When I began, the story was to have been a simple one about Narcissus. I started with that image of the boy looking into the water. Then swimming every day as I do, I thought, it's absurd to limit him to the tight mythological plot—being trapped in his own image, in a single pool. This man loves swimming! So in my first version I just let him out and he swam in an immense number of pools—thirty of them! But then I began to narrow it down, and narrow it down, and something began happening. It was growing cold and quiet. It was turning into winter."[5]

This story received as much critical attention as just about any of his novels or other stories. Cheever himself laughed off various Marxist and Freudian interpretations, though. The Freudian ones do, however, possess some compelling evidence insofar as Neddy Merrill is certainly a modern projection of the mythic Narcissus, who pursues his own image and finally dies. Water is certainly a classic Freudian symbol for the womb and suggests that Neddy is trying to return to the womb-like security of his household. A Jungian interpretation, though, avoids some of the limitations of Freudian ones and can help the reader understand the stages and significance of Neddy's "heroic" journey, since that is precisely the structure the narrative follows.

Scholars Hal Blythe and Charlie Sweet nail down with utterly convincing evidence the deep mythic pattern that uncovers the nature of the irony in an essay entitled "Cheever's Dark Knight of the Soul: The Failed Quest of Neddy Merrill."[6] They assert that Cheever's story contains virtually all of the archetypal patterns found in Western literature's most famous story: the quest for the Grail. They propose that Neddy Merrill combines the role of the failed Grail quester and the wounded Fisher King—the mythic king whose wounded condition turns his kingdom into a wasteland. They use as their source Jesse Weston's *From Ritual to Romance,* pointing out that Neddy Merrill possesses the characteristics of virility and local legendary status that make him the hero on a mythological quest. After pointing out modern versions of the obstacles on the mythic road toward the Grail—threshold crossings, social ostracism, rejection of former loved ones—they assert that Neddy is the Fisher King who fails his test primarily because of the selfish nature of his quest. "[H]e acts not for community, but for self," they argue. [H]is ultimate goal is purely egocentric," not spiritual (Blythe and Sweet, 348). They also identify modern examples of dark towers and Chapels Perilous, but point out even more important seasonal shifts that take place during the course of the story; autumn is changing into winter and Neddy is aging perceptibly. Most important, Neddy as Grail quester "fails to ask the proper questions and to find suitable answers" (Blythe and Sweet, 349). At the conclusion of the quest, the knight is found worthy only if he asks the right questions; and if he does so, he is granted a heavenly vision, and the "freeing of the waters" heals both the wounded king and the land. At the conclusion of Cheever's story, Neddy returns home to find it abandoned and empty; he has failed in his quest.

One fascinating avenue of study of "The Swimmer" relates to the significance of names in the story. The surnames of the families whose pools Neddy swims in represent, according to Robert Morace, an "ironic reversal of Odysseus' homecoming."[7] The names become various ports of call and also a catalogue of Neddy's friends, who are transformed into enemies as the story comes to its depressing conclusion. Michael Byrne, in his essay "The River of Names in 'The Swimmer,'" relates the list of names to "the famous litany of guests at Gatsby's parties" and notes the association to "social and psychological violence and conflict" in names such as "'Hammers,' 'Crosscups' and 'Bunkers'."[8] Byrne additionally detects an ethnic arrangement of names, from the Scottish, English, and German to the Jewish and the Irish. Neddy finally circles from Scots to Scots; that is, he started his journey at the Grahams and concludes it at the Clydes.

Byrne also notes the multifaceted significance of water, not only as the medium through which Neddy moves but as it is embedded in his first and last names. Neddy, like Narcissus, begin with the letter *N,* and Cheever admits the connection. The name Merrill comes from the name "Murial," which means "sea-bright." The first part of the name also derives from the French *la mer*, meaning "sea," and *mère*, meaning "mother." Other names are attached to water and the sea, such as Lear, which means "dweller by the sea," and Halloran, meaning "stranger from beyond the sea." The last name Clyde is the name of one of Scotland's longest and most important rivers (Byrne, 327).

Closer examination of the other names in this all-important catalogue of friends who become enemies not only reveals additional water references but also shows that all the other names refer to geographical places, many of which are adjacent to some body of water. Neddy Merrill's trip begins at the Westerhazy home and moves in a southwest direction. In that sense, he is moving in an ironic pattern from the "west" of Westerhazy to the southwest, so the trip is, as Morace suggests, an ironic odyssey and a confused one, since Neddy is very hungover—as expressed in the "hazy" part of Westerhazy. The etymological origin of the name Hammer, the second pool he visits, refers to "one who lives beside a stream." He then moves on to the Lears, "an old British river name," to the Howlands, a name that comes from the Welsh *Howell*, which refers to a "well" or "stream." Next he visits the Crosscups, who, with the Howlands, are away. The satiric reference to "cups"—that is, to one of the oldest manifestations of the Grail as a cup of immortality and its absence—shows Cheever's sly sense of humor. At the Bunkers (whose name does not bear any direct reference to water), he is received as royalty and with great affection, as a hero who was expected. And the name Bunker, aside from its obvious reference to a protective place used in combat, actually means "a reliable, good-hearted person," which Mrs. Bunker most certainly is. Neddy is kissed by eight or ten women and shakes hands with as many men who ply him with gin and tonics, certainly an allusion to the temptations of Odysseus by the Sirens and the inhabitants of the Land of the Lotus Eaters. These undaunted celebrants deflect him from his primary task, which is to follow the Lucinda River, his mythopoeic amalgamation of the fifteen pools that he has named after his wife, Lucinda. The name Lucinda comes from the name Lucy, which means "light." Neddy is following the light, the sun, as it and he fade into darkness. The name Lucy also refers to St. Lucy, the patron protector of Dante. Dante prayed to her because she was also the designated patron of people with eye problems, which plagued Dante throughout his life. There is little doubt that Neddy Merrill begins to experience severe "vision" problems as he concludes his journey in darkness. The Dantean allusions multiply as the story progresses.

At the Levys (a "levee" keeps a river from overflowing) he meets his first serious obstacles. The Hebrew name from which Levy derives, Levi, means "joining," which is somewhat ironic since the family is not at home. But it is at the Levys that the story takes a dramatic turn in which natural and supernatural forces begin to impede Neddy from his "heroic" progress. The seventh pool, normally a lucky number, is the place where he encounters several obstacles that Cheever uses in comic ways. There is a private property sign next to the entrance, with a parodic serpentine threshold guardian—"a green tube for the *New York Times*"— posted at the driveway. Neddy also arrives at the Levys just before a frightening storm drives him into their gazebo, a kind of modern Chapel Perilous, which gives him safe haven during the storm.

He progresses to the Welchers' pool, which is dry, a situation comically alluding to the term *welsher* as one who fails to meet his obligation— that is, to provide Neddy-Narcissus with water for his egoistic swimming contest. Additionally, the name Welch or Welsh refers to a "foreigner" and is also the English word for a Celt. One of the most famous Celtic-Welsh heroes was Peredur, who was the Welsh version of Parsifal-Percival, the Arthurian "innocent fool" who was the only successful quester for the Grail. The dry pool also reinforces the wasteland condition of sterility and lifelessness that Neddy begins to experience in increasingly painful ways. He is upset because "this breach in his chain of water" has fractured the coherence of his mythic journey, where "he felt like some explorer who seeks a torrential headwater and finds a dead stream" (*SJC,* 606). Again, Cheever evokes the failed attempts of the mythic Fisher King to find water—the source of life and healing.

The next part of his pilgrimage quite clearly finds Neddy entering its Dantean phase when he attempts to cross the threatening Route 424. He experiences great difficulties because the traffic will not permit him to cross the highway, and several drivers jeer at him. One even throws a beer can at him. Some think him "merely a fool," a description resonating with the Grail knight as the "innocent fool." Even the route number 424 suggests the retrograde, circular movement that his journey is taking. Only the charity of "an old man, tooling down the highway at fifteen miles an hour, let him get to the middle of the road, where there was a grass divider" (*SJC,* 607). This dangerous threshold crossing, aided by a "wise guide," alludes to the beginning of Dante's *Inferno,* where the traveler finds himself "in the middle way" entering "a Dark Wood." This Dantean threshold crossing is a prelude to Neddy's entrance to the Inferno-like Lancaster Public Pool, which is, by the way, the ninth sta-

tion on Neddy's fifteen stops during his trip and is, like the ninth circle
of hell, at the bottom of the Inferno. On the temporal level, Neddy's
growing anxiety over losing his youth and becoming middle aged (the
middle way) modernizes the Dantean allusions. Neddy also realizes that
it would be impossible to turn back simply because he had gone too far,
an echo of the prohibition that relegates all of the damned to hell for all
eternity.

The entrance into the Hades of the Lancaster Public Pool places
Neddy directly in a modern-day Inferno. The name Lancaster has a possible historical allusion to a famous English sixteenth-century sea explorer, Sir James Lancaster, and is consistent with the water metaphor of the
journey. The nine letters in the name also add to its symbolic significance. What Neddy encounters at the threshold of the pool are long lists
of rules and regulations and the general chaos of the damned of Dante's
descent into hell: "the sounds were louder, harsher, and more shrill, and
as soon as he entered the crowded enclosure he was confronted with reg-
imentation" (*SJC*, 608). The imagery Cheever uses throughout this scene
evokes the hellish Gustave Doré–like atmosphere: He "washed his feet
in a cloudy and bitter solution, and made his way to the edge of the
water. It stank of chlorine and looked to him like a sink. A pair of life-
guards in a pair of towers blew police whistles at what seemed to be regular intervals and abused the swimmers through a public address
system" (*SJC*, 608). This scene replicates Dantean images throughout
the *Inferno*, where pairs of bat-like fiends regularly abuse the regimented
phalanxes of the damned verbally and with the most disgusting actions.
"Neddy remembers the sapphire waters at the Bunkers with longing";
the most painful aspect of being among the damned is the remembrance
of happy times while they were alive. Cheever contrasts the heavenly
"sapphire waters" with Lancaster's water, which he calls "this murk,"
corrosive, sulfuric, and dangerous. Neddy reminds himself that this part
of his journey "was merely a stagnant bend in the Lucinda River," which
reminds him that he is "an explorer, a pilgrim" (*SJC*, 608).

He now enters directly into the "Dark Wood": "By crossing the road
he entered the wooded part of the Halloran estate," a deeper descent in
the ninth circle. The name Halloran possesses a number of interpretive
possibilities, but its first meaning is Irish for "beyond the sea," and in
this case it delivers Neddy from the hellish Lancaster Public Pool. The
Hallo part of the name could refer, ironically, to "hallow" or "holy" but
also to "hell." Both interpretations work because they represent an even
deeper descent into the Inferno of self-knowledge. The Hallorans are

wealthy and live exactly the way they wish and feel perfectly free to sit around their pool naked. They also have the only "natural" pool, which is fed by a brook. The water in the pool was "the opaque gold of the stream." The gold and the green in the story intermix, alchemically, to suggest that an important mystical transformation is taking place. A beech hedge enshrines their Ovidian-like pool and becomes a location of spiritual metamorphosis. Neddy first begins to doubt his senses when Mrs. Halloran expresses sympathy for his misfortunes, something he seems completely unaware of. It is at the Hallorans where Neddy becomes conscious of the physical and emotional metamorphoses he has undergone: "He was cold and tired and the naked Hallorans and their dark water had depressed him . . . His arms were lame. His legs felt rubbery and ached at their joints . . . Leaves were falling down around him and he smelled wood smoke on the wind" (*SJC,* 609). The story began on "one of those midsummer Sundays" and now it's autumn and Neddy is lost in the imperceptible changes of the seasons. He is not regaining his potency as the Fisher King does but is reverting to his former wounded condition. He confesses to needing a drink, a not-so-subtle allusion to the youth-reviving capacities of the Grail.

The next house he visits is inhabited by Eric Sachs, a "wounded hero" who has no navel because of radical abdominal surgery, an additional allusion to the wounded Amfortas—the Fisher King. Indeed, the name Eric means "rich leader of a realm," but his present realm is blighted, a word Cheever uses several times to characterize the landscape during the last third of Neddy's pilgrimage. Eric is also a name associated with famous Viking leaders who regularly "sacked" Britain and Ireland. Eric's wife is, ironically, Helen, but not the noble one of Troy; Helen Sachs is nursing her husband's wounded condition and won't permit any alcohol on the property. Neddy has no luck in getting a drink at their place, even though their name alludes to a strong Spanish wine. Now that Neddy has fully entered hell, like Dante, he observes the fallen heroes in their very unheroic condition.

Earlier Homeric allusions surface as George Hunt notes in his brilliant interpretation of "The Swimmer," which he called Cheever's version of *The Odyssey.* Just prior to starting his journey, Neddy had "slid down his bannister that morning and given the bronze backside of Aphrodite a smack" (*SJC,* 603). Besides being a blatant act of hubris, his action also foreshadows a bad end for Neddy-Odysseus, "because Aphrodite was the champion of the Trojans and Odysseus was a wily Greek; this goddess does not suffer indignities gladly or without reprisal" (Hunt, 280).

The tone and direction of Neddy's journey turn very ugly in his unannounced visit to the Biswangers, the next stop on his river journey. Grace Biswanger, who is anything but graceful or polite, calls him "a gate crasher," indicating another threshold crossing. This threshold reveals Neddy's growing awareness of the metamorphosis he is undergoing—from hero to outcast. Though he manages a quick swim in their pool, he recognizes his transformation into the foreigner, the exile, and the outsider.

The next station on his swim to Calvary is the culmination of his humiliation and rejection. It is, appropriately, the thirteenth pool, and it belongs to a past mistress, Shirley Adams. Again, Cheever's gnomic sense of humor plays with the possibilities of the mythic gender reversal that fits perfectly with the ironic Odyssey that Neddy is pursuing, and also adheres to their reversal of roles. He, the fallen Adam, is no longer in charge, though he persists in the illusion because "he broke it off." She, however, has taken charge, and when he asks her for a drink, she responds with: "I could but I won't. I'm not alone" (*SJC*, 611). Just previous to her rejection, she enacted another of the mythic Adam's primal roles as the namer of the world by articulating with stunning accuracy Neddy's delusional immaturity:

"What do you want?" she asked.
"I'm swimming across the country."
"Good Christ. Will you ever grow up?"

Christ, mythically, is the fully mature and realized Adam who enacted redemption in the selfless act of crucifixion. And by that act, Christ-Adam established the communion of saints and salvation for all. It is in this climactic scene that Cheever dramatized the infinite distance between the idealized message of Christian love manifested in the Holy Grail (the symbol of communion and community) and the egoistic, solipsistic definition that Neddy articulates so perversely in language directly out of ancient and medieval wound literature: "If he had suffered any injuries at the Biswangers' they would be cured here. Love—sexual roughhouse in fact—was the supreme elixir, the pain killer, the brightly colored pill that would put the spring back into his step, the joy of life in his heart" (*SJC*, 611). Cheever has never been as obvious as he is here when he substitutes the sublime aspects of the Grail—its curative powers to heal spiritual wounds—with blatantly sexual roughhousing as the modern elixir that temporarily mollifies erotic desire. Echoing the seasonal recurrence of spiritual regeneration—Easter—Cheever reduces it to an aphrodisiac ("a brightly colored pill") that puts "spring back into his step." Just before Neddy dives into Shirley Adams's pool, he "wondered if she was still wounded" (*SJC,* 611). He notices though, that he has been replaced by a younger man, that cycles continue but without him. Neddy's narcissism has moved into its inevitable pathological state of solipsism to such a degree that he has lost contact with any definable reality and is, existentially, lost. Without the defining protection of his aggressive sexuality, his domination over women, Neddy loses the ontological basis of "his" reality.

Neddy's obvious problem is, and has been, his drinking. He has been consuming his own, personal "Grail"—martinis, Scotch, whiskey—for so long that he has entered a stage of profound denial; like many alcoholics in their late stages, he has lost contact with reality. He asks himself: "Was his memory failing or had he so disciplined it in the repression of unpleasant facts that he had damaged his sense of truth?" (*SJC,* 602). Though many critics view this story as semi-metafictional or fantastic, a basic examination of it as an obvious descent into alcoholic insanity from years of prolonged drinking seems the one that many critics overlook. Cheever's brilliant mythologizing of the event gives readers Homeric, Dantean, and Ovidian ways of understanding its complex structure; but it also enables them to discern the narcissistic solipsism that late-stage alcoholics exhibit just prior to death or permanent custodial care. Alcoholics at this critical juncture of their illness often wander around imagining themselves some sort of mythic hero that nobody but they recognize. Early in the story, Neddy "had a vague and modest idea of himself as a legendary figure" (*SJC,* 603–4). As long as the alcoholic continues to drink, he is able to sustain his heroic delusion. But Neddy cannot get a drink from Shirley Adams, and he states, after her refusal: "Well, I'm on my way" (*SJC,* 610).

And he is on his way, by way of the alcoholic withdrawal that is severely weakening him, to a terrifying confrontation with reality: "He began to cry" (*SJC,* 611). He does finish his odyssey but is barely able to swim the length of either the Gilmartins' or the Clydes' pool. He descends into the pool by steps and a ladder, unable to dive. Only when he looks up into the late autumn night sky and sees that the constellations of midsummer are gone does he begin to see a world radically transformed from the one he left. Cheever's hero returns not to the triumph and victory of a welcoming and grateful community but, rather, to a dark, empty house. The classic Jungian symbol of the soul or psyche is that of a house, and certainly Neddy Merrill is facing for the first time in his life the depth of his emptiness. He resembles T. S. Eliot's anti-hero J. Alfred Prufrock at the terrifying conclusion of that great poem's last lines: "We have lingered in the chambers of the sea . . . / Till human voices wake us, and we drown." Once reality—"human voices"—begins to intrude, Neddy's descent into hell will be complete.

Certainly Hunt is correct in pointing out the story's obvious mythic parallels in other literary returning heroes: in Tennyson's "Enoch Arden" and "Ulysses," in Joyce's *Ulysses,* and in the drastically contracted time span in Ambrose Bierce's "An Occurrence at Owl Creek Bridge" and William Golding's *Pincher Martin* (Hunt, 282). Cheever's time warp in "The Swimmer" is explainable as a symptom of the serious physical, mental, and spiritual disintegration caused by prolonged alcoholic drinking. Certainly no other story Cheever wrote contains more interpretative possibilities than "The Swimmer." Cheever used many of the sophisticated literary techniques developed for this story in *Bullet Park,* the novel about Neddy Merrill's hometown.

Three other stories from *The Brigadier and the Golf Widow* that also deal with water are "The Seaside Houses," "The Ocean," and "The Angel of the Bridge." In "The Ocean" the ocean is briefly alluded to as a symbol of feminine chaos; it is not an active agent in the narrative. In "The Angel of the Bridge," the protagonist experiences panic attacks as he crosses over the Hudson River so that water becomes a symbol that threatens to swallow him up; he fears that, like Icarus, he will disappear into its depths. "The Seaside Houses" is a story that traces an Icarus-like fall from a condition of ignorance into knowledge that permanently alters the narrator's naive view of life.

"The Seaside Houses" is, among other things, a retelling of "The Enormous Radio" and is, for all intents and purposes, the same story, but one that takes place on a seashore, not in a comfortable Upper East Side apartment near Sutton Place. The narrative opens with one of Cheever's most ruminative meditations on the nature of the impulses that draw people to the sea. The narrator, Mr. Ogden, muses over the ritualistic aspects of seaside vacations; it seems that this ceremonious journey has been imprinted on the human unconscious and can be deciphered in dreams. He also suggests that being so close to the power of the sea, its chaotic but permanent process of creation/destruction and the profound responses it evokes, somehow sensitizes him to the ghostly presences of previous inhabitants of the seaside houses he rents each year. Cheever, along with Poe, Hawthorne, and Henry James, had a great gift for detecting the haunted and haunting residue of old houses' past occupants.

The name of the house the Ogdens rent is Broadmere, a name that is a metaphor for the revelations that take place during Mr. Ogden's stay there. The name Broadmere could be taken to mean "mother" or "sea," from the French, both of which are the source of life. Cheever is also punning on the sound of "mirror" in the name, because the protagonist begins to detect himself in the desiccated image of Broadmere's former inhabitant, Mr. Greenwood. The name of the seaside house, then, focuses all of the motifs of the story into a unified metaphor with at least three aspects. Broadmere is the broad sea, that is, the mythic sea of consciousness that Mr. Ogden finds himself a part of as he comes into the knowledge that he is another version of the desperate, ironically named alcoholic, Mr. Greenwood. In fact, Ogden becomes a secret sharer of Greenwood's ruin by pursuing various clues that lie about the house intimating Greenwood's descent into his own inferno. Ogden becomes so involved in tracing his descent that he becomes a virtual doppelgänger, or alter ego, of Greenwood; and in pursuing Greenwood's fate, he discovers his own. Ogden gradually takes on the characteristics of Greenwood and even, he fears, begins to dream his dreams after he accidentally observes him, a mean-spirited, shaking alcoholic, in a bar near Grand Central Station. The conclusion of the story finds an alcoholic Ogden with a new wife named Magda who is dyeing her hair orange, a habit she practices weekly. Ogden has entered the fallen world in which he and his new wife, who resembles a whore, inhabit another, but much seedier, seaside house; the name Magda comes from the most famous whore in history, Mary Magdalen.

"The Seaside Houses" demonstrates Cheever's ability to handle psychological scenarios in increasingly sophisticated ways. The house, a classic Jungian symbol of the unconscious, combines with dreams and the sea to symbolize Ogden's discovery that he and Greenwood are virtually the same person, a realization that simultaneously informs and terrifies him. What he learns at the story's conclusion is that his former wife's cries in her sleep—"Why have they come back? What have they lost?"—refer not to the former inhabitants of the house but directly to him. Ogden describes Greenwood in the bar as a type, and in so naming him, later discovers that he has also defined himself as simply another predictable, self-pitying drunk.

"The Ocean" has very little to do with the ocean, except in an overheard conversation in a bar where the protagonist, Mr. Fry, hears a man

condemning women. The reason Mr. Fry listens so attentively is that the
anonymous speaker is describing his wife as someone who he suspects
could actually murder him in his sleep, a fear that Fry also has about his
wife, Cora, who he thinks has been trying to murder him by putting
insecticide in his food and lighter fluid in the salad dressing. The man in
the bar says women are "the most miserable creatures in the history of
the world. I mean they're right in the middle of the ocean" (*SJC*, 575).
The ocean in this story serves as an unspoken metaphor for the unconscious, dream, and myth on which the complex narrative rests.

The key to understanding the story is the mythic structure that surfaces as Mr. Fry describes his fears and desires for himself and for his
family, especially his daughter, Flora, who has been "abducted" (albeit
willingly) by "a sexual freak" named Peter. The major project for Mr. Fry
is to get Flora back home, at least for temporary visits, to Bullet Park.
The situation resembles the story of the rape and the abduction to the
underworld of Persephone-Kore, daughter of Demeter, by Hades-Pluto
in Greek mythology.

The story opens with Cora Fry insisting on watering the flowers in her
garden in the middle of a heavy rain, an act that identifies Cora as
Demeter, the goddess in charge of keeping the seasons going and the
crops coming. Flora (Persephone) has been brought by Peter (Hades-
Pluto) to his underworld pad in the ironically named Eden Building on
the Lower East Side. In a twist to the Greek myth, Cheever has Mr. Fry
attempt to "abduct" his daughter by offering to pay Peter to disappear
for about six months so that Flora may come back home to what is in his
view the genuinely Edenic Bullet Park.

As Mr. Fry enters the Eden Building to retrieve his daughter, he hears
the barking of dogs, suggesting the three-headed guardian of the threshold of Hades, Cerberus; he also envisions himself as "an avenging angel,"
as he views the archangel Michael guarding the threshold with a flaming
sword. He finds Flora and Peter indulging in quasi-satanic activities—
they are decorating a skeleton they had bought from a medical supply
house with rare and beautiful butterflies. Flora is dressed in black and
Peter resembles "a minor apostle in a third-rate Passion Play" (*SJC*, 579).
Again, Cheever's use of names helps the reader understand his characters. Mr. Fry goes to the trouble of telling us that Flora was educated in
Florence, Italy, a name which means "city of flowers." He even specifies
the school in Florence from which she graduated, the Villa Mimosa,
mimosa being a delicate plant whose ball-like clusters of small flowers
respond to both light and touch. The word *mimosa* comes from the Latin

"mimus," meaning "mime," a description of the plant's imitation of animal sensitivity. Flora, ironically, does not respond to light but to the dark touch of the priapic Peter.

The story concludes, after Mr. Fry's unsuccessful attempt to return his daughter to Bullet Park, with a semidream vision of Cora in their bedroom. The only significant journey in the story is Mr. Fry's descent into the lair of Hades-Pluto and his failure to bring Flora back home. Mr. Fry wants his daughter to bring some love and affection into the household and to save his life if his paranoid suspicions that Cora is trying to murder him are true. His reveries bring back their first meeting in the bloom of youth at a wedding in a garden, a recurring location associated with Cora throughout the story. But before sleep, he looks upon her, as she prepares for bed, with a mixture of love and fear and wonders whether he is embracing a potential murderer. He understands that she is a product of his fecund imagination, a mythic figure who becomes "a goldfish, a murderess, and how when I took her in my arms she was a swan, a flight of stairs, a fountain, the unpatrolled, unguarded boundaries to paradise" (*SJC*, 583).

Mr. Fry awakens at three in the morning radiant with love, and after moving about the house painting the word "luve" all over the premises he enters a visionary realm between waking and sleep where he sees himself in an idyllic, Henry James–like English village searching for Flora and Cora, then moving to a Georgian house where he joins a party. Still unable to find his wife and daughter, he returns in this Eden-like scenario to the lovely meadow and sparkling brook and "fell into a sweet sleep" (*SJC*, 583). The story concludes in the only safe and secure paradise that Mr. Fry's imagination allows him to inhabit, a visionary, and possibly mad, landscape where Cora and Flora will be waiting for him, a conclusion that resonates with the dour ending of "The Swimmer," except that Mr. Fry's imagination-as-hallucination might protect him from the insanity of his devastated domestic life.

Few of Cheever's stories have so vividly presented such negative treatments of women as "The Ocean," a narrative portraying a wife who is probably trying to murder her husband and a daughter who refuses to return home to save her father. Cheever's use of obvious mythic female deities does not soften his persistently antifeminine attitudes, especially when the protagonist of "The Seaside Houses" ends his days with the goddess-as-whore, Magda. In contrast, "The Angel of the Bridge" presents the female in an angelic light. "The Angel of the Bridge" is also a story about an older brother who the protagonist neurotically believes has always been their mother's favorite. Cheever uses the brother to compare and contrast their increasingly debilitating phobias. In fact, the entire family suffers from phobias of various kinds. The seventy-eight-year-old mother is so terrified of planes that she is unable to fly to Toledo, Ohio, to visit old friends. The narrator's brother is so frightened of elevators that when his company moves to the fifty-second floor of a new office building, he quits his very lucrative job and finds work in a third-floor office.

Part of Cheever's genius is his ability to choose one crucial condition—phobias in this story—and construct an entire and often humorous story around it. Once the family phobias are exposed, the narrator traces a map of the local geography in terms of what bridges he can and cannot bear to cross. That grid of terror becomes the attenuated world he is forced to operate within throughout the story until he meets an angelic presence that releases him from his phobia. Biographer Scott Donaldson points out that Cheever himself suffered phobias about bridges, especially the Tappan Zee Bridge, a fear that effectively kept him from visiting close friends who lived in Rockland County. There was a correlation, though, between the intensity of the phobic reaction and his increasingly heavy drinking.

The narrator's phobia also becomes a backdrop against which he analyzes the possible difficulties that are disturbing his normally happy life. Though he visits his family doctor and receives little help, he tries to psychoanalyze his past life to understand the origins and causes of his bridge phobia. His mother, now a woman in her late seventies, embarrasses him as she flaunts herself at the skating rink at Rockefeller Center each Sunday afternoon, "dressed like a hat-check girl, pushing some paid rink attendant around the ice, in the middle of the third-biggest city of the world" (*SJC*, 491). But he shares with his mother, he later admits, her yearning for the innocent world of St. Botolphs, his boyhood home. In his desperate attempt to understand his phobia, even to blame something for it, he muses over the possibility that his sublimated Oedipal feelings toward his mother may, in some way, have activated his dread that the bridge will collapse when he is on it. Though Cheever uses the motif of the fall constantly throughout his fiction, this story becomes one of his most trenchant explorations of how it manifests itself in his increasingly neurotic life.

The narrator probes more deeply into the hidden message that his fear reveals and suggests that it "was an expression of my clumsily concealed horror of what is becoming of the world . . . And it was at the highest point in the arc of a bridge that I became aware suddenly of the depth and bitterness of my feelings about modern life, and the profoundness of my yearning for a more vivid, simple, and peaceable world" (*SJC,* 495). At the very moment when he is able to articulate the dynamics of his phobia, he also realizes that he cannot go home again: "Go back to St. Botolphs, wear a Norfolk jacket, and play cribbage in the firehouse? There was only one bridge in the village, and you could throw a stone across the river there" (*SJC,* 495).

At the very apex of his terror, as he pulls over to the side of the Tappan Zee Bridge, a young woman jumps into the car, a hitchhiker, and sings him across the bridge. She is carrying a small harp because she is a folksinger in various coffeehouses in and around New York City. As she begins to sing some of her songs, he forgets his phobia and is so charmed by her voice that he easily crosses the bridge and, effectively, loses his fear of both the Tappan Zee and the Triborough Bridges (he still refuses to go near the George Washington). The story verges on the magical realism of writers such as Márquez and Cortázar, but before most North Americans had read them: "She sang me across the bridge . . . and the water below us was charming and tranquil. It all came back—blue-sky courage, the high spirits of lustiness, an ecstatic sereneness . . . I drove on toward the city through a world that, having been restored to me, seemed marvelous and fair" (*SJC,* 479). The narrator has found, through the agency of the song—that peculiar sacramental power that art sometimes provides—a regenerated Eden of his lost innocence in which he feels one with the beauty and harmony of the world.

Though "The Angel of the Bridge" is principally about overcoming a specific phobia, it is also one of Cheever's most articulate expressions of a free-floating existential dread that he was feeling during the early 1960s, much of which concerned his drinking and the family problems it was causing. The narrator's fear can also be attributed to his terror at falling into a bottomless abyss that he sees in the collapse of the old verities, the devastating commercialism that was eating up the landscape, and the misery, drunkenness, and general dishonesty of "modern life." Certainly Cheever's next novel, *Bullet Park,* will be the culminating statement of the bitter disappointment he was feeling about life in the United States during the 1960s.

Chapter Six

"Lethal Eden": *Bullet Park* and *The World of Apples*

Three stories from *The Brigadier and the Golf Widow* foreshadow many of the themes and spiritual conflicts that John Cheever treats in his highly controversial third novel, *Bullet Park* (1969). "The Ocean" shows Mr. Fry trapped between his wife, Cora, an emerging femme fatale, and his daughter, Flora, who refuses to return from her happy Hades-Eden with her phallocratic lover, Peter, to protect her father from his murderous wife. "The Seaside Houses" is about the fatal spillage of Mr. Greenwood's unconscious into Mr. Ogden's consciousness as Ogden begins to see that they are, symbolically, the same person. Both characters are lost and lack the spiritual resources that can save them from alcoholism, madness, suicide, or religious conversion. With "The Angel of the Bridge," however, comes a redemptive outside agent, that of the angelic folk musician who sings the protagonist across the "abyss" of the Tappan Zee Bridge. *Bullet Park* tests, among many things, the power of the imagination to redeem its two major characters from a mechanistic, desacralized, and meaningless cosmos.

Bullet Park and many of the stories in *The World of Apples* constitute his bitterest indictment of the increasingly corrosive effect of the brainless technological "progress" taking place during the middle and late 1960s in America, not the least of which was the Vietnam War and the toll in human lives it exacted. Perhaps the drunken litany of the crimes of technology recited by Rev. Applegate in *The Wapshot Scandal* best sums up the plight of its victims: "Let us pray for all those killed or cruelly wounded on thruways, expressways, freeways and turnpikes. Let us pray for all those burned to death in faulty plane-landings, midair collisions and mountainside crashes. Let us pray for all those wounded by rotary lawn mowers, chain saws, electric hedge clippers and other power tools. Let us pray for all alcoholics measuring out the days that the Lord hath made in ounces, pints and fifths" (*WS,* 301).

The pervasive encroachment of technological advancement, the legacy of William Blake's "dark Satanic mills," becomes a major obstacle for both Paul Hammer and Eliot Nailles in their mutual quest to simplify life down to its least destructive elements. Both men discover that modern civilization has become a dehumanizing, demythologized, existential wasteland, and that their response to this condition is frenetic getting and spending, drunkenness, obsessive pill-popping, and a growing terror of facing the daily enterprise. As Hammer and Nailles are waiting for the 7:56 at the Bullet Park commuter station, a neighbor, Harry Shinglehouse, is sucked under the wheels of the Chicago Express and disappears forever, leaving only an expensive and "highly polished brown loafer" as evidence of his transitory existence. For Eliot Nailles the train station becomes a demonic version of the stations of the cross that adorn the side aisles of Catholic churches and trace Christ's journey to Calvary to be crucified for the sins of humanity. Nailles becomes so traumatized by Shinglehouse's death and his own son's fall into despair that he resorts to taking drugs to work up the courage to board the train and report to his own personal Calvary, where he has devoted his life as a chemist to improving "Spang," a mouthwash.

Critical opinions are sharply divided over the literary merits of *Bullet Park,* ranging from Benjamin DeMott's outright dismissal of the novel's structure as "broken-backed" and "tacked together" (40) to John Gardner's high praise. Gardner called the critics of *Bullet Park* "dead wrong" and stated, unequivocally, that "The Wapshot books, though well-made, were minor. *Bullet Park* . . . was major—in fact, a magnificent work of fiction."[1] Gardner further explains that, unlike the Wapshot novels, it is not concerned with the manners and mores of society. Rather, it is a philosophical novel concerning the darker aspects of chance and fate. Samuel Coale, however, best encapsulates the novel's theme and subject matter by calling it Cheever's "Lethal Eden" (Coale 1977, 95).

Using Coale's mythic reading of *Bullet Park* as a starting point, one can understand the crucial events that culminate in Cheever's clearest statement of his attitude toward Western civilization and its obvious apocalyptic trajectory as it closes out the chaos of the 1960s. This is Cheever's first genuinely existential novel, because it not only treats the moral dislocations of the second half of the twentieth century but directly addresses the fracturing of America's traditional values and beliefs. Chance, fate, and destiny are primary themes as major characters find themselves helplessly entangled in inexplicably desperate situations. Scott Donaldson, agreeing with Samuel Coale, proposes that *Bullet Park* can be best understood through Cheever's use of Greek myth and the

Bible: "From the first his work has carried resonances from Greek myth and the Bible. But these resonances penetrate deepest in his most recent fiction—*Bullet Park,* the stories in *The World of Apples* (1973), and most of all his novel *Falconer*" (Donaldson 1979, 193). Lethal Eden has become lethal because it lacks a center, and Cheever is so adamant in his declamations of its essential emptiness that *Bullet Park* becomes an allegory, but without the moral and philosophical perspective that gives allegory its instructive force.

Nowhere does Cheever use the devices of allegory as blatantly as he does in *Bullet Park,* starting with the title of the novel, all of the place names, and the vast majority of the names of the characters. The controlling metaphor of the place names is that of the machine and the emotionless technology that buries everybody in its wake; the machine is not only in the garden, it has completely taken it over. The violence inherent in the name Bullet Park does more than suggest the violence that waits just beneath the surface politeness of this suburb; it defines the very nature of the location. The names of the major characters, Eliot Nailles and Paul Hammer, so clearly label them that they could walk around with signs on their necks. Indeed, Cheever himself points out quite clearly the significance of names and their function in the novel early in the first chapter. Eliot Nailles overhears Paul Hammer tell the pastor of Christ Church their name: "We're the Hammers." Nailles is immediately disturbed over the odd chance that two families named Hammer and Nailles would live in the same, small suburban community: "Nailles claimed not to be a superstitious man but he did believe in the mysterious power of nomenclature. He believed, for example, that people named John and Mary never divorced."[2] In short, what establishes meaning issues not from any moral or spiritual center but from the coincidence of two names loaded with symbolic significance, especially in a place called Christ Church. Instead of using names to reveal origins or ancient meaning the way Cheever usually does, he turns the pattern upside down. In *Bullet Park* names signify nothing until chance juxtaposes them. Hammer then interprets the coupling as fate or destiny, not chance, and envisions himself in a reenactment of the crucifixion of Christ. Names—words—make meanings, and most of the characters in the novel unconsciously act out the identities that their names have allotted them or, more often than not, cursed them with.

One of the patterns that develops throughout the work is the comic way many of the names establish a satirical text. Paul Hammer moves into a wealthy section of Bullet Park called Powder Hill; the place becomes, then, an indicator of the source—gun powder—of the violence that accumulates in the novel. To further add to the satirical pattern, the name of the real estate agent who sells Hammer his house is, appropriately enough, Mr. Hazzard. Nailles belongs to the Gorey Brook Country Club, and Rev. Ransome is the pastor of Christ Church, a name that suggests Christ's ransoming himself for the sins of humankind on Calvary and the conservative critic and poet John Crowe Ransom, certainly a good, southern Christian gentleman whose "new criticism" canonized certain poems and poets as the last remaining symbols of historical coherence in the demythologized world of the 1930s, 1940s, and 1950s. And Nailles's first name, Eliot, suggests the poet T. S. Eliot and his similar pilgrimage toward truths he found in the structures and strictures of Anglo-Catholicism after his conversion in 1929. Much of John Crowe Ransom's new critical approach to literature comes directly out of T. S. Eliot's early literary criticism, especially "Tradition and the Individual Talent" (1919), and its prescriptions for establishing a specific cultural tradition based on a Western classical–Christian view of history.

Some of the important female figures also add to a darkly comic view of *Bullet Park*'s themes. Paul Hammer's mother is named Grace-Gretchen, a midwestern woman who becomes a dedicated Socialist and who also becomes pregnant by a wealthy drunk named Franklin Pierce Taylor, Paul Hammer's father. Since Paul is a bastard, his father won't permit him to use his name, and they decide to call him Hammer because at the moment of their discussion a gardener walked by the window carrying a hammer. Again, chance determines nomenclature which, in turn, conditions the behavior of the named. Cheever reverses one of the roles of the archetypal gardener, Adam-as-Namer, by trivializing the process and permitting chance, a glance out a window, to determine Paul's name and thus his fate. Hammer's mother, Grace, also becomes the prophetic conduit to the divine will—the function of grace in the Christian scheme—in determining his primary role in life. It is she who, acting in a semioracular role, bestows her son's vocation on him when she proposes crucifixion as punishment for the sins of capitalistic greed. The profile of the victim would be "an advertising executive . . . a good example of a life lived without any genuine emotion or value" (*BP,* 166). When Paul asks his mother precisely what action she would take, she states: "I would crucify him on the door of Christ's Church . . . Nothing less than a crucifixion will wake that world" (*BP,* 166).

The overall structure of the novel is divided into three parts. Part 1 deals with the life of Eliot Nailles and the formulation of his social and

religious value system, while part 2 details the life of Paul Hammer and
the various sources of his growing apocalyptic vision of the world and
what he sees as his evolving role in its destiny and awakening. Though
they occasionally run into each other and are Bullet Park neighbors in
the first two parts of the novel, they actually begin to become friends in
part 3. The comically obvious coincidence of their names—Hammer and
Nailles—also becomes the controlling metaphor of the book's blatantly
allegorical format and message. The Paul in Paul Hammer certainly
alludes to Christianity's foremost formulator of the restrictive attitudes
of Pauline Christianity toward the body, sexuality, and feelings. Saint
Paul unapologetically favored the soul or spirit over the downward pull
of the body and established Christianity's fear and loathing of the flesh,
a theological disposition that Saint Augustine absorbed and articulated
brilliantly in his *Confessions.* Pauline Christianity eventually evolved into
classic Calvinism that became the spiritual ground of America's contribution to Western progress, the Puritan or Protestant ethic. Cheever's
Pauline vision of America's origins and destiny finds its clearest
metaphor in the implied crucifixion that Hammer and Nailles symbolize, a crucifixion that such a value system and life-style demand. The
natural wants and needs of the body are suppressed by a work ethic that
requires some economic sign of success, God's favorable blessing, before
any real enjoyment may be experienced or acknowledged.

Saint Paul is the "hammer" that drives Paul Hammer to such polarized
behavioral extremes. Joy or satisfaction automatically turns into guilt as
he hammers his way through life, searching for an appropriate victim to
crucify as he simultaneously, and unconsciously, crucifies himself to a life
that oscillates between cyclic orgies of self-indulgence and self-abnega-
tion. Hammer becomes a metaphor for the unconscious self-destruction
that such a life-style embodies. Lewis Harwich, a character mentioned
only in passing, becomes an objective correlative documenting the horrif-
ic consequences of the Protestant ethic. Hammer reads the account of a
terrible accident in the Bullet Park newspaper: "Mr. Lewis Harwich was
burned to death last night when a can of charcoal ignitor exploded and
set fire to his clothing during a barbecue party in the garden of his home
at 23 Redburn Circle" (*BP,* 14). Eden has, indeed, become lethal in its
Dantean twenty-third circle of its modern-day inferno.

Nailles-nails, of course, becomes the instrument of crucifixion that
only Hammer can activate. Metaphorically, it is the hammer of Saint
Paul, that peculiar combination of self-loathing and passion, that Nailles
becomes the victim of on exterior and interior levels. Once the scales fall

from his eyes as he witnesses his son, Tony, descend into a spiritual torpor that debilitates him completely and sends him to his bed permanently, Eliot Nailles becomes his own worst enemy and finds that he needs drugs to get him through his hellish daily descent into the city. The Protestant ethic has utterly failed him when he begins to view his work as shallow, commercial, and empty; his religion satisfies none of his existential questions or yearnings; and his doctors show themselves to be helplessly ineffectual and at times contribute to the severity of his problems rather than to their solution. It is, in fact, his own doctor, Dr. Mullin, who prescribes the tranquilizing pills, Miltown and Nembutal, which Nailles must henceforth take to function during his waking hours and knock himself out at night.

The names of minor characters are as allegorical as those of the major characters because they share with them the quality of objects. But they also possess similar aggressive—even war-like—characteristics. The perpetually wounded yet randy Wickwires, who surface intermittently throughout the novel, appear with broken limbs, black eyes, and bruises about the head and shoulders, are victims of their own drunken behavior. Mrs. Wickwire makes her last appearance at the final party at the Lewellens in a wheelchair. Their desperate attempts to get their week going after a long weekend of partying and drinking at the beginning of *Bullet Park* is one of Cheever's most hilarious routines. They finally resort to a semimilitaristic sexual coupling despite massive hangovers, an aggressive maneuver that enables Mr. Wickwire to start for work: "finally he dresses and racked by vertigo, melancholy, nausea, and fitful erections he boards his Gethsemane—the Monday-morning 10:48" (*BP,* 9). Their name combines the mechanistic with the sexual. Hammer's disturbed wife, Marietta, was named Drum before she became a Hammer, a coincidence of names that contributes to the verbal drumming she gives him at their first and presumably last dinner party. Drums, like wicks and wires, are used as objects of war and serve to spur soldiers to war-like behavior. Marietta Drum-Hammer, once she begins to drink heavily, becomes embarrassingly bellicose in the extreme as she viciously attacks her husband, Paul, accusing him of every kind of malfeasance from adultery to being a drunken, isolated doormat.

Although he appears only to disappear, Harry Shinglehouse, the fellow Bullet Park commuter, is sucked under the Chicago Express before the horrified gaze of both Hammer and Nailles. Shinglehouse is, of course, another object blown away by high winds, but shingles are the very things that protect suburbanites from the ravages of nature. Along with drums, wicks and wires, strings and kites play important roles in demonstrating the way Hammer's alcoholic imagination projects significance into harmless, common objects. Paul Hammer experiences a major epiphany on a beach as he is being "cruised" by a homosexual, or so he imagines. He is convinced, in his semihysterical state, that a "faggot" is trying to seduce him. And one must not forget that his psychiatrist had earlier diagnosed Hammer as a repressed homosexual. Hammer "escapes" a potential homosexual seduction by joining up with a middle-aged man and his wife and two children and shows them how to fly their kite in the proper way. This incident shows Hammer, once again, reading deeper meanings everywhere and concluding that the kite and the string have become redemptive objects saving him from such a life: "but the filament of kite line in my fingers, both tough and fine, that had quite succinctly declared my intention to the faggot seemed for a moment to possess some extraordinary moral force as if the world I had declared to live in was bound together by just such a length of string—cheap, durable and colorless" (*BP*, 145). Hammer's penchant for joining up becomes a pattern through the novel to such an extent that he actually changes his name, temporarily, from Hammer to Levy, a name that actually means "joining" in Hebrew.

Cheever's handling of major symbols has never been more skillful. Both Hammer and Nailles are involved in great existential journeys to find certitude and meaning in an empty, relativistic world. Hammer travels throughout America and Europe and finally discovers his vocation in life—to immolate the anti-Christ as manifested in the typical American businessman, the primary reason he decides to move to Bullet Park. Nailles, on the other hand, has been a true believer, as has his wife, Nellie, in the promise of the American dream. They are long-time inhabitants of Bullet Park, and the first part of the novel shows them discovering the fragility and, finally, the disappearance of the beliefs and practices on which they have built their lives. Their fall, then, consists of moving from a condition of ignorance into one of knowledge concerning their actual life in a modern wasteland of American social and ethical values. There is nothing sacred anymore; everything has been profaned by the lack of a moral and spiritual center.

For centuries, Western civilization has used the legend of the Holy Grail to embody concepts of redemption, wholeness, holiness, and healing. Nailles and his family attend Christ's Church and receive the Holy Eucharist, communion, in an act that symbolizes their participation in the Communion of Saints and, thus, a sacramental condition that tran-

scends and ameliorates the assaults of time. Cheever again uses the figure of the Eucharist, the Grail—Christianity's most sacred symbol—and
transforms it into a mouthwash, Spang. Cheever has created a mechanistic and therefore demonic version of the Grail by making it a substance
that one drinks not to gain entrance into a sacramental condition of holy
communion with God and one's fellows but to spit out. There is no true,
sacramental transfiguration only a prophylactic sanitizing that creates
the appearance—the aroma—of cleanliness and sanitation.

Significantly, it is Nailles's son Tony who drives his father to nearly
murdering him when Tony throws the cosmetic emptiness of his father's
lifelong profession in his face after Eliot has been badgering him into
looking for some kind of "meaningful" occupation: "He said he might
want to be a thief or a saint or a drunkard or a garbage man or a gas
pumper or a traffic cop or a hermit. Then I lost my patience, my woolly
blanket, and said that he had to get off his ass and do something useful
and he said: 'What? Like pushing mouthwash?' Then I lifted up my putter and I would have split his skull in two but he ducked" (*BP,* 116). And
it is directly following this scene that Tony takes to his bed and stays
there.

Earlier in the novel, Eliot Nailles had experienced a devastating revelation that counterpoints Hammer's kite and string epiphany. For
Nailles, the symbol of meaning and coherence is a bridge, an object that
joins seemingly unconnectable points. The suction-death of Harry
Shinglehouse threw Eliot into spiritual vertigo, an ontological crisis:
"Nailles's sense of being alive was to bridge or link the disparate envi-
ronments and rhythms of his world, and one of his principal bridges—
that between his white house and his office—had collapsed" (*BP,* 62). He
then characterizes his train trip into the city as stations, as in the stations
of the cross: "Station by station he made a cruel pilgrimage into the city"
(*BP,* 63). Recurring motifs and images of the Grail, and other Christian
symbols in the Roman Catholic and Anglican churches, transform the
lives of Nailles and Hammer into unconscious reenactments of Christ's
passion. The stations of the cross, the agony in the Garden of
Gethsemane, the scourging at the pillar of the American materialistic
enterprise system, and the crowning of thorns in the mental anguish
that both Hammer and Nailles undergo, constitute lives that move inexorably to Calvary's summit. Indeed, Nailles's life has become so painful
that he requires another kind of Grail-like curative, tranquilizers
(Miltown) and sleeping pills (Nembutal). Again, like the merely cosmetic function and effects of Spang, these pills temporarily benumb his con-

sciousness of the living hell that his life has become. Though the effects of these so-called curatives are supposed to be temporary, the need to take them becomes permanent, and his drug addiction becomes the center of Nailles's life: "The tranquilizer gave him the illusion that he floated upon a cloud like Zeus in some allegorical painting . . . When the train came in he picked up his cloud and settled himself in a window seat. If the day was dark, the landscape wintry, the little towns they passed shabby and depressing, none of this reached to where he lay in his rosy nimbus" (*BP,* 119).

The principal source of Eliot Nailles's pain is the increasingly troubled relationship between him and his son Tony. Though Tony sees through the hypocrisy of his father's devotion to Spang and scorns his materialistic values, Tony is also deeply divided over the Puritanical attitudes of his parents over sexual matters regarding him, though not themselves, and is mystified by "the carnal demands, encouragements, exclamations and cheers he heard so often from his parents' bedroom" (*BP,* 33). In addition to his perplexity over his parents' bifurcated sexual attitudes and behavior, he is frustrated by his father's inability to show him affection by fostering some kind of paternal intimacy between them. Instead of expressing his love, he merely gives him gifts: "The only reason you love me, the only reason you think you love me is because you can give me things" (*BP,* 115). And though Tony is embarrassed and confused by his parents' vivid sex life, his father, on discovering Tony's collection of pornographic pictures of half-naked women, does not hesitate to destroy it. Tony uses an expensive tape recorder, a gift from his father, to record his bitter feelings about his parents' sexual behavior. Had Eliot Nailles turned on the tape machine, he would have heard Tony's expressions of frustration and anger: "You dirty old baboon, you dirty old baboon. For as long as I can remember it seems to me that whenever I'm trying to go to sleep I can hear you saying dirty things. You say the dirtiest things in the whole world, you dirty, filthy, horny old baboon" (*BP,* 37). And, making the hypocrisy worse, Eliot holds up his adoration of the Broadway musical *Guys and Dolls* as an example of aesthetic perfection that embodies the American sublime.

The most radical event in Tony's teen years is, however, his difficulty with his highly neurotic and sexually hysterical French teacher, Miss Hoe. Of course, a "hoe" is another object in the evolving catalog of objects that make up virtually all the characters in the novel. But this pedagogical "hoe" does not result in a fruitful educational harvest with her student. After she decides that Tony must drop off the football team so he can improve his French grade, Tony calmly states: "You know I could kill you . . . I could strangle you" (*BP,* 80). Miss Hoe immediately becomes hysterical and runs to the principal's office claiming that: "He threatened to kill me," a claim that becomes, after the police arrive: "He tried to kill me" (*BP,* 81). And Tony perceives how language creates reality, a lesson that dramatically deepens his depression.

In the final scene before Tony takes to his bed permanently, he and his father are playing miniature golf and having a paternally directed philosophical discussion as Eliot tries to explain to him why he must not quit school. Tony says he wants to become a social worker, a profession where he may be able to escape the "phoniness" of middle-class life, a word used here in the same way it is used by Holden Caulfield in J. D. Salinger's *Catcher in the Rye.* Contrary to his father's wishes, Tony does not want a college degree, which, he insists, is "just a phony scrap of paper" (*BP,* 114–15). The argument between father and son intensifies to the point where Tony berates his father's work life and Eliot raises his phallic putter in an act of potential murder. Tony then becomes an emotional and psychological invalid and takes to his bed.

The only way Tony can articulate the nature of his condition is by comparing it with a house of cards and the oppressively contingent feeling that this image evokes: "I feel terribly sad. I feel as if the house were made of cards. When I was a little kid and sick you used to make me card houses and I'd blow them over. This is a nice house and I like it but I feel as if it were made of cards" (*BP,* 45). Tony's overpowering sense of melancholy counterpoints Hammer's notoriously quixotic *cafard.* Paul Hammer defines *cafard* as "melancholy . . . a form of despair" (*BP,* 172); Cheever himself defined it in his journals as "this immortal longing, this mysterious and stupendous melancholy" (*J,* 135).

With wit and insight, Cheever uses Tony's condition and his father's response as vehicles to explore the ways Americans then treated their spiritual and psychological problems. While the source of seventeen-year-old Tony's suffering is spiritual, Eliot is determined to try traditional middle-class medical remedies. He brings in his physician, Dr. Mullin, who prescribes tranquilizers; they only make Tony's condition worse. Eliot then tries a psychiatrist, Dr. Bronson, who after a fifty-minute visit with Tony in his bedroom (a comic reference to psychiatrists' traditional fifty-minute hour) is convinced that Tony should be hospitalized in a sanitarium called Stonehenge and be given electroshock therapy. After rejecting this horrible proposal, Eliot, now desperate, brings in a specialist "on somnambulatory phenomena," a recovering alcoholic who connects Tony to various machines while indulging in a nonstop monologue on his battle with alcohol addition and who sends the family a bill for $500.

Among the possible trades and vocations other than social work that Tony enumerated to his father during their dramatic confrontation on the miniature golf course, he mentioned that he might want to become a drunkard or a garbage man or a saint or a hermit—foreshadowings of what he could become. He has, in true adherence to his namesake, become a hermit. Saint Anthony of the desert, a fourth-century Egyptian monk and the founder of monasticism, decided at age twenty that the world was a wasteland of temptation and sorrow and went to live alone in various districts of lower Egypt. He is recognized as the first of the great "desert fathers." Such historical and religious allusions are not minor. What eventually cures Tony is meditation, and meditation is precisely what the desert hermits spent most of their time doing.

Tony's cure comes from a Jamaican healer, Swami Rutuola, whom Tony's mother, Nellie, learns about from her maid, Mary Ashton (an apt name that combines the divine intercessor, the Blessed Virgin Mary, with a clear symbol of the wasteland condition in which Bullet Park and America are spiritually buried). Nellie, whose given name is Mary Ellen, descends into the Hades of the poorest slum of Bullet Park to seek healing from Swami Rutuola. Like Christ's mother, Nellie acts as an intercessor between two very different worlds. The Swami is, among all of the characters in *Bullet Park,* perhaps the kindest and most decent. He agrees to see Tony immediately and refuses compensation for his "healings." Cheever structures an inverted Dantean descent when Nellie arrives at the home of the Swami, which is above a funeral home and is called the "Temple of Light."

On meeting Tony, Swami Rutuola openly and honestly details his own descent into the dark night of the soul—his stay in prison where he was beaten so severely by fellow inmates that he lost the sight in his left eye, the eye in Gnostic lore that possesses mystical insight. After his release from prison, the only work he could find was cleaning toilets in the men's room at Grand Central Station, where he began to understand the depth of desperation that human beings express in the obscene graffiti they inscribe on walls. He came to understand "how lonely and horny mankind is" (*BP,* 130). One night, a middle-aged man collapsed there and begged the Swami not to let him die alone, his greatest fear. Rutuola then carried the man up to the empty great concourse of Grand Central and directed his attention to the enormous illustrated advertisement for cameras showing a brightly lit pastoral scene of a family on a beach with gorgeous snow-covered mountains in the background. He encouraged the dying man to concentrate on the image, an Edenic one, and got him to recite a mantra that consisted of repeating the word *valor* over and over until the man felt better and was able to get a cab to a hotel. Rutuola's meditative technique, a mantric litany of the word *valor,* demonstrates his ability to tap the potential valor or courage that the word embodies and make that power available to the collapsed man.

Cheever seems to invite an ironic comparison between the different responses that these "therapies" evoke when he names the doctor at Nailles's mother's nursing home, Dr. Power, who reports that his comatose mother repeats her own unconscious mantra: "I'm living in a foxhole" (PB, 26). The verb form of *valor* is *valorize,* a word not used in the late 1960s the way it is in recent critical discussions, meaning to assign value to or to create meaning in an indifferent and nonteleological universe. Rutuola helped the collapsed man by encouraging—or valorizing—him to continue living by focusing his attention on an Edenic scene—a fiction—that became a possibility or promise that he might someday attain. The dynamics of Rutuola's "promised land," that a better and more satisfying life is always possible, is the exact opposite of Hammer's sentimental or nostalgic—and impossible—yearnings for a past that can never be reassembled or "valorized," only remembered with increasing sorrow and regret.

Swami Rutuola uses the same meditative method with Tony that he did with the man in Grand Central Station, but he explains his methods in greater detail. He immediately tells Tony that he believes in the efficacy of prayer, but not in a traditional Christian sense: "I believe in prayer as a force and not as a conversation with God and when my prayers are answered . . . I honestly do not know where to direct my expressions of gratitude" (*BP,* 136). Rutuola's emphasis on the inner light, or source of energy and healing, immediately releases Tony from ingrained and traditional religious obligations involving formalized prayers and precarious attempts to somehow contact and converse with an ultimate listener, God, whose "responses" are riddled with doubt and confusion. Rutuola proceeds to teach Tony nothing less than the first prelude or step in the spiritual exercises of St. Ignatius Loyola: composition of place.

The Swami calls himself "a spiritual cheerleader" who possesses a varied reservoir of cheers, an adumbration of Roland Barthes's concept of a "reservoir of images" with which artists sustain themselves in creating their work: "I have all kinds of cheers. I have love cheers and compassionate cheers and hopeful cheers and then I have cheers of place" (*BP*, 136). He then carefully lays out what, according to the Ignatian Method of Meditation, is known as composition of place; that is, the Jesuit novice, before attempting to speak to God, imaginatively prepares—creates—a fictive place in which he may encounter the divine. But the place that Rutuola is enabling Tony to create involves uncovering the power of the soul, by means of the imagination, to heal itself. The imagination, then, becomes a means of grace in the Emersonian sense, not to speak to an ultimate listener outside the self but to contact the origins of self-identity in their most profound activity—the creation of one's own world, recognized as such, which satisfies the soul's deepest needs.

By teaching Tony the dynamics of composition of place, or "place cheers," Rutuola is also teaching him what James Hillman calls "healing fictions"—that is, how, with assistance, the soul can heal itself with its own powers by telling itself stories, creating fictions that protect it from the unbearable realities of living in a demythologized world. Wallace Stevens, in defining the concept of nobility in ancient Greek art, also defined the same redemptive power of the imagination as "a violence from within that protects us from a violence without. It is the imagination pressing back against the pressure of reality."[3]

Rutuola then leads Tony in a repeat-after-me-step-by-step creation of a "healing fiction" about a young man sitting by the sea waiting for his beloved, who will return shortly. The story concludes with a reassuring coda: "I am sitting under an apple tree in clean clothes. I am content" (*BP*, 137). After repeating a litany of "love" cheers and "hope" cheers, Tony appears to be on his way out of his debilitating dark night of the soul and actually gets out of bed and takes a few faltering steps, like the resurrected Lazarus emerging from the tomb: "Oh I feel like myself again . . . I'm not sad any more . . . I'm all better, Daddy . . . I'm still weak but that terrible sadness is gone. I don't feel sad anymore and the house doesn't seem to be made of cards" (*BP*, 138–39). By using the power of his imagination in creating useful and convincing fictions and by learning the crucial relationships between words, actions, and meaning, Tony has discovered that he possesses the key in determining his identity or who he is. He is empowered by the possibilities that his present actions possess as projected by his fictions in creating a life that he may now inhabit.

Comparing Hammer's feeling of melancholy with Tony's and contrasting their ways of dealing with its debilitating effects becomes the heart of the novel's theme and shows Cheever addressing and engaging the agonizing philosophical and moral issues of the day. Hammer reveals the way he responds to his *cafard,* or massive despair, by taking long, circuitous journeys throughout the United States and Europe. Hammer's mother, Gretchen-Grace, makes sure that beneath all these searches for release, Paul possesses a purpose in life; that is, to crucify the archetypal American capitalist and awaken the world. Of course, Paul Hammer's namesake, St. Paul, struggled with his own recurring *cafard,* which he called "a sting of the flesh." But once Paul converted to Christianity, he was no longer seriously threatened by it. Paul Hammer, though, has no redeeming conversion to relieve him of his particularly virulent brand of melancholy and its sudden and unexpected appearances.

He does explain, however, the effect it has on him and the psychological strategies he uses to overcome it. He defines his *cafard* as "a form of despair that sometimes seemed to have a tangible approach. Once or twice, I think, I seemed to glimpse some of its physical attributes. It was covered with hair—it was the classic bête noire—but it was as a rule no more visible than a moving column of thin air" (*BP,* 172). Most important, however, is that in detailing successful techniques in overcoming it, he also reveals its source: "My best defense, my only defense, was to cover my head with a pillow and summon up those images that represented for me the excellence and beauty I had lost" (*BP,* 172). By covering his head with a pillow, Hammer is quite obviously returning to the most satisfying memory of all, the womb itself, revealing an Oedipal dilemma that signals his unconscious Thanatos, or death wish. His private, solipsistic meditative methods are the exact opposite of those of Tony Nailles, whose healing fictions create or compose a place in which he can dwell in the possibility of future promise. Paul Hammer's ruminative techniques can only evoke images from a fallen world, an irretrievable and, therefore, unredeemable past of sentimental nostalgias that crucify him between a pristine, Edenic past and the unbearable fallen world of the present.

Hammer lists the archetypal images and delineates in great detail their comforting power but, unlike Tony Nailles, is unable to transform them into useful, healing fictions. His sole response is to suffer their lost beauty. He presumably summons from the depths of his unconscious image reservoir three recurring and never-changing scenarios: the image of a mountain, certainly Mount Kilimanjaro, with a Bronze or Iron Age village resting at its foot; a fortified medieval town resembling Orvieto or Mont-Saint-Michel or the grand lamasery in Tibet; and, finally, "a

river with grassy banks . . . the Elysian Fields." All of these images
seemed to represent "beauty, enthusiasm and love" (*BP,* 172–73). They
remain permanent, unchanging, and are exterior to Hammer's bleak
inner life. He is never able to interiorize them into useful forms of "healing" fictions. Instead, they coerce him into travelling to the actual loca-
tions, desperately hoping that he will experience some kind of mystical,
healing encounter. In short, he must concretize these metaphors into
actuality.

His severely attenuated imagination resembles that of T. S. Eliot in
that both of them experience life as an event of overwhelming loss, and
only the massive memory of some kind of ideal past—the monolithic
Christianity of the Middle Ages, for example—could focus their lives
meaningfully. But T. S. Eliot, to save himself from his recurring break-
downs, felt compelled to convert to the Anglican religion, an institution
that made permanent the values and beliefs that could save him from
the spiritual sterility of the modern wasteland condition following World
War I. Paul Hammer shares T. S. Eliot's terror of the imagination's penchant for fantasy, fiction, and solipsism which will not permit Hammer
to engage in the mythopoeic stirrings that revivify Tony Nailles's life and
comfort him. Tony's fictions, because they are his own, and he knows it,
possess the power to transform him because he allows them to do so.
Hammer's fantasies and memories exclude him, so he is forced to actual-
ize them by literally going to Orvieto to inject himself into his fantasies—to make them "real"—an act that portends madness and
eventual death.

One of the most revealing scenes in *Bullet Park* is Paul Hammer's visit
to the Museum of National History in New York City. He can define his
peculiar Eden only when he recognizes it, which he does at the museum
by remembering his visit some fifteen years earlier. His present visit
becomes significant only in relation to a former memory as they coalesce
into a comforting, permanent image: "Here in the stale and cavernous
dark was a thrilling sense of permanence. Here were landscapes, seasons,
moments in time that had not changed by a leaf or a flake of snow during my lifetime. The flamingoes flew exactly as they had flown when I
was a child. The rutting mooses still slinked through the blue snow
towards the pane of glass that separated them from chaos and change,
and not a leaf of the brilliant autumn foliage had fallen" (*BP,* 210).
Nothing could be further from the transforming epiphany of Tony
Nailles's healing fictions than Hammer's recognition and embracing of
T. S. Eliot's evocation of stasis as paradise: "At the still point of the turn-

ing world."[4] Hammer's enemies are the same as those of his namesake, St. Paul, and T. S. Eliot: chaos and change, the heart of his existential terror.

Hammer uses, in addition to his chaotic trips all over the Western world searching for "yellow rooms"—an evocation of the womb—gin for its ameliorating effects. But gin also becomes the agency of stasis, a Grail that has the same effect as the static tableau in the museum. Gin freezes time and makes the world his own, enabling him to create "permanent" solipsistic fantasies.

Hammer further elucidates the backward direction of his imagination as memory when he defines his own peculiar form of love and regards himself as one, somehow, above the vulgar crowd of weaklings who fall in love with actual people: "My fault was that I had thought of love as a heady distillate of nostalgia—a force of memory that had resisted analysis by cybernetics. We do not fall in love—I thought—we reenter love, and I had fallen in love with a memory" (*BP*, 214). He then explains, since his wife refuses to have sex with him, that he must resort to "the reveries of an adolescent, a soldier, or a prisoner" and feels forced to invent "dream girls" to fuel his masturbatory fantasies: "Like all lonely men, I fell in love—hopelessly—with the girls on magazine covers and the models who advertise girdles . . . These were women I had never seen" (*BP*, 215). Hammer's truncated spiritual world functions only at the level of sexual fantasies from "girlie" magazines, a habit that underscores his life-long narcissism that will not permit him to acknowledge the genuinely new. If he has spent his life reentering love, then he has never lost it; there has been no fall, no new knowledge and experience and, therefore, no need for redemption. Certainly the classic narcissist never actually experiences guilt because he has never become conscious of falling into sin; he is always a victim of some wicked exterior agency.

On Hammer's last trip to escape his overwhelming sense of despair, he experienced a genuine feeling of community. It happened in Rome as he observed a memorial procession passing by, and he deeply felt himself one with a group of silent mourners. He was so touched that he joined the procession for the deceased communist delegate named Mazzacone and was especially moved by the placards, which read "PACE" (peace), "SPERANZA" (hope), and "AMORE" (love). Hammer was moved to tears: "There was no question of drying my tears . . . and as soon as I began to march I felt the cafard take off" (*BP*, 218). He marched with the mourners for three blocks in silence, except for the "shuffle and hiss of shoe leather, much of it worn, and because of our numbers, a loud, weird and organic sound, a sighing that someone with his back to the parade might have mistaken for the sea" (*BP*, 218). Hammer, then, narcissistically analyzes the arbitrary nature of his grief: "This grief which, in my case, we accidentally shared, reminded me of how little else there was that we had in common. I felt the strongest love for those strangers for the space of three city blocks" (*BP*, 218).

Once again, Hammer can respond emotionally only to a sentimental past, a nostalgic memory that reinforces the grief, the existential emptiness these mourners share among themselves. The name of the deceased communist delegate, Mazzacone, underscores Hammer's identification with him: *mazza* in Italian means "sledge-hammer," "club," or "mace," and *cone* means "cone," a fairly obvious phallic object. Hammer can be deeply moved only by another "hammer," this time a sledge-hammer. Only an unconscious image of himself moves him to tears, which are really tears of self-pity. The mixture of the phallic and the narcissistic establish beyond question the solipsistic nature of Hammer's closed world, and enables him, the following summer, as he is resting on a beach, to remember "that my crazy old mother's plan to crucify a man was sound and that I would settle in Bullet Park and murder Nailles. Sometime later I changed my victim to Tony" (*BP*, 219).

The radical contrast between Tony Nailles's recovery and Paul Hammer's psychic regression shows Cheever expanding and deepening his fictions beyond the obvious allegorical contexts of *Bullet Park*. On one hand, Hammer's narcissism keeps him from seeing himself as an isolated and, therefore, impotent instrument—a hammer without nails—but on the other, it empowers him to crucify Tony. His self-involvement blinds him to the self-destruction he is actually fashioning as he plans the murder of Tony Nailles. Because he possesses a bleak spiritual life composed mainly of vague, sentimental yearnings for an irretrievable past, he feels compelled to commit an act of murder that will awaken the capitalistic world to its own self-consumption and transform him into the savior of that world.

Tony Nailles's healing results from what he learns from Swami Rutuola regarding methods to create and recreate himself within his own changing stories or narratives. The poet George Quasha delineates the vital connection between the imagination and the soul's spiritual health as it is expressed in what he calls healing fictions: "healing is a life process that begins with our acceptance of our fictive realities and authorial roles within them, the acceptance, that is, of myself as the arena I create for specific independently originating psychic forces." Quasha, in

defining the important work of James Hillman in identifying the fictive
with the spiritual, adds: "The psychological context of Hillman's work
offers a permission to take one's own stories with the same authority
assigned to great fiction . . . Psychological freedom is compositional; the
private mind composes itself and inhabits an art-space."[5]

Because Paul Hammer views his life as a crucifixion between the
polarities of what painter Francis Bacon called "the brutality of fact" and
an arbitrary, meaningless set of chance coincidences without an interven-
ing human imagination as spiritual arbiter, he is compelled to fulfill the
destructive role that his mad mother imposed upon him. Gretchen-
Grace Oxencroft is one of Cheever's darkest yet subtlest archetypal
women. As an inversion of Gretchen, Goethe's "eternal feminine" in
Faust, she becomes not the agent of an upward striving to improve herself and the world but the opposite: a nihilistic, fatal woman who leads
Paul to damnation. Though she sometimes calls herself Grace, she is
anything but.

Part 3 of *Bullet Park* shows Hammer befriending Eliot Nailles so that
he may get close to the recovered Tony, his intended sacrificial victim.
He plans to execute Tony by immolating him on the altar of Christ's
Church. His mistake is that he gets drunk for exactly the wrong reasons:
"not for courage or stimulation but to make the ecstasy of his lawlessness
endurable" (*BP,* 234). Once he is released from his habitual condition of
spiritual stasis—ecstasy means "out of stasis"—he loses control and his
first act is to inform Swami Rutuola that he plans to murder Tony. Real
freedom for Paul is immediately transformed into the most obvious self-
destructive behavior.

The conclusion of the novel comes very close to melodrama when
Eliot Nailles breaks through the door of Christ Church with a chain saw.
The self-indulgent narcissist Hammer, who insists on finishing his cigarette, is found weeping in the front pew of the church: "Nailles lifted his
son off the altar and carried him out into the rain" (*BP,* 242). Cheever
concludes the novel in an objective journalistic reporting of the facts:
"Paul Hammer, also of Bullet Park, confessed to attempted homicide
and was remanded to the State Hospital for the Criminally Insane . . .
He carried Nailles to the church with the object of immolating him in
the chancel. He intended, he claimed, to awaken the world" (*BP,* 243).
Hammer had finally been given an opportunity to confess his sins, which
was the first time he had gotten sufficiently outside himself to see what
he had become. There are widely divergent critical opinions on the tone
of the last sentence of the novel. Eden is restored insofar as Tony is back

in school and his father "Nailles . . . drugged—went off to work and everything was as wonderful, wonderful, wonderful, wonderful as it had been" (*BP,* 243). Certainly the four "wonderfuls" indicate that Eliot is once again safely ensconced on his tranquilized cloud "like Zeus in some allegorical painting . . . where he lay in his rosy nimbus" (*BP,* 119). Only Tony has been transfigured owing to the spiritual lessons of Swami Rutuola. The repeated "wonderfuls" also resonate with one of the most popular American television shows, another "Temple of Light," throughout the 1950s, 1960s, and 1970s: *The Lawrence Welk Show.* The show became a veritable icon of and for the American middle class, who heard, over a twenty-seven-year period, Welk's incessant refrain, his response to each and every act presented on his show as "wonderful, wonderful, wonderful, wonderful."

The World of Apples

Though the critical reception of *Bullet Park* was mixed, *The World of Apples* fared better. Scott Donaldson, though, found only a few of the stories approaching the excellence of Cheever's earlier masterpieces like "The Swimmer," "Goodbye, My Brother," and "The Country Husband" (Donaldson 1988, 269). Three or four, though, out of a collection of ten do stand out in terms of their perceptive delineation of character and their ability to evoke resonating mythic parallels from Greek and Roman mythologies. Several also concern themselves with sexual obsession combined with the fear of aging and death, phobias Cheever himself was battling during the late 1960s and early 1970s. The title story of the collection is Cheever's "Death in Venice" combined with his portrait of the artist as an old man, the story of an American expatriate poet who has lived in Italy for many years.

The poet, Asa Bascomb, shares physical characteristics and psychological affinities with several famous poets, such as Robert Frost, Ezra Pound, and William Butler Yeats. Bascomb shares Frost's snow-white hair, his New England roots, pastoral subject matter, and Yankee stubbornness, but Pound's expatriate figure is obvious. He has settled in a small village at the foot of Monte Carbone (Mount Charcoal), south of Rome, a name that ironically mirrors the charcoal remains of Bascomb's sexuality, which are dramatically reignited when he stumbles on a couple fornicating in the woods near Monte Felici (Mount Happiness). He finds himself so traumatized by the compelling starkness of the scene that he can only produce the most obscene kinds of poetry for the next ten days, giving them titles like "The Fart That Saved Athens" and "The Confessions of a Public School Headmaster." Even taking his housekeeper, Maria, to bed—his wife has been dead for ten years—does little to relieve him of his late-Yeatsian sexual frenzy. He finally resorts to making a pilgrimage to Rome, hoping that some contact with high culture will exorcise his compulsive demons. He stays where he always stays, at the Hotel Minerva, the Roman equivalent of Athena, the patron of artists, but finds himself, like his German counterpart, Gustave von Aschenbach in "Death in Venice," drawn to the sexual underground as he enters a public men's room and observes a male prostitute displaying his wares. Bascomb's imagination, however, in true Ovidian fashion (this story is about both metamorphosis and water) transforms an obscenity into an almost spiritual message: "he seemed to old Bascomb angelic, armed with a flaming sword that might conquer banality and smash the glass of custom" (*SJC,* 618).

He returns home more sexually desperate than ever from his second failed pilgrimage, a cultural one, and determines to make a religious pilgrimage, even though he is not a believer, to a local holy place known as Monte Giordano (Mount Jordan), an allusion to Christianity's most sacred river, in which Jesus Christ was himself baptized. He intends to pray to the patron of the holy mountain, the Sacred Angel of Monte Giordano, for release from his degrading sexual compulsions. On his way to the holy mountain, he befriends a dog and encounters an old man who invites him into a shelter during a storm; Bascomb envies the peace and serenity of the old man and also comforts the trembling dog, who is terrified by the thunder and the rain. It is comically ironic that one of the most common names for dogs in Italy is Giordano—like Spot and Rover in America—though this dog is unnamed. Both the dog and the old man are more than anonymous and accidental presences, particularly since the dog's fear of water foreshadows the watery baptism that concludes the story and releases Bascomb from his sexual distractions. The unnamed old man also resembles the ghost of Yeats, whom T. S. Eliot meets during an air raid in London in part 2 of "Little Gidding" from the *Four Quartets.* The Yeatsian ghost relates to Eliot the agony of growing old and the lacerating pain of remembered shame and guilt, mostly sexual, that unexpectedly returns in old age. And it is for exorcism of his priapic possession that Bascomb humbly enters the sanctuary of the Sacred Angel of Monte Giordano.

After donating the Lermontov Medal he had received from the Soviet Academy of Arts to the skeptical priest at the church, he begins his

homeward journey. Cheever's choice of the Lermontov allusion cleverly
fits the precarious spiritual conditions that Bascomb finds himself torn
between, because two of Lermontov's most famous poems are "Demon"
and "Angel"—certainly apt metaphors describing Bascomb's dilemma.
Bascomb had earlier discovered the origin of his belated sexual reawak-
ening in his New England Calvinist repression: "Was it merely some
ancient fear of Daddy's razor strap and Mummy's scowl, some childish
subservience to the bullying world? . . . and had he allowed the world
and all its tongues to impose upon him some structure of transparent
values for the convenience of a conservative economy, an established
church, and a bellicose army and navy?" (*SJC*, 619). In short, he sees
himself as a classic product of America's most common cultural formulator, the Protestant or Puritan ethic, the avowed enemy of the instinc-
tual expression of the body.

It is, however, on his second entrance into the woods—his first in a
forest near Mount Felici where he came upon the copulating pair and
lost his innocence—that he discovers the means of his redemption. The
last act he had performed at the church on Monte Giordano was to pray
to and for the souls of his spiritual/literary ancestors: William Faulkner,
Dylan Thomas, Hart Crane, F. Scott Fitzgerald, and especially Ernest
Hemingway, all of whom had destroyed their lives because of their various obsessions with alcohol and sex rooted in their own Calvinistic guilt.
Both Hemingway and Crane actually committed suicide, thoughts of
which had plagued Bascomb earlier in the story. That night Bascomb
awakens from a dream-vision in a hotel bed with four brass angels
guarding the bedposts and finds himself "in that radiance he had known
when he was younger. Something seemed to shine in his mind and limbs
and lights and vitals" (*SJC*, 622).

The residue of his dream-vision in which he felt himself in a youthful
radiance became a visionary metamorphosis that required a natural
counterpart for its complete fulfillment: "on the next day, walking down
from Monte Giordano to the main road, he heard the trumpeting of a
waterfall. He went into the woods to find this" (*SJC*, 622). As he views
the waterfall, he suddenly remembers a scene from his childhood where
he observed an old man stripping naked and entering into a similar
waterfall on the Vermont farm where he had been raised. The man bel-
lowed with pleasure as he stepped into the icy torrent and Bascomb realizes that that old man was his father, but only after he has left the scene.
He then replicates his long-dead father's actions and enters this Italian

version of the cleansing waters of the River Jordan as he "stepped naked into the torrent, bellowing like his father" (*SJC*, 623).

Of course, Bascomb undergoes a natural baptism and enters the cold bath not to Calvinistically extinguish the fires of youthful ardor and sexual desire but to celebrate the body's physicality. Two of the essential phases in Joseph Campbell's mythological journey of the hero are "the call to adventure" and "father atonement," both of which Bascomb fulfills as he answers the call of the waterfall and imitates his long-dead father, realizing that he has "become" his father both spiritually and physically. This scene constitutes one of Cheever's most brilliant visionary scenarios, perhaps his most impressive, especially in his ability to unify his actual father with his angelic literary fathers and juxtapose them with the life-denying forces of the Puritan ethic. Cheever transforms the Puritanical long walks and cold showers into Bascomb's spiritual pilgrimages and waterfall baptism that become authentically redemptive: "he seemed at last to be himself . . . and in the morning he began a long poem on the inalienable dignity of light and air that, while it would not get him the Nobel Prize, would grace the last months of his life" (*SJC*, 623). Cheever's last sentence contains the most important detail that concludes the story's major theme; that is, that Bascomb's body had responded for the most crucial of reasons—that death was imminent and the body insisted on a valedictory acceptance and celebration of the persistence of life.

Another story from *The World of Apples*, "Mene, Mene, Tekel, Upharsin," records a tale about the persistence of the imagination, in this case as found and documented on the dark walls of men's rooms. Cheever's unnamed expatriate hero revisits America on business and is able to view it more objectively after having lived overseas for many years; he returns to a world that deeply disturbs him. After a difficult and circuitous flight during which the old DC-7 almost goes down in mid-Atlantic, he finally arrives at Idlewild and then New York's Grand Central Station. He descends into the men's room, a threatening place mentioned occasionally by Cheever throughout his journals and stories, and experiences a revelation somewhat like the one Swami Rutuola of *Bullet Park* had in the same location.

What the narrator observes not only in Grand Central Station but in men's rooms in Union Station in Indianapolis and on the train heading back east is the graffiti on their walls. The texts he notices are not the obscene imperatives or invitations of common graffiti but lengthy narrative texts whose literary style and banal subject matter offend his sense of decorum. He also examines the medium on which the first two texts are written—the quality of the marble and the patterns he detects within the stone itself. Cheever had never built a story—and it is barely a story at all—in such a way as to call attention to its structure as a structure.

Mythically, of course, this story is another descent into one of Cheever's favorite threatening places, an underworld of buried texts hidden from the common eye that cry out for explanation, interpretation, and understanding: why are they there and what do they mean? In short, the narrative rests upon a variety of palimpsests, those ancient written documents whose original texts can sometimes be detected beneath more recent ones. Cheever uncovers a series of palimpsests not only within the narratives but also in the medium, the light brown marble itself, as he details the "Paleozoic fossils beneath the high polish and guessed that the stone was a madrepore" (*SJC,* 554). The word *madrepore* refers to a particular kind of marble, "mother-stone" or, for purposes in this palimpsest-like story, an ur-text or "mother-text." Indeed, the title of the story becomes more than a clever biblical allusion; it is the mother-text on which the story is structured and most clearly explains its meaning. The title of the story alludes to the Book of Daniel's narrative of Belshazzar's feast during which a spectral hand appears and writes a mysterious message on the wall in Hebrew, which the barbaric Babylonians do not understand. Belshazzar was the son of the wicked Babylonian king Nebuchadnezzar, who imprisoned the Jews during the legendary Babylonian captivity. The prophet Daniel had been summoned, in this earlier story, to interpret three dream-visions that had disturbed and mystified Nebuchadnezzar. Daniel's interpretation of the dreams greatly pleased the king, but he failed to heed their prophetic content and fell from power a year later. In the later story, Belshazzar, having drunk too much wine during the feast, orders his servants to bring out the sacred vessels of the captive Jews and use them in their orgy, an act of sacrilege and idolatry. A mysterious hand then appears and inscribes on the wall the Hebrew words: "Mene, mene, tekel, upharsin." Again, the prophet Daniel was brought in to interpret the message and rendered the following translation: "Here is the interpretation: mene: God has numbered the days of your kingdom and brought it to an end; tekel: you have been weighed in the balance and found wanting; u-pharsin: and your kingdom has been divided and given to the Medes and Persians."[6] The literal translation of the Hebrew, without Daniel's prophetic interpretation, is "to number, to number, to weigh, to divide." As in his earlier apotheosis, Daniel was robed in purple and given a gold chain, but Belshazzar was assassinated that very night by the Medes.

Cheever's nameless narrator is, obviously, a Daniel working within the story as it takes on the characteristics of a hermetic-Gnostic text. He insists on the cultural importance of the wall texts and searches for funds from various organizations to analyze the texts he has discovered in the American underworld, where the truth of its condition is obscured and mired in men's rooms throughout the nation. Cheever's three texts form a palimpsest of ancient, Victorian, and modern narratives and counter-point the three prophetic dream-visions of Nebuchadnezzar and the gnomic, three-word message on Belshazzar's wall. The Daniel-narrator of the story regards these modern wall inscriptions as dire signals of the imminent moral collapse of America. His interpretation suggests that the sacred and the profane had become virtually interchangeable, a proposition Cheever developed at length throughout *Bullet Park*. The narrator also observes that pornography is readily available in the lurid paperbacks he sees on the bookracks in the train stations and muses over their significance: "What had happened, I suppose, was that, as pornography moved into the public domain, those marble walls, those immemorial repositories of such sport, had been forced, in self-defense, to take up the more refined task of literature" (*SJC*, 558). And from his thoughtful theory on their meaning and significance, he articulates what he has discovered: "Our knowledge of ourselves and of one another in a historical moment of mercurial change" (*SJC*, 559). These moral, social, and spiritual palimpsests must be "diagnosed" as modern instances of "the writing on the wall." He, like Daniel, theorizes and interprets: "If these fancies were recorded and diagnosed, they might throw a brilliant illumination onto our psyche and bring us closer to the secret world of the truth" (*SJC*, 559).

Little could Cheever have known that this story adumbrates in fictive form the kinds of literary exercises that "new historicists" would be using twenty years later to "diagnose" the moral and social components of the American psyche. The narrator garners no interest at all in his important project, even among his six friends who work for various foundations. In fact, one of them says he is "out of touch" and another finds his idea "repulsive." Later, as he plans to return to Europe, finding the anti-intel-lectual denial of America unbearable, he discovers that it was not the "impropriety" of his discovery that repelled one of them but "its explo-siveness that disconcerted him, and that he had, in my absence, joined the ranks of those new men who feel that the truth is no longer usable in solving our dilemmas" (*SJC*, 560).

Cheever had never before so purposefully structured a narrative about narratives—texts whose content is also about the relationships between and among texts. Even though it is not necessary to understand or translate the title to grasp the theme of the story, once a reader discovers, via another Daniel, the meaning of the title, the story immediately assumes much greater thematic significance by bringing together nine different texts—six outside the story—that "tell" the same story. The title is the hermetic text—the hidden key, the "mother-stone"—which, once known, reveals the full meaning of the story.

The prophetic narrator decides that to escape the willful ignorance of America regarding "the writing on the wall," he must return to Europe, but not before reading another message on another men's room wall while waiting for a plane to Orly Airport. It consists of a line from Keats's sonnet "Bright Star": "would I were steadfast as thou art—not in lone splendor hung aloft the night." The line becomes an apt departing image as he boards his plane for Paris, "the city of light."

The story "Artemis, the Honest Well-Digger" shares important themes with both "The World of Apples" and "Mene, Mene." Water is the redemptive agent in both "Apples" and "Artemis" and all three characters "dig" into important areas—Asa Bascomb into the source of his sexual obsession, Artemis into the ground for water, and the unnamed narrator into underworld texts. Asa Bascomb and Artemis Bucklin also share the same initials. The buck in *Bucklin* most likely alludes to the deer-bucks associated with the Greek virgin-goddess, Artemis-Diana, patron of the hunt. And Artemis, a young buck himself, is hunting for a future wife who is a virgin, a clever juxtaposition that Cheever uses for satiric purposes throughout the story.

Though not literally a virgin, Artemis is looked upon by older women as possessing those clean-cut, buck-like attributes that make him a highly desirable sexual object. Two of his lovers in the story are modern-day nymphs. The first seductress is Mrs. Filler, the unsatisfied wife of a college professor: she "had a big butt and a big front and a jolly face . . . and had been elected apple-blossom queen in her senior year" (*SJC*, 653). A midwestern "wife of Bath," Mrs. Filler—who can never be fully fulfilled—is sexually starved and behaves in nymphomaniacal ways when she first meets Artemis. Even though Artemis is ill, Mrs. Filler insists on visiting him in his sick bed and begins to caress his chest and shoulders. But then, reversing roles, she "hits pay dirt" as she digs down under the covers: "Do you always get hard this quickly? It's so hard" (*SJC*, 656). As ex-apple-blossom queen, she plays Eve to Artemis's naive Adam. They also comically switch roles as she performs oral sex upon him in his pickup truck; the well digger looking for gushers is transformed: "You want me to tell you when I'm going to come? . . . Big load on its way . . . Big load's coming down the line" (*SJC*, 657). The "honest" in the story's title refers not to his truthfulness but to the Renaissance use of the word denoting virginal chastity. Mrs. Filler so pressures Artemis that he begins to think seriously about taking a vacation.

Artemis's other nymph-like lover, as sexually voracious as Mrs. Filler, is Maria Petroni, whose name combines the water from Marie (*la mer*) with Mary Magdalen before her conversion. Her surname, Petroni, humorously suggests its Italian source *petra*—"stone" or "rock"—the medium through which Artemis must drill to find water, and the great documenter of Roman orgiastic decline, Petronius Arbiter. Indeed, Maria confesses to the innocent Artemis that her greatest sexual experience was having seven men in one evening: "There was a lot of drinking and then we all got undressed. It was what I wanted. When they were finished, I didn't feel dirty or depraved or shameful" (*SJC*, 653). Both Mrs. Filler and Maria Petroni are modern embodiments of ancient Greek and Roman fertility goddesses like the virginal Artemis-Diana. The father of Cheever's Artemis had mistaken the gender and vocation of Artemis and named his son, he thought, after the patron of artesian wells and well diggers.

Artemis escapes the clutches of both "nymphs" by taking a vacation to the Soviet Union during the last days of Nikita Khrushchev's reign but continues his search for the American archetypal wife: the girl on the oleomargarine package. He meets and falls in love with his guide to Moscow, Natasha Funaroff. After returning to America, he and Natasha carry on an extensive correspondence, "texts" that become the occasion for some of Cheever's bitterest satire on the paranoid fantasies of some U.S. State Department officials who misinterpret their love letters and regard them as secret messages that threaten America. As in "Mene, Mene," the story concludes with an Ovidian dramatization of how harmless texts are metamorphosed into subtexts of international intrigue. Because these bureaucrats have nothing better to do, they order Artemis to their offices in Washington and demand that he explain certain "coincidences" found in their letters. It seems that a number of references in them corresponded to some troop and submarine movements that had similar names and numbers: "Earlier she wrote that you and she were on a wave of the Black Sea. The date corresponds precisely to the Black Sea maneuvers" (*SJC*, 670). After refusing to participate in blatant acts of disinformation, Artemis goes back home, grateful for the return of "the healing sound of rain to hear, at least there was that. Water, water" (*SJC*, 671). Water and the other elements ground Artemis in a reality far from the one in which love letters become subtexts or hidden messages that undermine American democracy. The innocence that Artemis loses during his story is not his virginity but his naive vision of the way the world operates.

One of the most imaginatively developed stories in *The World of Apples* is "The Geometry of Love," a story that returns to the comfortable world of suburban Remsen Park. The narrative opens as Charlie Mallory, a free-lance engineer, accidentally runs into his wife, Matilda, in the toy department of Woolworth's. She immediately accuses him of spying on her, and her recurring accusations begin to drive Charlie to desperate acts. As he looks out his office window in New York city, a frequent habit for Cheever's troubled characters, he sees "a small truck advertising EUCLID'S DRY CLEANING AND DYEING. The great name reminded of the right-angled triangle, the principle of geometric analysis . . . What he needed was a new form of ratiocination, and Euclid might do. If he could make a geometric analysis of his problems, mightn't he solve them, or at least create an atmosphere of solution?" (*SJC*, 595). The engineer, Charlie Mallory—whose initials, "CM," also designate the geometric method of measuring lines, centimeters—then begins to draw lines that "represent" his wife and two children. Much of the remainder of the narrative shows Mallory refining his method of geometrically organizing the confusion and disorder of daily life.

Charlie confesses that he is driven to structuring his world in this way because other ordering structures, such as his religion, fail to make the world cohere. But his fatal flaw from the beginning is that he mistakes the map for the territory, an attitude that limits his vision of the world to lines and surfaces. His totally linear view of existence cannot abide chance, coincidence, or change. Likewise, he has also mistaken his geometrical creations—his fictions—for reality and has thus failed to recognize the fictiveness of his fictions. His ability to map his troubles into geometric theorems enables him to bear the chaos of the quotidian, but

he also becomes Ovid-as-geometer as he transforms himself into someone who can now regard Matilda's quixotic mood swings "with ardor
and compassion. He was not a victor, but he was wonderfully safe from
being victimized" (*SJC,* 597). Most important, though: "He was able to
carry the conviction of innocence, with which he woke each morning,
well into the day" (*SJC,* 597). In short, his linearizing imagination
enables him to regenerate his own semipermanent Edenic condition and
dwell in it most of the time. In fact, his experience becomes so successful
that he considers writing a book about it and calling it *Euclidian Emotion:
The Geometry of Sentiment.*

With practice comes proficiency and he employs his method so successfully that while on a train trip to Chicago he makes "the monumen-
tal gloom" of Gary, Indiana, almost disappear "by translating the
components of the moment into a parallelogram" (*SJC,* 597). His
method puts depressing scenery "away from him until it seemed harmless, practical, and even charming" (*SJC,* 597). His semi-alchemical
method of transforming the elements of reality into mathematical mea-
surements continues to protect him from sordid family squabbles in
Chicago and Matilda's capricious mood swings. But it is on a second trip
through Gary, Indiana, that the city simply vanished due to "that theo-
rem that had corrected the angle of his relationship to the Indiana landscape" (*SJC,* 600).

Part 5 of the story, the last act in this tragedy, finds Charlie Mallory in
critical condition after ten inches of his intestine has been removed.
Matilda visits him in the hospital only to remind him of how fortunate
he is to have the best doctors and facilities that New York City has to
offer. After spilling hot soup all over him, she brings him a shaving mirror, a fatal act, because he sees himself for the first time since the operation: "His emaciation forced him back to geometry, and he tried to
equate the voracity of his appetite, the boundlessness of his hopes, and
the frailty of his carcass" (*SJC,* 602). When Matilda arrives home, the
cleaning woman informs her of Charlie's death. Charlie Mallory's call to
adventure in linearly "straightening out" the disorder of the world had
come from an advertisement for EUCLID'S DRY CLEANING AND DYEING. It
had also become a prophetic instance of an abstraction becoming real.
Charlie transformed himself into Euclid and attempted to "dry" clean
the wet, changing world into abstract theories, and his effort to "dye" or
change the world into his own theoretical abstractions literally "dyed" or
killed him.

Cheever creates an Ovidian parable illustrating the self-destructive hubris that such absurd propositions bring down on their creators; they would rather die than live in the imponderable natural cycles of process and change. Love and the other verities that Cheever celebrates can never be reduced to such theoretical formulations, really scientific fictions, because they consolidate spiritual, emotional, and physical truths into the mysteries of human existence.

Chapter Seven

Confinement and Release: *Falconer* and *Oh What a Paradise It Seems*

Falconer

The theme, tone, and structure of John Cheever's penultimate novel, *Falconer* (1977), are dramatically different from those of *Bullet Park,* the chief reason being that Cheever wrote *Falconer* as a sober man. After a devastating alcoholic collapse and, subsequently, a month's stay at the Smithers Alcohol Rehabilitation Center in Manhattan, he returned home 6 May 1975 and began a difficult but ultimately successful recovery program. He never touched a drop of alcohol again and died a sober and reasonably happy man seven years later. With the consistent help of Alcoholics Anonymous, John Cheever, at the age of sixty three, became the first of his generation of writers to sober up and not die the agonizing alcohol-related deaths suffered by the majority of the writers a generation earlier: Sinclair Lewis, F. Scott Fitzgerald, William Faulkner, Ernest Hemingway, Thomas Wolfe, and many, many more. As Scott Donaldson notes: "When Cheever quit drinking, he quit taking pills: no Valium to get through the day, no Seconal to bring on sleep. Instead he drank large quantities of ice tea and chain-smoked cigarettes. (In the spring of 1979, he finally shook off his addiction to tobacco.) He chose not to sedate himself, and stuck to that choice with a remarkable fierceness of will" (Donaldson 1988, 292). John Updike recalled seeing the first page of the manuscript of *Falconer* in Cheever's typewriter in Boston in the early fall of 1975, when Cheever's drinking had made both teaching and writing impossible. Updike noted that "from month to month the page in the typewriter never advanced" (Donaldson 1988, 293). Cheever immediately resumed working on *Falconer* after his release from Smithers and made rapid progress on it, producing an astounding seven pages a day. Cheever himself stated that *Falconer* was, among many things, about "confinement."

Cheever had been deeply interested in the idea of prisons and had taught at Sing Sing from 1971 to 1973. As he told *Saturday Review* interviewer John Firth: "All my work deals with confinement in one shape or another, and the struggle toward freedom."[1] Cheever's major source of confinement, or imprisonment, was certainly his alcoholism and, to a lesser extent, his reliance on the drugs prescribed by various physicians and psychotherapists. He frequently alludes to his increasingly destructive drinking in his journals, particularly in the early 1970s; his preoccupation with his alcoholic enslavement becomes one of the four or five major motifs around which the journals are built. In a revealing interview with novelist John Hersey, Cheever designates other metaphors for confinement: "*Falconer* is *not* Sing Sing. I used the imaginary prison of Falconer principally as a metaphor for confinement. It would be the third large metaphor I've used. The first is St. Botolph's, a New England village which has the confinement of traditional values and nostalgia; the second was the suburban towns, Bullet Park and Shady Hill, again areas of confinement; and the third is Falconer. *Not* Sing Sing . . . Fiction is not crypto-autobiography."[2]

Undoubtedly, one of the literary models for the novel was one of Cheever's favorite books, Dante's *Inferno*. *Falconer* opens with the main character's descent into Hades, the living hell of prison life. Mythically, the descent into Hades plays crucial roles in both Virgil's *Aeneid* and Homer's *Iliad,* but it also participates in the New Testament's "Harrowing of Hell" as Christ releases faithful souls from bondage the day before his own resurrection. Shady Hill, a modern Hades, has become its Judeo-Christian equivalent. *Falconer's* sculpted threshold guardians of Liberty wearing "a mobcap and carrying a pike," and Justice "blinded, vaguely erotic in her clinging robes and armed with a headsman's sword," greet the entering prisoners and remind them what brought them to this hopeless place. The nadir of Joseph Campbell's multifaceted journey of the mythological hero is what he calls "the belly of the whale"—that is, the hero is confined, trapped, or imprisoned in an ultimately destructive mechanism. Jack Abbott, the brilliant recidivist protégé of Norman Mailer, entitled his book on prison experience *In the Belly of the Beast* (1981), a title that combines mythic resonances with the sadistic agendas that a Calvinist society wreaks on its prison populations. Indeed, *Falconer* can be analyzed quite comprehensively using Campbell's mythic categories as Ezekiel Farragut, its protagonist, recalls encounters with fatal women, especially his spectacularly cruel wife, Marcia, and is aided by wise guides and magic flights—miracles—attaining, finally, a quasi-glorious apotheosis of freedom in the novel's concluding pages.

Once again, the brother conflict takes center stage. Zeke Farragut is in prison because he has killed his brother, Eben, in a drunken-drugged rage; *Falconer* can certainly be read as a permanent resolution of the brother conflict, which first arose in Cheever's highly praised story, "Goodbye, My Brother," some thirty years earlier. Zeke's punishment for murdering his brother is his confinement in Falconer prison in Cellblock F, which is under the absolute control of the morbidly obese and ironically named Tiny. With *F* being the sixth letter of the alphabet, Cellblock F becomes the sixth circle of *The Inferno,* the location of the City of Dis, the capital of hell itself. The flaming red towers of Dis are surrounded by great walls of iron as are Falconer's walls and towers. Even Virgil is powerless in Dis because human reason cannot cope with the essence of evil, and only divine assistance enables Dante and Virgil to continue their journey. So, too, heroin addict Zeke Farragut must rely on some sort of miracle to help him bear the burden of his existence in Falconer.

The name of the prison suggests a particularly oppressive species of bird that humans imprison and then train to destroy others of its kind at great distances from the falconer; the natural destructive impulses of the bird are sharpened under the so-called rational training they receive from their human captors. Cheever could not have found a more appropriate name for the kinds of activities that take place under the euphemism of prison "rehabilitation." A recurring image that becomes a motif shows Zeke Farragut closely observing the behavior of several different species of birds through the prison bars. He yearns for their freedom of movement and discovers why prisoners are obsessed with birds of all sorts. They become moving symbols of free flight as well as geographical signals, like the blackbirds that document the presence of a nearby swamp. Shortly after his arrival at Falconer, he observes a prisoner feeding bread crumbs to a dozen pigeons in a quasi-Eucharistic image that "had for him an extraordinary reality, a promise of sameness . . . the image of a man sharing his crusts with birds had the resonance of great antiquity."[3] Indeed, the metaphor of birds extends throughout the entire prison system and defines, in prison argot, both power and sexual relationships among the inmates. A "chickenhawk" refers to an older man sexually preying on younger and more vulnerable inmates known as "chickens," though in the case of Jody's love relationship with the older

Zeke, Jody designates Zeke as "Chicken," ostensibly because he has seduced Zeke and defined their relationship.

Hawks or falcons also tear their victims to pieces in much the same way that the prison system metaphorically tears its victims to pieces. A scene in chapter 2 shows the sadistic deputy warden, Chisholm, arriving on the scene, stating: "I hear you got a withdrawal show scheduled . . . The floor show's about to begin" (*F,* 53–54). Chisholm and two other guards sadistically enjoy watching Farragut go through the excruciating process of withdrawal, brought on because the authorities have withheld his methadone treatment. The deputy warden—the falconer—permits Farragut, the masochistic falcon-chicken, to tear himself to pieces in his agony: "He fell and beat his head on the floor, trying to achieve the reasonableness of pain. Pain would give him peace. When he realized that he could not reach pain this way, he began the enormous struggle to hang himself" (*F,* 54).

The bird metaphor extends throughout the novel, though in sometimes strange manifestations. Though not an actual bird, the helicopter that delivers Cardinal (another kind of bird) Thaddeus Morgan to the prison to say mass and award the eight inmates their certificates from Fiduciary University becomes an almost comic metaphor for the Holy Spirit—traditionally represented as a dove—descending into the prison courtyard and "delivering" Jody into freedom. Zeke himself, in meditating on the habits of red-winged blackbirds, an image that evokes ecclesiastical Roman Catholic figures, notes the correspondences among flocks of birds, leaves, and paper: "So in the autumn he watched the birds, the leaves and the Fiduciary University announcements moving as the air moved, like dust, like pollen, like ashes, like any sign of the invincible potency of nature" (*F,* 90). The deus ex machina of the Cardinal's helicopter is one of the major miracles of the novel, which some critics objected to, though one of the novel's most enthusiastic supporters, John Gardner, found it charmingly appropriate and called his review of the novel "On Miracle Road."[4]

Though Gardner suggests that a novelist like Tolstoy would give the reader the Cardinal's reason for helping Jody to escape, none are needed if one detects the allusion to another nineteenth-century French novel, Victor Hugo's *Les Miserables,* in which the Bishop of Digne saves the young Jean Valjean from prison even after catching him stealing from his house. Not only does he not prosecute Valjean, he gives him the stolen articles and exhorts him to donate the proceeds to the poor and needy. Cardinal Thaddeus Morgan acts in a similarly solicitous manner when he actually takes Jody to a clothing store across the street from his episcopal house and buys him his first civilian suit. The Cardinal safely delivers Jody into freedom and becomes his symbolic father. Farragut hears from DeMatteo, the broken-hearted chaplain's assistant (and Jody's "other" lover, who arranged for his escape), that Jody has married under the name H. Keith Morgan. Both of the Cardinal's names enrich the novel's themes, since *Morgan* comes from the German *morgen* meaning "dawn," "morning," or "daybreak" and defines Jody's resurrection into a new life of freedom and love. The Cardinal's first name, "Thaddeus," refers to St. Jude Thaddeus, the renowned patron of hopeless causes that require miracles for their solutions.

Another Chicken, the most important in the novel, Chicken Number Two, becomes the direct agent of Zeke Farragut's transcendence—his "miraculous" flight to freedom from Falconer. Farragut agrees to take care of the dying Chicken Number Two in his first act of charity in the novel. And it is while attending to Chicken's failing health that he conceives his escape scheme, that of replacing Chicken's body with his own after the prison guards leave a burial sack in Chicken's open cell and then depart. Of course, this mode of escape is lifted directly from Dumas's prison masterpiece, *The Count of Monte Cristo,* in which Edmond Dantes escapes by placing himself in the burial sack meant for a fellow prisoner he had befriended.

All three prison narratives—*Falconer, The Count of Monte Cristo,* and *Les Miserables*—share the theme of resurrection by miraculous means with clergymen acting in their human rather than their ecclesiastical roles. As Jody takes on the identity of Cardinal Morgan by disguising himself as a priest and later adopting his name, so too, Farragut takes on the identity of Chicken Number Two by disguising himself and symbolically dying so that he may attain transcendence and "return to life"—the world of freedom. If caught, Zeke would have died in prison, because escape attempts add substantially to prison sentences. Both Zeke and Jody attain what Joseph Campbell calls in his scheme of his journey of the hero "apotheosis," or the exaltation to divine rank, enabling them to return to the world of common day as "masters of two worlds"—that is, the world of confinement and an enhanced appreciation of their freedom because of their prison experience. In Christian terms, they both undergo forms of Christ's ascension and the Virgin Mary's assumption. Zeke also becomes Chicken Number Three (with Chicken Number Two and Chicken Number One before him now dead), or the third person of the Holy Trinity, the Holy Spirit, traditionally represented as a dove in

Christian iconography. The Holy Spirit is the divine spirit who delivers and sustains the faithful, by means of grace, into the eternal life of God.

Zeke attains another and unexpected kind of freedom when he and Jody become lovers. The love that develops between them is selfless and has little to do with issues of possession and power that sometimes sully passionate relationships. Though Jody claims he is not a homosexual and is not interested in homosexuals—a claim that Tiny seriously questions—Jody does not hesitate to seduce Zeke and "transports" him to an abandoned water tower for their romantic trysts two or three times a week. Their meetings take place in a traditionally mythic place of transcendence, a tower, where Zeke finds a kind of love he had never before experienced, a transcending, transformative love that requires nothing from him but willing surrender.

Zeke, as he anticipates the sound of Jody's squeaking sneakers, vividly recalls six former lovers: Jane, Virginia, Dodie, Roberta, Lucy, and Helen, with Jody the lucky seventh in Farragut's amatory pantheon. Part of Jody's compelling attraction is that he truly understands the dynamics of the sacred, as he explains to Zeke the significance of the Mass and how it will enable him to escape by making him invisible: "At mass you don't look at the other acolytes. That's the thing about prayer. You don't look . . . you don't go around asking who's the stranger on the altar. This is holy business and when you're doing holy business you don't see nothing. When you drink the blood of Our Savior you don't look to see if the chalice is tarnished or if there's bugs in the wine. You get to be transfixed, you're like transfixed. Prayer. That's why it is. Prayer is what's going to get me out of this place" (*F*, 102–3). What Zeke understands about his love for Jody is that it too is "holy business" and transforms him into the kind of human being he never dreamed he could become.

Though Cheever consistently denied autobiographical connections in his work ("fiction is not crypto-autobiography"), there is little doubt that his involvement with Alcoholics Anonymous and the honesty that sobriety demands helped him become discreetly open about his homosexual relationships with several younger men during the last years of his life. In many ways the spiritual centers of *Falconer* are Zeke Farragut's long, meditative ruminations on his lifelong fear and rejection of homosexual feelings, and the Cuckold's narration of his one, passionate homosexual experience with a young hustler named Michael. Zeke, though willing to admit to other inmates that he loves Jody deeply, refuses to see himself and Jody as a homosexual "couple"—that is, "the boy with an older man" stereotype that disturbed Zeke (and John Cheever) all of his life. But there is no doubt that Jody is "the beloved" in their relationship.

Zeke Farragut confronts what Paul Hammer in *Bullet Park* never could: that his passionate attraction to Jody might merely be a form of narcissism or, even worse, a sentimental infatuation with his lost youth. Jody had called attention to Zeke's beauty after one of their erotic trysts in the abandoned tower: "'Shit, man, you're beautiful. I mean you're practically senile and there isn't much light in here, but you look very beautiful to me . . . ' It seemed that he [Zeke] had always known that he was beautiful and had been waiting all his life to hear this said. But if in loving Jody he loved himself, there was that chance that he might, hell for leather, have become infatuated with his lost youth . . . He missed his youth, missed it as he would miss a friend, a lover" (*F,* 109–10). From the fear of confusing true love with self-pity over his lost youth, Zeke descends even further into a maelstrom of despair as his mind equates "unnatural" homosexual love with a deathwish close to Freud's concept of Thanatos: "while kissing, as he had, the tight skin of Jody's belly, he might have been kissing the turf that would cover him" (*F,* 110). These deepest of dark thoughts bring Zeke into a condition of existential emptiness so disorienting that he momentarily does not know where he is and must ask Tiny one of the most profound questions of his life: "'Hey, Tiny . . . Where am I?' Tiny understood. 'Falconer Prison . . . You killed your brother.' 'Thanks, Tiny.'" Once Tiny's words establish a reality, Zeke is able to anchor himself, for a while, in a verbal universe where he can then address "his troubling sense of otherness . . . the sense of being simultaneously in two or three places at the same instant . . ." (*F,* 111).

From Farragut's disturbing ontological swings between nonexistence and being in several places simultaneously, he begins to experience recurrent reveries and dreams of a woman, a beach, and a song that he could not understand or interpret until, while reading Descartes, he experiences an emptying of self so terrifying that he loses contact with where and who he is. Once he loses his sense of identity, he descends utterly into the Nietzschean "abyss" where objects and the bifurcated self lose any and all connection to words. Even though he was in the act of copying down a meaningful sentence from Descartes—trying to record significance—his effort brought on a frightening condition of Cartesian dualism: "He did not know himself. He did not know his own language. He abruptly stopped his pursuit of the woman and the music and was relieved to have them disappear. They took with them the absolute experience of alienation, leaving him with a light nausea" (*F,* 115). As

Cartesian dualism slides into Sartrean cosmic giddiness, Farragut is forced to reevaluate the spiritual scaffoldings upon which his life rests. Though Zeke had considered "transcendent experience to be perilous rubbish" with "the exception of organized religion and triumphant fucking," his disturbing episode of near psychotic otherness brought him closer to an understanding of the importance of his love for Jody and how love establishes a ground of significant meaning.

Farragut's visionary experience, even though a dark "via negativa," also demonstrates to him how "the moraines of consciousness" combine with memory and desire, dream and reverie, to establish a ground of being and therefore knowable forms of reality: he clearly discovers who he is, what he has done, and why he is where he is. And at his deepest point in hell he begins his ascent from the "belly of the whale," because in recovering himself he is now able to experience an authentic "other" as he willingly listens, for the first time, to the Cuckold's tragic tale of homosexual love and identifies with the poignant and, at times, comic scenario.

Cheever's positioning of the Cuckold's narrative in the novel is crucial for several reasons. For one thing, Farragut has, up to this point, felt a greater revulsion toward him than any other prisoner in Cellblock F because he and Cuckold share middle-class backgrounds and values—wives, children, and homes. And Farragut is revolted by the Cuckold's "protuberant vulnerability—produced, it seemed, by alcohol and sexual embarrassment" (F, 116). It is also clear that he hates him for some of the same reasons that he hates himself, as Farragut has unconsciously identified himself with those same abhorrent qualities. But what most disturbs Zeke about the Cuckold is his open identification of himself as a figure of abject aloneness: "I was the kind of lonely man you see eating in Chinese restaurants. You know? . . . always this lonely man. Me. We never eat the Chinese food, we lonely men. We always have the London broil or the Boston baked beans in Chinese restaurants" (F, 116). Throughout Cheever's life he vigorously disclaimed any identification with "this lonely man in the Chinese restaurant" over and over because he greatly feared, perhaps more than anything else, that he would end up such a pitiful and forlorn figure. Cheever—through Zeke—finally confronts himself as that figure in the Cuckold.

But the Cuckold is also a mythic figure, a doppelgänger or double, because he and Zeke share not only middle-class status, but their Cuckoldry and their young male lovers, both hustlers but capable, nonetheless, of selfless love. These young males are also major threshold figures who transport both men into new dimensions of sexual love. The Cuckold also represents the most fearfully threatening aspect of Zeke's identity, homosexual passions that can become either destructive or redemptive. Before Zeke's transfiguring sexual experience with Jody, those feelings and the Cuckold's personality were repellent; but after Jody, Zeke must revise his attitudes toward homosexuality and the Cuckold. Since the Cuckold is a doppelgänger, Zeke's feelings of hostility are really about himself. When the Cuckold first asks Zeke to listen to his homosexual tale, Zeke responds contemptuously: "'I've got a cab downstairs, waiting to take me to the airport,' said Farragut. Then he said, sincerely, 'No, no, no, I don't mind if you talk, I don't mind at all'" (*F,* 116). By unexpectedly accepting the Cuckold, Zeke begins to accept himself and becomes capable of opening himself up even to those whom he had earlier scorned; he begins to understand that what he hated in the Cuckold was himself.

The Cuckold finishes his tragic tale of homosexual love as he tells Zeke that Michael, his hustler-lover, had been stabbed twenty-two times by a murderer whom the police never found. Coincidentally, Zeke Farragut had received twenty-two stitches when the deputy warden smashed him over the head with a chair as he tried to escape Cellblock F after his withdrawal symptoms became unbearable. Cheever further extends the symbolic mirror images of the doppelgänger, the Cuckold and Zeke, by using the number 22 to parallel their couplings and their common plights.

Once Zeke is psychologically opened up by the Cuckold's story, he is ready to descend into and explore the very bottom of hell, a location known at Falconer as "the Valley." And, significantly, it is the Cuckold who, now functioning as a mythic wise guide, tells Zeke about this dark place: "The Valley was a long room off the tunnel to the left of the mess hall. Along one wall was a cast-iron trough of a urinal. The light in the room was very dim . . . The Valley was where you went after chow to fuck yourself . . . There were ground rules. You could touch the other man's hips and shoulders, but nothing else . . . If you finished and wanted to come again you went to the end of the line. There were the usual jokes. How many times, Charlie? Five coming up, but my feet are getting sore" (*F,* 124–25). The Valley is unquestionably the bottom of Dante's *Inferno* and is depicted in Dantean images as rows of desperate men masturbate in public, loveless solitude.

The bottom of Dante's *Inferno,* the ninth circle, is a place of self-mutilation, a kind of masochistic circle jerk, but the reason Dante's ninth circle is frozen in ice is that it lacks the heat of love and genuine passion. Cheever, like Dante, categorizes types of sinner-masturbators as "the frenzied and compulsive pumpers, the long-timers who caressed themselves for half an hour . . . the groaners and the ones who sighed, and most of the men . . . would shake, buck, catch their breath and make weeping sounds, sounds of grief, of joy, and sometimes death rattles . . . Farragut went here regularly after Jody was gone" (*F,* 125). Bereft of love and resorting to the consolations of the Valley, Farragut unexpectedly discovers a light in the forlorn darkness of postorgasmic despair: "It was majestic; even in prison he knew the world to be majestic" (*F,* 126). Surprised by joy in such spiritually destitute circumstances, Farragut is able to tolerate another brutal visit from his wife, Marcia, to whom, after she inquires whether he has found any boyfriends in prison, he openly admits he has: "I've had one . . . but I didn't take it up the ass . . . When I die you can put on my headstone: 'Here lies Ezekiel Farragut, who never took it up the ass'" (*F,* 128).

Just after Marcia leaves, Jody makes his last visit, a celibate one, to bid Zeke goodbye, and at "Lights Out" later that evening, Zeke hears random explosions of thunder that "seemed to explain that heaven was not an infinity but a solid construction of domes, rotundas and arches" (*F,* 130). His epiphany reveals the majesty of the world, even in the Valley at the bottom of hell, and combines with his love for Jody in transforming the world from an infinitely empty cosmos into a clearly human location that humanizes the yawning existential void. More than most critics, John Gardner understood Cheever's ability to probe the mind's ability to make meaning out of nothingness and its power to see "not only the fashionable existential darkness but the light older than consciousness which gives nothingness definition" (Gardner, 259).

Though Zeke proudly boasted to Marcia that he never "took it up the ass," he did delicately insert a ballpoint pen up his anus after stealing it from a distracted prison doctor so that he might record the sadistic details of the humiliating withdrawal episode that entertained the deputy warden and his minions. Zeke spends a great deal of time and energy choosing a medium upon which to record his narrative and decides that the heavily starched sheets of his infirmary bed will serve the purpose well. His intention is to detail the atrocities in three letters, commit them to memory, and, after he returns to Cellblock *F,* type them up and send copies to the governor, his bishop, and one of his old girlfriends. It is during Zeke's recording of his hellish prison experience that he takes on both the demeanor and dimensions of his namesake from the

Old Testament, the great prophet, Ezekiel, whose sixth-century B.C. circumstances somewhat resemble Farragut's.

Ezekiel was one of the four major Hebrew prophets who shared exile with his fellow Israelites during the Babylonian captivity after the fall of Jerusalem. Both Ezekiel Farragut and the prophet Ezekiel are spokesmen for their imprisoned condition. God transported Ezekiel during a dream-vision and put him down on a desert plain full of bones and asked him: "Can these bones live again?" That same question certainly defines Zeke Farragut's condition in Falconer Prison. But the answer that God gave the biblical Ezekiel was that those bones can live again and be re-membered into living, breathing bodies if the Israelites do not despair during their captivity and have faith that they will be delivered. But one condition must be met: the Israelites must acknowledge their complicity in their captivity by the Babylonians; that is, accept their role in their fate. If they would accept and adhere to Ezekiel's prophecies and promises, God would transform their wasteland condition, their captivity, into a regenerated Garden of Eden (Ezek. 36:31–35). God instructed Ezekiel to write these things down on leaves of tablets in the same way that Farragut is recording his experience on his starched-stiffened sheets. Both prophets are re-membering—that is, bringing the past together into a coherent narrative—and recording the disasters for posterity so that they might not recur. Such acts eventually prove redemptive because their lessons were adhered to and followed. Indeed, Farragut's long, prophetic letters to the governor, his bishop, and an old lover are his first serious responses to Tiny's recurring, Jeremiah-like lamentations: "Oh, Farragut, why is you an addict?" Concurrent with Cheever's writing of *Falconer,* he was himself attending A.A. meetings and reciting a similar curative mantra heard at A.A. meetings everywhere: "My name is John and I am an alcoholic."

Certainly Zeke Farragut's drug addiction would seem to indicate that his spiritual "bones" could never live again, and Falconer would forever remain a desert where bones could never be re-membered into something living. Zeke's initial struggles in recording in writing—creating a text that records his desperate plight—become his first participatory steps in his own self-redemption from his life in hell. But, it is his redemption from drug addiction, which he only discovers after the fact, that enables him to understand that he is clean and has been physically, psychologically, and spiritually resurrected from the Hell of his own personal confinement. This cleansing took place during a three-day prison revolt at Amana Prison, during which inmates at Falconer were locked up in their cells so that they couldn't start their own revolt. Although prison officials had been giving Farragut placebos for over a month, he suddenly realizes, in a panic, that he has not received his methadone treatment for three days. Zeke's three-day "entombment" is analogous to Christ's entombment, which led to His resurrection on the third day.

Of course the name Ezekiel had always been a favorite of John Cheever's. The patriarchal Ezekiel Wapshot founded the American branch of the Wapshot family in the Wapshot novels, and this Ezekiel had his source in Ezekiel Cheever, from whom John Cheever claimed to be descended. The last important Ezekiel was one of Cheever's most beloved black Labrador puppies—called Zeke for short. Cheever also tried, without success, to persuade his son Benjamin to name his first son Ezekiel.

The beginning of chapter 5 of *Falconer* shows prison officials enacting what they consider radical prison reform after the devastating riots at Amana Prison. They have decided to change the colors of the inmates' uniform from gray to green, and Zeke sings a few bars of the Old English carol "Greensleeves" to a bemused Cuckold. Chicken Number Two had earlier sung his final song, which, in keeping with the prison-bird metaphors used throughout the novel, becomes his swan song at the conclusion of chapter 4. His song was a lament in the tradition of Old Testament prophet, Jeremiah, who recorded the despair of the Israelites after the fall of Jerusalem, which resulted in the Babylonian captivity. The message of Chicken's lament is that the slaughter at Amana (really Attica Prison) was so brutal and senseless that it resists song in any form; the only proper response to its savagery is silence. For purposes of charting Zeke Farragut's rebirth, green is certainly the most appropriate color to replace gray, the color of ashes and death. Though Zeke is unaware that he has been weaned from his drug addiction, he finds himself singing for the first time in Falconer; and his rendition of "Greensleeves" constitutes a song of praise and celebration of a freedom that Zeke is not yet aware of but that counterpoints the despair of Chicken's final lament.

Cheever also uses Grail motifs in somewhat the same way he used them in *Bullet Park,* particularly by substituting commercial elixirs for spiritual ones. Zeke is in prison because of his addiction to heroin-as-Grail, and the guard Tiny keeps his inmates under control during the Amana Riots by giving them high-quality marijuana as a kind of benumbing sacramental tranquilizer. The prison medical staff, Farragut discovers, has also been substituting placebos for his methadone medication. (The word *placebo* comes from the Latin verb "placeo, placo" meaning "to sooth or calm." Though stunned by the discovery of the placebos, and his unintentional "cure," he becomes keenly conscious, for the first time, of Chicken's quickly disintegrating condition when he touches him: "Chicken's hold on his arm seemed desperate. Chicken seemed truly old and feeble" (*F,* 200). For only the second time in the novel Farragut is able to get outside himself long enough to decide not to tell Chicken that he is clean; he has organized his priorities according to someone else's needs for once. Instead, he puts his arm around Chicken and helps him to his cell. Just after this act of selfless love, a young priest mysteriously enters the cellblock with Holy Communion—the Holy Grail as spiritual sustenance, not a placebo— and Zeke, who has been torpid all day, gratefully kneels down in his cell and humbly receives the Eucharist. Without even making a conscious effort, he vividly recalls the liturgical responses of his early youth and recites them in a firm and manly voice: "Holy, Holy, Holy." Significantly, Zeke's first two acts after he realizes he is clean—that he has been redeemed and liberated from his addiction—are a gratuitous act of charity toward Chicken and a willing reception of the Holy Eucharist. In short, his Christ-like act of love made him worthy of the Eucharist and enabled him to participate in sacralizing (making holy) the fallen and hopeless world of Falconer: "'Heaven and earth are full of Thy Glory. Praise be to Thee, O Lord.' When he had been blessed with the peace that passes understanding, he said, 'Thank you, Father,' and the priest said, 'God bless you, my son'" (*F,* 200–201).

Cheever was very familiar with Grail lore and used it extensively throughout *Bullet Park* and many of his stories, especially "The Swimmer." An important motif in the Grail lore concerns the questions that both the Grail quester and the various threshold guardians of the Grail ask each other. The "question" is the final phase of the "quest" for the Grail and its truth, since both words come from the same etymological root. The redeeming Grail questions that release the rain that reinvigorates the wasteland are those questions that demonstrate selfless love and concern for the plight of the wounded Fisher King. So Zeke Farragut becomes the "innocent fool"—he does not know how and when his wounded condition was healed—when he begins to care for the mortally wounded Chicken Number Two.

Zeke insists on bathing Chicken and discovers, to his amazement, that Chicken's emaciated body is covered with old, fading tattoos— texts, both verbal and pictorial. His body is a medieval tapestry and an illuminated manuscript inscribed and interwoven with motifs of ancient heroes on Grail-like quests. Zeke delineates a portrait of a horse named "Lucky Bess" on Chicken's chest, and on his left arm "there was a sword, a shield, a serpent and the legend 'Death before Dishonor'" (*F*, 203). On Chicken's back, Zeke observes the words of Dante's *Inferno:* "Most of the back was a broad mountain landscape with a rising sun, and below this, forming an arch above his buttocks . . . in faded and clumsy Gothic lettering: 'Abandon all hope, ye who enter here.' Serpents sprang from his groin and wound down both legs, with his toes for fangs. And all the rest of him was dense with foliage" (*F*, 203).

Key to the healing powers that the innocent fool of the Grail legend generates are the questions he must both ask and answer, which suggests that the Grail quester's primary goal is self-knowledge. As Zeke bathes Chicken and prepares him for death, he asks him a seemingly innocuous question, why is he selling his getfiddle, and Chicken answers: "For two cartons of menthos." But then Chicken unexpectedly asks Zeke the Grail question, the one question that no one has dared ask and that Zeke fears more than any: "Why did you kill your brother, Zeke?" (*F*, 203).

Once that all-important question is asked, Farragut's past floods over him. As he attends the dying Chicken and peers into the gate of hell of Chicken's buttocks and, spiritually, into the inferno of his wrecked past, he knows he must face his crime and admit his guilt once and for all. Cheever was himself undergoing, as he was writing *Falconer,* his own spiritual cleansing process during his frequent attendance at A.A. meetings, where he painfully trudged through the brutal honesty of A.A.'s Twelve Steps. The two Steps that demand the most assiduous honesty are Steps Four and Five. Step Four reads: "Made a searching and fearless moral inventory of ourselves," a process that Farragut has finally begun as a result of Chicken's crucial question and that demands an absolute commitment to uncovering and facing those past actions that have, in short, ruined Zeke's life. The Fifth Step follows logically: "Admitted to God, to ourselves, and to another human being, the exact nature of our wrongs." At this point in the novel, Farragut admits to God—via the mysterious priest who brought communion—and to himself and to another human being, Chicken Number Two, the exact nature of his "wrongs." His recitation replicates exactly the traditional narrative structure that takes place at A.A. meetings in which speakers tell what their lives as drinkers were like, what happened that caused them to stop drinking, and what their lives have become after they are clean and sober. Zeke must finally "confess" by telling his entire story, with its complicated ramifications from the troubled history of the family, and come to understand how those issues resulted in his murder of his sadistic, alcoholic brother, Eben.

The story that Zeke tells is a composite of the many family histories which Cheever used repeatedly over a forty-year period, resulting in typical Cheeveresque icy mothers, drunken fathers, and hateful brothers. What is new in *Falconer* is that Cheever has combined his two most painful autobiographical crises into the novel's climactic scene. There is little doubt that Eben Farragut, Zeke's brother, is as demonically and gratuitously cruel as any character in Cheever's fiction. Eben's name most probably derives from another Ebeneezer, the Scrooge of Dickens's *A Christmas Carol,* but Cheever's Scrooge is a hopelessly sadistic drunkard whose alcoholism has transformed him into something closer to the picture of Dorian Gray hidden in the attic; that is, an actively delusional, sodden, self-indulgent narcissist. The earliest prototype for Eben goes back to the Calvinist monster Lawrence Pommeroy of "Goodbye, My Brother." The anonymous narrator, a prototype of Zeke Farragut, attempts to murder his brother with a large root but manages only to bludgeon him to his knees on a gorgeous Atlantic beach. What sparked both violent responses was an older brother's brutish insistence on forcing a younger brother to face, point blank, the most threatening kind of family truths. After Zeke chides Eben for his cruelty toward his wife and begs him to explain why he chooses to live the stupid life he lives, Eben declaims:

> "Because I love it" . . . Then he bent down, raised the old Turkey carpet and kissed it with his wet mouth.
>
> Zeke, disgusted, responds: "I'll be any kind of freak or addict before I'll be mistaken for you. I'll do anything before I'll kiss a rug."
>
> "Kiss my ass," said Eben.
>
> "You've got Dad's sense of humor," Farragut said.
>
> "He wanted to kill you," screamed Eben.
>
> "I bet you didn't know that. He loved me, but he wanted you to be killed. Mother told me. He had an abortionist come out to the house. Your own father wanted you to be killed."
>
> Then Farragut struck his brother with a fire iron. The widow testified that Farragut had struck his brother eighteen to twenty times, but she was a liar, and Farragut thought the doctor who corroborated the lie contemptible" (*F,* 211–12).

The old story of Cheever's father inviting the abortionist to dinner surfaces once again in his fiction, but this time as the climactic scene in one of his most highly acclaimed novels. In one Freudian literary stroke, as it were, Cheever dispatches both the most hateful and threatening aspect of his actual brother, Fred, and also symbolically "murders" his own father, another Fred, who seriously considered having him murdered in his mother's womb. Cheever brings together and terminates long-standing brother/father conflicts on which he had built virtually all of his novels up to and including *Falconer*.

Once Chicken Number Two hears Zeke's story, he clearly understands and articulates his fate: "I'm dying, Zeke, I'm dying . . . I can feel that I'm dying . . . I can feel that I'm dying, but it ain't done my brain no harm" (*F*, 213). Zeke will shortly become Chicken Number Three after Number Two dies; Zeke's resurrection depends entirely on the older inmate's death, a mirror of the way natural cycles work. Cheever counterpoints Zeke's involvement in the deaths of his two older "brothers" when Chicken Number Two becomes his older prison brother. Though he caused his blood-brother's death, he now attends to Chicken Number Two, assisting him in his journey from life to death in an act of selfless love. By taking Number Two's place in his burial sack, Zeke becomes Number Three and will shortly undergo a visionary transport that will deliver him from his death-in-life existence in Falconer to the freedom of the outside world.

Zeke crawls into the womb of the burial sack and seals himself up, but not before remembering to bring along a razor blade so he may cut himself out of it—perhaps recalling that all-important detail from Dumas's *The Count of Monte Cristo,* in which Dantes cuts himself out of the burial sack after he is thrown into the sea. Farragut hyperconsciously experiences passing through two gates, which become mythic threshold crossings in his movement toward rebirth and, in keeping with the womb-like metaphor of the journey, remarks, "He had never, that he remembered, been carried before . . . The sensation of being carried belonged to the past, since it gave him an unlikely feeling of innocence and purity" (*F*, 218). His feeling of pure innocence evokes the womb experience and adumbrates an imminent rebirth into fresh freedom that could not take place without his freely given act of love in attending the dying Chicken Number Two.

Once Zeke is outside the walls of Falconer, he cuts himself out of the sack but in the process also cuts his fingers and his thigh with the razor. The thigh wound authenticates him as a mythic hero, placing him in a long succession of wounded heroes. The thigh wound also locates him precisely in the tradition of Grail questers who were always wounded somewhere in the thigh area but who also attended wounded kings (like Amfortas in the Teutonic myths) with mysteriously festering wounds around and about the thigh. As later critics discovered, those thigh wounds were actually sexual wounds that centuries of Judeo-Christian emendations mythically displaced to other parts of the body, though Hemingway recenters their sexual significance in Jake Barnes's groin injury in *The Sun also Rises.*

Cheever's obstetrical language also clearly suggests the birthing process and the early developmental movements of an infant: "He put one foot in front of the other . . . his foot was wet with blood, but he didn't care." Cheever then, almost humorously, adds a musical accompaniment to the felicitous rebirth: "Then he heard a piano. It could, that late at night, have been a child, but the fingers seemed stiff and ungainly and so he guessed it was someone old. The music was a beginner's piece" (*F,* 221). Zeke's musings over the melody cleverly combine motifs of birth and death, youth and age, as he himself begins a new life.

Zeke immediately meets a version of himself, an old one, in the form of a slightly drunken man who has been evicted and is wandering around in the rain looking for a home. Zeke charitably helps the man carry some of his belongings onto a bus. His freely given act of love earns him a free bus trip, an offer of a temporary home with the man, and, most important, a raincoat; that is, symbolic armor to protect him from the actual rain and disguise him from the police. The Hemingway-like rain also becomes an appropriate metaphor for a new life. As Zeke gets off the bus at the next stop, he thanks the charitable stranger, who voluntarily gives him his phone number at work, which becomes Zeke's "lucky" number: "Stepping from the bus onto the street, he saw that he had lost his fear of falling and all other fears of that nature. He held his head high, his back straight, and walked along nicely. Rejoice, he thought, rejoice" (*F,* 226). In transcending this fear, Zeke Farragut finally learns to feel at home in the world, a freely moving, transfigured character rejoicing in his transcendent freedom, or what George Santayana called "animal faith." Psychologist James Hillman defines "animal faith" as "faith in the world: that it is there, that it won't give way underfoot when you take the next step, that you just know which way to turn and how to proceed. It's the faith your hands and your feet have."[5] Of course, these were the very same kinds of spiritual lessons that Cheever was himself discovering in his increasingly satisfying sobriety in Alcoholics Anonymous, where he was learning to live life untrammeled by the guilt and fear of his terrible years of alcoholic confinement.

Oh What a Paradise It Seems

The second novel Cheever wrote in sobriety was *Oh What a Paradise It Seems,* published in 1982, the year he died. Cheever had intended it to be a long, major work and had begun it in 1980. It was during a stay at his beloved Yaddo in October 1980, though, that he experienced a terrifying grand mal seizure. A short time later doctors discovered he had cancer of the kidneys, which, even though they removed his cancerous right kidney, metastasized into cancer of the bone. The cancer treatments weakened him, but he continued to work on a considerably shorter version of *Paradise.*

Oh What a Paradise It Seems continues the tone and mood of gratitude that concludes *Falconer,* even though Cheever suspected he was a dying man. Though *Paradise* is quite short—about a hundred pages—Lemuel Sears, the protagonist, and his beautiful younger lover, Renée Herndon, are compelling literary characters. The major emphasis in the novel is on serious environmental issues; namely, the transformation of Beasley's Pond, a beloved local recreational lake, into a trash dump by greedy entrepreneurs. Cheever combines the preservation of Edenic innocence with larger ecological issues, making *Paradise* an ecological parable or allegory about the proper relationship between humans and the earth they are supposed to be caring for.

Lemuel Sears, a wealthy New York City businessman in his sixties, is deeply disturbed to discover the befouled condition of Beasley's Pond on his third visit to the upstate community of Janice, New York, where his daughter lives and where he had previously enjoyed skating on the pond in the winter months. No longer skatable, the pond now contains, among other refuse, "the shell of a ten-year-old automobile and a little closer to him a dead dog. He thought his heart would break."[6] Sears writes a scathing letter to the local newspaper and also contacts his law firm to investigate the ecological tragedy.

The narrative also concerns Lemuel Sears's highly successful love life with both female and male lovers. Sears had married twice, and both of his wives are dead. His first wife of twenty years was the beloved Amelia, a seeming perfect wife and mother. Estelle, his second wife, was a glamorous but rather shallow woman who prided herself on her clairvoyant powers; she died by accidentally falling in front of a commuter train in a suburb of Philadelphia. Estelle shared similar characteristics with other chthonic Hecate figures such as Miss Deming of "The Music Teacher" and Joan Harris of "Torch Song." Like Harry Shinglehouse of *Bullet Park,* who met a similar fate, "nothing was found of her but a scrap of veiling and a high-heeled shoe" (*P,* 62). Though Sears has had many female lovers since the death of his second wife, his affair with Renée Herndon is his most intense relationship to date. He meets her frequently after her Alcoholics Anonymous meetings, though she never tells Lemuel exactly what the meetings are about. And Lemuel, being the gentleman that he is, never directly asks her.

During one of their harmless spats, Lemuel experiences a brief but intense homosexual love affair, the first in his life, with the elevator operator in Renee's building, a middle-aged man named Eduardo who is the happily married father of two college-age sons. Although Lemuel's erotic affair is in every way successful, he feels compelled to seek the advice and counsel of a Dr. Palmer, a psychiatrist whom Lemuel refers to as "a homosexual spinster" (*P,* 54). Dr. Palmer, whose name suggests masturbatory solutions to dangerous relationships, does little to help Lemuel work through his homosexual crisis. Sears finally concludes that there is nothing harmful in his relationship with Eduardo and that, in fact, it is as normal as any other love relationship. Eduardo's job as an elevator operator comically suggests his role of erotic wise guide in enabling Lemuel to attain new heights not only of sexual passion but of genuine affection.

The other, more important narrative in *Paradise* concerns Lemuel Sears's hiring an ecological specialist, Horace Chisholm, to take legal steps toward getting Beasley's Pond cleaned up. Two other couples, inhabitants of Janice, are Betsey and Henry Logan, and their next-door neighbors, the desperate Sammy and Maria Salazzo. Names, once again, can be used as allegorical signals, since Horace Chisholm's first name evokes the venerable Latin poet, Horace, who frequently wrote about his country estate as an Edenic place where he felt close to the vital energies of nature and spent his most contented hours. Betsey and Henry— Elizabeth and Henry—have names that allude to English royalty at the height of the English Renaissance, a golden age in which spiritual, political, and artistic institutions worked together to improve the quality of the lives within the realm. And it is that very agenda that the Logans, especially Betsey, relentlessly pursue throughout the novel. The Salazzos, whose surname derives from the Italian word for "to bleed," become willing participants in continuing the degradation of Beasley's Pond. The local crime organization puts Sammy in charge of collecting ("bleeding") substantial amounts of money in the form of payoffs for permission to dump anything into the pond. As a result, the Salazzos' financial condition improves greatly.

The conflict between these next-door neighbors reaches a climax during a minibattle that mirrors the one between the ecologist and the polluters, when Betsey Logan confronts Maria Salazzo in the local supermarket, Buy Brite. With the crowd cheering her on, Betsey bars Maria from using the express lane with her week's worth of groceries. The Logans become, then, defenders of the rights of the common folk in confronting the Salazzos, who symbolize the corrupting influences of outsiders. Betsey pushes her civic responsibilities even further when, after discovering that the Salazzos are directly responsible for the continued poisoning of Beasley's Pond, she decides to become a poisoner herself. She leaves a bottle of teriyaki sauce on a shelf at Buy Brite containing enough ant poison to kill a family. Pasted to the bottle is a message that reads "Stop poisoning Beasley's Pond or I will poison the food in all 28 Buy Brites." Her tactic so alarms the community that the dumping stops and the Salazzos leave town forever. Cheever cleverly uses ant poison to underscore the fact that humans, like ants, kill their own kind.

Meanwhile, Horace Chisholm's efforts to stop the dumping have met with tremendous opposition from the WASPish town fathers who employ McCarthy-like tactics unabashedly. Chisholm is mysteriously run over by a car after rescuing the Logans's baby, Binxie, who was accidentally left on the side of the road. During the course of the hearing that Lemuel Sears has financed, Cheever vividly articulates the destruction that polluting the pond will eventually cause. He uses the pond as a local metaphor for what brainless technology is causing everywhere in the so-called civilized world and clearly locates the root of the fall in man's failure to recognize the "holy" relationship between man and nature; the words *holy* and *whole* come from the same etymological root. The rapacious greed of the entrepreneurs has blinded them to the damage they have inflicted on his Eden—the "Paradise" of the novel's title— as Horace Chisholm charts the lethal path of chemical pollution: "As they moved from the wetlands to the charming brook he recited the diseases these chemicals produced in men. Rickets. Blindness. Brain tumor. Impotence. Sterility" (*P,* 89). Sears sees these natural resources as "the bridge that spans the mysterious abyss between our spiritual and carnal selves" (*P,* 89). If *Bullet Park* can be designated Cheever's "Lethal Eden," then *Paradise* can be labeled "the lethalizing of Eden."

Once the corruption is uncovered, steps are taken to reverse the polluting process as Lemuel Sears establishes the Beasley Foundation. Sears, at home in the warm embraces of Renée Herndon, experiences an almost visionary revelation of the vital importance of his accomplishment as it is viewed against a much larger cosmic and spiritual backdrop: "What moved him was a sense of those worlds around us, our knowledge however imperfect of their nature, our sense of their possessing some grain of our past and of our lives to come. It was that most powerful sense of our being alive on the planet. It was that most powerful sense of how singular, in the vastness of creation, is the richness of our opportunity. The sense of that hour was of an exquisite privilege, the great benefice of living here and renewing ourselves with love. What a paradise it seems!" (*P,* 105).

What an infinite distance separates the bitter, recriminating tone of *Bullet Park* from the humble gratitude of a man who knew he was dying. There is little question that the quality of Cheever's sobriety shines through the rhetoric and limpid style of *Paradise* as it records a full, sensual reengagement with life's physicality—he repeats the word "sense" five times in one paragraph—and a recognition that Paradise-Eden is a condition of the spirit that one is responsible for once it discerns the connection between nature and love: "Sears spoke with an enthusiasm that sprang from the fact that he had found some sameness in the search for love and the search for potable water" (*P,* 104.)

Cheever concluded his literary career in a mode of wonder, awe, and gratitude, and recorded his valedictory observations by grounding them in a sense of life as "an exquisite privilege." Such words demonstrated the rich spiritual life of a sober man fully conscious and appreciative of the serenity that sobriety brings.

Chapter Eight

One Day at a Time: The Letters and the Journals

The Letters of John Cheever, edited by his son Benjamin, were published in 1988, the same year of Scott Donaldson's biography. Both works provide enormous amounts of biographical information on John Cheever's life, while giving two individual perspectives from which to judge his life. Much of the information in the letters can also be found in Donaldson's biography. What is new in Benjamin Cheever's editing is the highly instructive and extensive commentaries he weaves throughout the letters. The comments form an alternate or corresponding text, which adds details and facts but also includes Benjamin Cheever's opinions and interpretations concerning the content of his father's letters and, therefore, his life. He is also painfully honest about how he was affected and, at times, hurt by his father's difficult and complex personality.

The letters show, for the most part, the public face of John Cheever, though he does not hesitate to talk openly about his debilitating problems with alcohol, his ongoing conflicts with his wife, Mary, or his increasingly problematic homosexual feelings, which he euphemized as "difficult propensities."[1] Benjamin Cheever states that it was these 1974 letters of his father to the novelist Allan Gurganus that became the "first concrete and irrefutable evidence of bisexuality in this book" (*L,* 299), though his father had fleetingly alluded to some homosexual behavior in a letter to his Russian translator, Tanya Litvinov, in 1971 or 1972. It is Benjamin Cheever's often puzzled responses that make the letters more than just letters. Indeed, almost as important as the letters themselves are Benjamin's sometimes extensive interactive engagement with their contents; his shocked and troubled reactions help readers understand and contextualize his father's sometimes aberrant behavior, particularly in light of John's classic bourgeois sexual attitudes: "In public he was an ardent heterosexual, and he told me that homosexuality made men vain, ungenerous, and ultimately ridiculous. If I had discovered that I was homosexual, I wouldn't have dared tell him. I would have expected him to throw me out of the house" (*L,* 300).

Many of Cheever's most revealing letters were written to other writers, such as Josephine Herbst, John Updike, and John Weaver, or to
writer-editors, like Malcolm Cowley and William Maxwell. But his attitude in them was, in a sense, a public one because he was conscious that
they would someday be published and read by thousands of his readers.
The letters map a chronological journey of a man moving through
increasingly troubled phases of his life, culminating in a dramatic alcoholic collapse in April 1975. They share the journals' obsessions with
five or six problem areas of his life that gradually take on the dimensions of Wagnerian leitmotifs: loneliness, drinking, problems with writing, troubling homosexual feelings, and family conflicts, especially with
his wife, Mary.

What distinguishes the letters from the journals is that the journals
reveal John Cheever's private self while the letters reflect the public one.
A similar radical contrast appeared when critics first compared the letters of Evelyn Waugh with his very different diaries. Waugh's diaries are
dark, depressing, and sometimes savagely cruel toward fellow writers
and family members, whereas his letters are witty, charming, and brilliantly sardonic. When the editor of the letters, Mark Amory, asked an
old friend of Waugh's to explain the great differences in the two works,
he was told: "No, no, you see he wrote his letters in the morning, when
he was sober. He wrote his diary at night when he was drunk."[2] Though
there is no evidence that Cheever was that emotionally bifurcated or
wrote when he was drunk, the radically different emotional dispositions
between the letters and the journals are clearly evident.

As Benjamin Cheever states in his introduction to *The Journals of John
Cheever* (1991), his father used them primarily as a private workshop:
"The journals were not initiated with publication in mind. They were
the workbooks for his fiction. They were also the workbooks for his life.
He'd buy a miniature looseleaf, fill it up, then buy another. The note-
book in use would sit on or near his desk. The lined sheets of filler were
easy to distinguish from the standard yellow foolscap he used for his stories and novels" (*J*, vii). There can be little doubt, also, as to how significantly the journals deepened and enriched the content of Cheever's
work and expanded his early, lean, realistic-naturalistic prose into one of
modern American literature's most elegantly ruminative styles. Close
scrutiny reveals a correlation between the developing prose style of his
journal entries of the late 1940s and early 1950s and the increasingly
sophisticated stylistic brilliance of the stories in *The Enormous Radio and
Other Stories* in 1953.

Robert Gottlieb, the editor of the journals, estimated that he used about one-twentieth of the approximately 3–4 million words that comprise the journals. The published journals run to 395 pages and cover every conceivable area of John Cheever's difficult, painful, but ultimately triumphant life. The journals could easily be labeled "The Spiritual Exercises of John Cheever," in which there is as much spiritual exorcising as there is imaginative exercising. Indeed, the act of revealing the nature and depth of his demons seemed to cleanse his soul in his never-ending quest to attain what he called "spiritual robustness." Few writers could make the daily enterprise of household duties so numinous or transform what Wallace Stevens called "the malady of the quotidian" into significant spiritual occasions. And Cheever could accomplish these quasi-alchemical transformations because he was creating his life as he was documenting it in words. He invented his life as an artist in complex methods of recording, remembering, musing over, and making meaning out of the detritus of the quotidian while simultaneously practicing his craft; that is, creating varieties of characters and settings that could, and often did, appear in a particular story or book he was developing. Gottlieb intended "to follow the line of Cheever's inner life as he wrote it down day after day, year after year; to reflect, in proportion, the conflicts and the satisfactions of the thirty-five or so years that these journals represent; and to reveal something of how he worked" (*J*, 397). Certainly few editors were more qualified than Robert Gottlieb, editor of the *New Yorker* and editor of Cheever's last five books published by Alfred A. Knopf.

The journals comprise, then, an intertextual mosaic of Cheever's ruminations, meditations, and remembrances, combined, at times, with early versions of characters and scenes from his fiction. He also periodically reread and reassessed earlier journal entries, a habit that contributed to a richer and more complex reworking of ongoing journal entries. His writing and life became, then, one enterprise, a symbiotic enrichment of his literary career in spite of years of devastating alcoholic excess, sexual desperation, and domestic strife. It is unlikely that Cheever could have continued to publish and maintain his literary reputation without the disciplined exercise that his faithful journal keeping demanded. In short, he kept his imagination alive and active by refining the quality of his conscious perception and by developing a range of expressive nuance that grew even during the writing of *Bullet Park* when, some critics complained, he had seemingly lost his sense of taste and smell, a common occurrence among chronic alcoholics.

At no time, however, did Cheever lose his connection to the potentially redeeming capabilities of nature as shown in the hundreds of journal passages that describe the healing effects of a walk in the woods. Whatever problems were troubling him, contact with nature by means of swimming, hiking, or ice skating usually gave him a larger perspective from which to view his condition. His devotion to his beloved dogs, especially Cassy and Flora, very often helped him forget, temporarily, some of his domestic conflicts. He used nature as a transcending medium to create order in the midst of chaos, much in the tradition of his New England predecessors, Emerson and Thoreau, though Whitman's ecstatic enthusiasm often finds its way into Cheever's more eloquent descriptions of nature's powerful presence. Likewise, Cheever's ability to evoke a sense of place was as important in the journals as it was in his fiction. He was able, like Hawthorne, to evoke the spirit of the houses he lived in and often, at times, the individual rooms in those houses.

But it is John Cheever himself, in a lengthy passage from 1968, who best outlines and analyzes the recurrent concerns of his life as he read two old journals:

> High spirits and weather reports recede into the background, and what emerges are two astonishing contests, one with alcohol and the other with my wife. With alcohol I record my failures, but the number of mornings (over the last ten years) when I've sneaked drinks in the pantry is appalling . . . Sentiment and intelligence seem more important than passion. There are many accounts of sexual and romantic ecstasy, but they are outnumbered by an incredible number of rebuffs . . . I urge myself a hundred times to be cheerful and keep my pecker up, and how puerile this advice seems . . . Do I appear to this world to be henpecked? I think not . . . And another disconcerting thing about the old journals is the recurrent mention of homosexuality. But why do I blame myself for this? Homosexuality seems to be commonplace in our time—no less alarming than drunkenness and adultery—but my anxiety on the matter is very deep and seems incurable. I suffer, from time to time, a painful need for male tenderness, but I cannot perform with a man without wrecking my self-esteem. What, then, is my self-esteem? It seems composed of imponderables—shifty things. It is, at worst, I suppose, a deep wish to placate Muzzy and Dazzy. It is, at its best, a sense of fitness that approaches ecstasy—the sense of life as a privilege, the earth as something splendid to walk on. Relax, relax. (*J,* 245)

At the time of this entry Cheever was working on *Bullet Park,* and this passage throws some light on Paul Hammer's sexual difficulties with his frigid wife and his fear and hatred of homosexuals. Three of Cheever's major thematic motifs, both literary and personal, are acknowledged here: his guilt-laden alcoholism, his never-ending complaints about his wife, and his mixed feelings over his homosexual needs. Several other recurrent concerns—his persistent sense of loneliness and his often harsh criticism of his own writing—occupy significant parts of the journals.

Cheever's sexual preoccupation throughout his journals deals with both heterosexual and homosexual matters. As early as 1951 he records what he calls "the hint of aberrant carnality" that pervaded New York City, and in 1960 describes some desperate and dangerous homosexual activity in the men's room at Grand Central Station as two men expose themselves to each other. Shaken by the experience, he confesses: "I seem threatened by an erotic abyss. The sensible thing is to stay out of such places" (*J,* 139–40). He refers guiltily again and again to his boy-hood homosexual activities. Guilt and apprehension alternate with erot-ic celebration after reading Philip Roth's *Portnoy's Complaint,* as he records the many places where he, too, masturbated. He also recalls some early adolescent homosexual activities with various school chums: "One rainy day at camp when the administration had broken down and we had nothing to do we all doubled up in bed. I first got an Irishman named Burke with a big prick and a very fatherly embrace. Then I switched over to F. for the second trip, but when we had come we dressed and, standing in the rain outside the tent, decided to swear off jacking off. I don't remember how long the resolve lasted, but my jack-ing off was mostly a genuine extension of love. Roth is always alone, and there is never any question in his mind about his maleness, although he does say he missed being a faggot by luck . . . the thought of being homosexual terrifies me, and I am frightened and ashamed to recall that G. sucked me off" (*J,* 247).

Earlier, in 1961, Cheever had cited his father's emotional coldness, lack of familial affection, and readiness to consider an abortion of his wife's second pregnancy as possible causes of his homosexual impulses: "My parents were not happy, and I was not happy with them. I was told that he meant to harm me, and I suppose I never forgave him. But my heart seems to have been open and I was innocently, totally in love with G. when I must have been ten or eleven. At twelve I was in love with J., at thirteen with F., etc. There was no possibility of requital for my feel-ings towards my father, and so I looked to other men for the force of censure, challenge, the encouragement that I needed, and was given this in abundance by W. But it seems, in retrospect, to have been almost entirely an improvisation. I have the character of a bastard" (*J,* 156–57).

Though Cheever never felt the need to rationalize his sexual pursuits, either heterosexual or homosexual, his erotic yearnings always seemed to be connected to his emotional needs and desires to give and receive genuine affection. As time wore on, though, he saw age as the enemy barring him from the possibility of a lasting and healthy homosexual relationship: "I think perhaps I should have an affair with a man. I will go to X and say, 'I'll let you have me,' and he will laugh and say, 'You're twenty years too late. You might, you just might have passed twenty years ago, but now you're nothing but a potbellied old jerk'" (*J,* 270). By the time he made these observations, at age fifty-eight, he had had a number of homosexual affairs, usually with younger men.

Fear of aging and of "the erotic abyss" did not, though, keep him from periodic visits to the men's room at Grand Central, a place notorious for sometimes blatant and dangerous sexual activity: "Fifteen or twenty men stand at the urinal at Grand Central. Their looks are solicitous, alert, sometimes wistful. They use the polished marble as a glass for pickups, and most of them are fondling or pulling their various-sized and -colored cocks. Why does the sight of fifteen or twenty men jerking off seem more significant than the string music in the Palm Court? One young and attractive man, the point of contact concealed by a raincoat, is making an accelerated jerking, as if he was approaching juice time. These are the darkest days of the year" (*J,* 281). There is little doubt that these kinds of scenes disturbed some readers of the *New Yorker* when they first appeared there in the early 1990s; there is also little doubt that Cheever used scenes such as these as models for "the Valley" of masturbation in *Falconer* many years later, but not before transforming them into something poignantly human and nonthreatening. Later, at age sixty-three, and shortly after returning from Smithers Alcohol Rehabilitation Center, his attitude toward his homosexual feelings are clear, direct, and without the cloying self-pity of his drinking years. In love with a man he called A., Cheever finds the courage, at Yaddo, to declare his love openly: "After dinner we walk around the lakes. I ask if he will be my lover, and he refuses, but kindly and politely. I have no response, certainly no pain. I enjoy his company and would enjoy his skin, but I miss neither. I could be unpleasant. I could call him a bore. Any unpleasantness at all would be wicked" (*J,* 312). His growing sobriety enabled him not to be devastated by rejection, a risk he did not hes-

itate in taking; and sobriety also helped him weigh, morally, several possible responses to his unsuccessful offer. He clearly chose to be mature
and reasonable and not to hurt either A. or himself: he will not be
"wicked."

Only with sobriety, though, was Cheever able to become open about
his homosexual relationships, and one friend and lover, Max Zimmer,
aided him greatly during the last weeks of his life, giving him both the
emotional love and care he needed and taking him to and from various
clinics and doctors for medical attention. Though terminally ill, Cheever
observes himself, at seventy, acknowledging erotic desires and engaging
in sexual activity: "It is interesting to observe that a man who is very
near death will lose none of his sexual ardor. If I said to you, 'I know an
old man who keeps in the crook of some tree photographs of naked
young men with stiff pricks,' what would you say?" (*J,* 387). Shortly
before his death, he asked a young man whom he calls R. to come visit
him and take him for a drive: "He is a pleasant young man about whose
way of life, whose friends, I know nothing and can imagine nothing.
Carnally the drive is very ardent, and we end up in a heap of brush
before lunch. I find my orgasm very gratifying and very important" (*J,*
394). Sex for Cheever, whether onanistic, heterosexual, or homosexual—
and his heterosexual activities far outnumbered his homosexual ones—
was never a trifling matter, and he felt compelled to record in his
journals how gratifying and important such experiences were to him.

In the introduction to *The Journals of John Cheever* Benjamin registers
his dismay, after his father had asked him to read the journals, at the
dark and unflattering portrait they painted: "This was not the witty,
charming man in whose guest bedroom I had been sleeping. The material was downbeat and often mean-spirited. There was a lot about homosexuality. I didn't quite get it, or maybe, I didn't want to get it . . . Few
people knew of his bisexuality. Very few people knew of the extent of his
infidelities. And almost nobody could have anticipated the apparent desperation of his inner life, or the caustic nature of his vision" (*J,* x). Next
to the damage that the cold indifference of his parents caused him and
its contribution to his dark vision of life, his endless struggles with alcohol clearly emerge as the second most important contributing cause of
his desperate inner life.

Alongside the agony of his own drinking was the added pain of his
brother Fred's long and painful alcoholic demise as he lost jobs, family,
and finally his life to alcohol. In 1962, John Cheever describes in painfully accurate details the physical and psychological damage that drinking

had had on his brother: "Fred comes. He is now a very heavy man, his girth so swollen that his naturally bellicose walk is close to a waddle . . . The more ruinous his life becomes, the more didactic, informative, and overbearing his manner. 'Now listen to me . . . Let me tell you . . . I know all about the Boston Safe Deposit and Trust Company' . . . in his determination to rally he has developed a crude mockery of cheerfulness. Everything is wonderful, simply wonderful . . . This is the harshness of despair" (*J*, 165). But what made Fred's death even more heartrending was that, during one of his sober periods, he helped John by taking him to Phelps Memorial Hospital for detoxification. Unfortunately, Fred Cheever was never successful in his genuine attempts to stop drinking.

Mary Cheever had worried about John's vast capacity for gin in the early 1950s, and Cheever never disclaimed his pathological reliance on alcohol, stating in 1958: "I am a solitary drunkard. I take a little pain killer before lunch but I really don't get to work until late afternoon" (*J*,94). And, in 1958, he actually looked up the telephone number of Alcoholics Anonymous while suffering from a hangover but changed his mind before making the call: "I open the bar and drink the left over whiskey, gin, and vermouth, whatever I can lay my shaking hands on" (*J*, 112). In 1966, contemplating the connections between drinking and self-destruction, he identifies himself with those fellow writers whose lives ended prematurely because of their suicidal alcoholic excesses or their actual suicides, as in the case of Virginia Woolf: "Thinking of Fitzgerald. I find there is a long list of literary titans who have destroyed themselves: Hart Crane, Virginia Woolf, Hemingway, Lewis, Dylan Thomas, Faulkner . . . Shall I dwell on the crucifixion of the diligent artist?" (*J*, 213). The same list, minus Woolf, appears in one of Cheever's greatest stories, "The World of Apples," as aging poet Asa Bascomb simultaneously contemplates suicide and prays to and for his literary saints. In the journals, however, Cheever further develops his quasi-morbid meditation and attempts to define the relationship between the artist's imagination, alcohol, and self-destruction: "The writer cultivates, extends, raises, and inflates his imagination, sure that this is his destiny, his usefulness, his contribution to the understanding of good and evil. As he inflates his imagination, he inflates his capacity for evil. As he inflates his imagination, he inflates his capacity for anxiety, and inevitably becomes the victim of crushing phobias that can only be allayed by lethal doses of heroin or alcohol" (*J*, 213).

The specific and recurrent index that demonstrates Cheever's absolute dependence on alcohol is his crisis over when he should begin drinking on any given day. What is an appropriate time to have the first drink? As early as 1962, he reveals that his need to drink begins at nine in the morning yet becomes "sometimes unmanageable at eleven-thirty. To describe the humiliation of stealing a drink in the pantry and the galling taste of gin . . . I have a drink at the Biltmore, when my hand is shaking so that it is difficult to get the glass to my mouth. A young man down the bar gives me a hang-dog look; when we succumb to alcohol we lose our self-esteem all the way down the line" (*J,* 175). By 1967, while sketching out fictional scenes, he projects himself into an idealized character "whose dependence on alcohol was extreme but who, through some constitutional fortitude, was able to ration his drinks, to exploit alcohol rather than having it exploit him. He never drank before noon and, after his lunch drinks, not again until five" (*J,* 234). Reality breaks through Cheever's fictive defenses as he tries to adhere to his rule not to drink before eleven: "Now Thursday morning. Twenty minutes to eleven. I am in the throes of a gruelling booze battle. I think a tranquillizer will retard my circulation. I could cut grass, but I am afraid of pulling my ankle. There is really nothing to do but sit here and sweat it out. I can write myself a letter. Dear Myself, I am having a terrible time with the booze. Ride it out" (*J,* 234).

A few passages later, he writes, "this is the journal of an invalid," as he confronts the detrimental psychological and physical effects of his drinking: "Vertigo on the station platform. Will the blacktop fly up and strike me between the eyes? I never know; but it never has. Vertigo in Grand Central. Walking in the city with my son, I stay close to my club in case I collapse there will be some place where I can be taken. Scrotum-grabbing vertigo on bridges, tunnels, and freeways" (*J,* 242). Five years later, after having given up trying to hold out until eleven, the list of his phobias has grown considerably as he struggles with a desperate need to pray; that is, to ask for relief from his addiction: "The situation is, among other things, repetitious. The hours between seven and ten, when I first begin to drink, are the worst. I could take a Miltown, but I do not. Is this the sort of stupidity in which I used to catch my brother? I would like to pray, but to whom—some God of the Sunday school classroom, some provincial king whose prerogatives and rites remain unclear? I am afraid of cars, planes, boats, snakes, stray dogs, falling leaves, extension ladders, and the sound of the wind in the chimneys" (*J,* 277–78).

In 1972, however, the effects of his alcoholic drinking prevented him from practicing his profession; physically he could no longer write: "My cruel addiction begins sometimes at five, sometimes later. Sometime before daybreak. On waking, I want a drink . . . Things worsen at around seven. Now I can think of nothing but the taste of whiskey . . . and I sit at the table sighing as my mother used to sigh. Also my brother . . . Yesterday my hands shook so that I could not type . . . I don't divorce, because I am afraid to—afraid of loneliness, alcoholism, and suicide" (*J,* 286–87). A short time after that journal entry, John Cheever, with his family's support, committed himself to the Smithers Alcohol Rehabilitation Center in New York City, where after an initial period of difficult adjustment he surrendered to the treatment and sobered up for the remainder of his life. He never drank alcohol again.

The journals from 1975 till his death detail Cheever's amazingly swift recovery and contain some of his most profoundly beautiful writing. Once sober, he bravely confronted such painful issues as loneliness, homosexuality, adultery, and, most important, how to live without the alluring consolations of alcohol and drugs. Although his initial experience with Alcoholics Anonymous was unexceptional—he had earlier characterized his first meeting as "dreary"—once he stopped drinking he found them to be enormously helpful in keeping him sober. He also made significant strides in understanding the damage that drinking had caused him and records, the day after he returned home from Smithers, the following lesson: "Laughter seems to be my principal salvation. Laughter and work. I seem unable to resurrect the months in Boston. The role alcohol played is inestimable . . . I cannot face the shame of having lost my moorings through drunkenness . . . I think of [John] O'Hara kicking the shit in his forties and continuing to work. He was about the only one" (*J,* 303).

Further along the entry, he perceptively delineates hurtful and helpful levels of euphoria and formally organizes his day around a thematic goal: "The set piece I'll aim at will be on liberty. There are three points of hazard. One is the euphoria of working at what I think of is the best of my ability; one is the euphoria of alcohol, when I seem to walk among the stars; one is the euphoria of total sobriety, when I seem to command time. That bridge of language, metaphor, anecdote, and imagination that I build each morning to cross the incongruities in my life seems very frail indeed" (*J,* 303). Once he realizes that time is not the enemy as long as he does not drink today—that time is on his side—he sees the possibility of real hope. Nowhere in the journals up to this entry has Cheever articulated so lucidly or maturely the thin line that separates self-destructive alcoholic euphoria from the life-generating euphoria of work and sobriety. But even more important, he discovers that his identity is dependent on his recovery, which resides in that "bridge of language" he creates each and every day. He has begun to understand that he is free to create his own life through his work as long as he chooses not to drink one day at a time. It also seems clear that Cheever is using the simple lessons he learned at Smithers and is successfully sorting out and addressing the agonizing moral and spiritual issues that had confined him within his tortured psyche for most of his life. It is no wonder that his next novel, *Falconer,* concerned itself with prison life.

By the thirteenth day out of Smithers, which was also his sixty-third birthday, he is exhibiting unmistakable signs of gratitude: "I feel as well as I've ever felt and thank God for this" (*J,* 305). By the time he begins a new journal, and after many A.A. meetings, he demonstrates that he had been closely listening to the repetitive but necessary lessons heard there; the most important fact of his life has finally registered: "I don't think I have anything to worry about other than alcohol" (*J,* 310). On his first sober trip to Yaddo, he discovers new lessons about how to live without alcohol, particularly in a place where he had done some of his heaviest drinking, and recognizes the gradual disappearance of some of his alcohol-related phobias: "I think of bridges I may be too frightened to cross, of my fear of throughways, but all of this is remote. My only unease is over the intensely intellectual nature of my pleasure. Alcohol at least gave me the illusion of being grounded. I count now on cutting and splitting wood, swimming in cool water, orgasms, and perhaps, gluttony" (*J,* 310–11). He quickly understood the subtleties involved in distinguishing between the illusion of alcoholic euphoria and the grounding evidence of what his body tells him in both pleasure and work.

Obviously the messages he heard at A.A. meetings were helping him stay sober and were spilling over into the writing of *Falconer* as Cheever mused over the novel's unconscious agenda: "I wonder if this book is not simply a testament of conversion. Conceal this." In the same entry, however, he contrasts the character and intensity of prayers said within the walls of traditional churches and those recited at A.A. meetings in their basements: "I do observe how loudly and with what feeling we say the Lord's Prayer in these unordained gatherings. The walls of churches have not for centuries heard prayers said with such feelings" (*J,* 320).

Depressing emotional preoccupations that had troubled Cheever for years seemed to simply disappear at age sixty-five and to be mysteriously replaced by a serenity that helped him accept life as it presented itself to him on a daily basis: "I do not seem to miss my youth. There is nothing so graceful as that" (*J,* 332), and this from the author of America's most poignant story of lost youth, "O Youth and Beauty!" After observing a poor young woman unsuccessfully trying to sell something to his barber, Cheever identifies with her courageous failure: "I think her experience—standing by the side of the road—is a part of all our lives. I cherish this. And so it is nearly dark, one has nothing at all, and one has everything. I will answer letters, light a fire, and read" (*J,* 332). By 1977, his attendance at A.A. enables him to identify with classes of people with whom he had never before come in contact: "And so we say the same; our confessions all deal with self-destruction and love. Look away from the body into truth and light! We find, in these church basements, a universality that cuts like a blade of a guillotine through the customs we have created in order to live peaceably. Here, on our folding chairs, we talk quite nakedly about endings and beginnings" (*J,* 337).

As a result of Cheever's broad range of experiences with fellow recovering alcoholics, he begins to question and reexamine the psychological and spiritual soundness of some of his old emotional reactions: "I buy groceries at an A&P strange to me. There is for some reason no music, and I miss this. The customers seem to me unclean, stupid, and gross, and I see that this level of perception—this seizure of morbid sensitivity—cripples my usefulness as a man. My sympathy for the young women at the checkout counters is outrageous. I want to gather them all up in my arms and take them off to Arcadia" (*J,* 343). In Cheever's drinking days he would have expanded "this seizure of morbid sensitivity" into something resembling the apocalyptic supermarket scene in *The Wapshot Scandal* or the surrealist conclusion of "The Death of Justina." Cheever realizes that he can no longer afford certain kinds of emotional self-indulgence because such seizures may contain self-pity mixed with unacknowledged feelings of class superiority. Alcoholics Anonymous kept Cheever firmly grounded in its world of absolute equality for all, regardless of occupation, status, or wealth.

Still, Cheever's prevailing loneliness never left him and, in fact, the mental and emotional clarity that sobriety brought him sometimes appeared to deepen and intensify his unmedicated sense of aloneness. But A.A. also kept that condition from turning into unconscious forms of self-destructive behavior by enabling him to reassess earlier mental habits in light of the damage they could do to his fragile sobriety. Even though he was undergoing painful cancer treatments in 1981, his understanding and appreciation of how the lessons of A.A. were working within him deepened significantly: "I go to A.A. and I am astonished to realize that this is not a social gathering. Why else should men and women meet with one another but to make friends or find lovers? But we are gathered together to save one another from alcoholic suicide . . . One might say that these people are failures, and they are indeed—I seek out evidence of their having failed—but these are my most important companions . . . We are gathered here because we are drunkards" (*J,* 379). For the first time in his life Cheever acknowledged that he was, indeed, part of the human race and identified with those who shared with him their struggle to save themselves from themselves, a project he had finally confronted with great and steadfast courage.

Notes and References

Chapter One

1. Scott Donaldson, *John Cheever: A Biography* (New York: Random House, 1988), 9; hereafter cited in text as Donaldson 1988.
2. Susan Cheever, *Home before Dark* (New York: Bantam Books, 1984), 2; hereafter cited in text as S. Cheever.
3. Struthers Burt, "John Cheever's Sense of Drama," *Saturday Review,* 24 April 1943, in *Critical Essays on John Cheever,* ed. R. G. Collins (Boston: G. K. Hall & Co., 1982), 23; hereafter cited in text.
4. Weldon Kees, "John Cheever's Stories," *New Republic,* 19 April 1943, 516–17.
5. Joan Didion, "A Celebration of Life," *National Review,* 22 April 1961, 255.
6. John Cheever, *The Stories of John Cheever* (Alfred A. Knopf, 1978), 467–69; hereafter cited in text as *SJC.*
7. George Garrett, "John Cheever and the Charms of Innocence: The Craft of *The Wapshot Scandal,*" in *Critical Essays on John Cheever,* 58.
8. Samuel Coale, "Cheever and Hawthorne: The American Romancer's Art," in *Critical Essays on John Cheever,* 204; hereafter cited in text as Coale 1982.
9. Benjamin DeMott, "A Grand Gatherum of Some Late Twentieth Century Weirdos," *New York Times Book Review,* 27 April 1969, 40; hereafter cited in text.

Chapter Two

1. Herbert Mitgang, "Behind the Best Sellers: John Cheever," *Conversations with John Cheever,* ed. Scott Donaldson (Jackson and London: University Press of Mississippi, 1987), 173.
2. According to a report by John F. Baker, "Academy Chicago Offers New Cheever Collection," *Publishers Weekly,* 20 December 1993, 9, the stories the Cheever family agreed to allow into print in *Thirteen Uncollected Stories of John Cheever* were those "that entered the public domain as of January 1994. The stories in the collection . . . were either copyrighted by magazines that eventually went bankrupt or were ones whose copyright had reverted to the author, but which Cheever didn't renew." The collection was edited by Franklin H. Dennis, who chose only those stories that had entered the public domain as of 1994 and would thus not be subject to litigation over rights. George W. Hunt, S.J., one of Cheever's most important critics and the author of the comprehensive 1983

study *John Cheever: The Hobgoblin Company of Love,* wrote a lengthy introduction to the volume that traces the development of Cheever's early style, his interest in socialistic ideas, and the unmistakable influence of Hemingway.

Sven Birkerts, who reviewed the volume in "A First Glimpse of Cheever Country" for the *New York Times Book Review,* 13 March 1994, 17, calls the stories "competent, solid," but says that "such a collection would not see the light of day if it did not have the Cheever name on the cover. . . . We hear few preliminary notes of the vioce that we recognize as Cheever's."

John Updike puts his response to these thirteen stories ("Posthumous Output, *New Yorker,* 30 May 1994, 107–10) in the context of a larger reprisal of Cheever's early work, particularly the stories in *The Way Some People Live* and the stories George S. Kaufman brought together as the play *Townhouse,* which he directed on Broadway. *The Thirteen Uncollected Stories* "begin with some formless, vaguely anticapitalistic effusions by a teen-ager," Updike writes, "and progress to some pat, hokey confections by a young man trying to survive the Depression by selling to the slick magazines." What he finds fascinating is seeing "a splendid talent grow its wings. The last two stories, published in a 1942 *Collier's* and a 1949 *Cosmopolitan,* display, if not quite the full-feathered sheen, many gleams" (108–9). Updike concludes with a request to the Cheever family to consider publishing "an edition of [Cheever's] uncollected stories more generous and orderly than this baker's dozen born of bitter litigation" (110).

3. John Cheever, "Expelled," *New Republic,* 1 October 1930; reprint, *New Republic,* 19 and 26 July, 1982, 35; hereafter cited in text as "Expelled."

4. John Cheever, *The Way Some People Live* (New York: Random House, 1943), 3; hereafter cited in text as *WSPL.*

5. *The Journals of John Cheever,* ed. Robert Gottlieb (New York: Alfred A. Knopf, 1991), 397; hereafter cited in text as *J.*

6. Frederick Karl, "John Cheever and the Promise of Pastoral," in *Critical Essays on John Cheever,* 209–19.

7. James O'Hara, "John Cheever," in *American Short-Story Writers, 1910–1945,* vol. 102 of *The Dictionary of Literary Biography,* ed. Bobby Ellen Kimbel (Detroit: Gale Research, 1991), 33.

8. Annette Grant, "John Cheever: The Art of Fiction LXII," in *Conversations with John Cheever,* 108.

Chapter Three

1. Donald Attwater, *The Penguin Dictionary of Saints* (New York: Viking Penguin, 1986), 69.

2. John Cheever, *The Wapshot Chronicle* (New York: Harper & Row, 1957), 11; hereafter cited in text as *WC.*

3. Dana Gioia, Millicent Dillon, and Michael Stillman, "An Interview with John Cheever," in *Conversations with John Cheever,* 75.

4. Charles Olson, "On Projective Verse," in *Selected Writings of Charles Olson,* ed. Robert Creeley (New York: New Directions, 1966), 16.

5. Samuel Coale, *John Cheever* (New York: Frederick Ungar, 1977), 73–74; hereafter cited in text as Coale 1977.

6. Scott Donaldson, "John Cheever," in *American Writers: A Collection of Literary Biographies,* ed. Leonard Ungar, supplement 1, part 1 (New York: Charles Scribner's Sons, 1979), 180; hereafter cited in text as Donaldson 1979.

7. John Cheever, *The Wapshot Scandal* (New York: Harper & Row, 1964), 107; hereafter cited in text as *WS.*

8. George Hunt, S.J., *John Cheever: The Hobgoblin Company of Love* (Grand Rapids: William B. Eerdmans, 1983), 127; hereafter cited in text.

9. Edward Arlington Robinson, "The Man Against the Sky," in *Collected Poems* (New York: Macmillan Company, 1944), 66.

Chapter Four

1. James O'Hara, *John Cheever: A Study of the Short Fiction* (Boston: Twayne Publishers, 1989), 36.

2. Robert Morace, "From Parallels to Paradise," in *John Cheever: A Study of the Short Fiction,* 138.

Chapter Five

1. William Peden, *The American Short Story: Continuity and Change, 1940–1975* (Boston: Houghton Mifflin, 1975), 37.

2. Lynne Waldeland, *John Cheever* (Boston: Twayne Publishers, 1979), 91–92.

3. Robert Graves, *The Greek Myths: I* (New York: Penguin Books, 1977), 89.

4. James Hillman, *The Dream and the Underworld* (New York: Harper & Row, 1979), 23–24; hereafter cited in text as Hillman, 1979.

5. Eleanor Munroe, "Not Only I the Narrator, but I John Cheever," in *Conversations with John Cheever,* 136.

6. Hal Blythe and Charlie Sweet, "Cheever's Dark Knight of the Soul: The Failed Quest of Neddy Merrill," *Studies in Short Fiction* 29 (Summer 1992): 347–52; hereafter cited in text.

7. Robert Morace, "John Cheever," in *Magill's Survey of American Literature,* vol. 1 (New York: Marshall Cavendish, 1991), 383.

8. Michael Byrne, "The River of Names in 'The Swimmer,'" *Studies in Short Fiction* 23 (Summer 1986): 327; hereafter cited in text.

Chapter Six

1.   John Gardner, "Witchcraft in Bullet Park," in *Critical Essays on John Cheever,* 258.

2.   John Cheever, *Bullet Park* (New York: Ballantine Books, 1990), 19; hereafter cited in text as *BP.*

3.   Wallace Stevens, *The Necessary Angel* (New York: Random House, 1951), 36.

4.   T. S. Eliot, *The Complete Plays and Poems* (New York: Harcourt Brace & World, 1971), 119; hereafter cited in text.

5.   George Quasha, "Publisher's Preface," in James Hillman, *Healing Fiction* (Barrytown, New York: Station Hill Press, 1983), x–xi.

6.   Dan. 5:26–29, in *The New English Bible* (Oxford and Cambridge University Presses, 1970); all biblical quotations are from this edition and are hereafter cited in text.

Chapter Seven

1.   John Firth, "Talking with John Cheever," *Saturday Review,* 2 April 1977, 22.

2.   John Hersey, "Talk with John Cheever," in *Conversations with John Cheever,* 114.

3.   John Cheever, *Falconer* (New York: Ballantine Books, 1977), 6; hereafter cited in text as *F.*

4.   John Gardner, "On Miracle Road," in *Critical Essays on John Cheever,* 80–84.

5.   James Hillman, *Inter Views* (New York: Harper & Row, 1983), 90.

6.   John Cheever, *Oh What a Paradise It Seems* (New York: Ballantine Books, 1982), 7; hereafter cited in text as *P.*

Chapter Eight

1.   *The Letters of John Cheever,* ed. Benjamin Cheever (New York: Simon and Schuster, 1988), 300; hereafter cited in text as *L.*

2.   *The Letters of Evelyn Waugh,* ed. Mark Amory (New Haven: Ticknor and Fields, 1980), viii.

Selected Bibliography

PRIMARY WORKS

Short-Story Collections

The Brigadier and the Golf Widow. New York: Harper and Row, 1964. Reprint. New York: Bantam: 1965.

The Enormous Radio and Other Stories. New York: Funk & Wagnalls, 1953. Reprint. New York, Harper & Row, Colophon, 1965.

The Housebreaker of Shady Hill and Other Stories. New York: Harper & Brothers, 1958. Reprint. New York: Macfadden Books, 1961.

Some People, Places, and Things That Will Not Appear in My Next Novel. New York: Harper & Brothers, 1961. Reprint. New York: Bantam, 1963.

The Stories of John Cheever. New York: Alfred A. Knopf, 1978. Reprint. New York: Ballantine Books, 1980.

Thirteen Uncollected Stories of John Cheever. Edited by Franklin H. Dennis. Chicago: Academy Chicago Publishers, 1994.

The Way Some People Live. New York: Random House, 1943.

The World of Apples. New York: Alfred A. Knopf, 1973. Reprint. New York: Warner, 1974.

Dennis, Franklin H, ed. *Thirteen Uncollected Stories of John Cheever.* Chicago: Academy Chicago Publishers, 1994.

Novels

Bullet Park. New York: Alfred A. Knopf, 1969. Reprint. New York: Bantam, 1970; Ballantine, 1978.

Falconer. New York: Alfred A. Knopf: 1977. Reprint. New York: Ballantine, 1978.

Oh What a Paradise It Seems. New York: Alfred A. Knopf, 1982.

The Wapshot Chronicle. New York: Harper & Brothers, 1957. Reprint. New York: Penguin, 1963; Bantam, 1964; Time-Life, 1965; Harper & Row, 1973; with *The Wapshot Scandal* in single volume, New York: Harper & Row, 1979.

The Wapshot Scandal. New York: Harper & Row, 1964. Reprint. New York: Bantam, 1965; Harper & Row, 1973.

Letters and Journals

*Good Tidings: A Friendship in Letters: The Correspondence of John Cheever and
    John D. Weaver, 1945–1982.* Edited by John D. Weaver. New York:
    HarperCollins, 1993.
The Journals of John Cheever. Edited by Robert Gottlieb. New York: Alfred A.
    Knopf, 1991.
The Letters of John Cheever. Edited by Benjamin Cheever. New York: Simon &
    Schuster, 1988.
Weaver, John D., ed. *Good Tidings: A Friendship in Letters: The Correspondence of
    John Cheever and John D. Weaver, 1945–1982.* New York: HarperCollins,
    1993.

SECONDARY WORKS

Book-length Biographies

Bosha, Francis J., ed. *The Critical Response to John Cheever.* Westport:
    Greenwood Press, 1994. Bosha's impeccably researched book is an indis-
    pensable, comprehensive survey of Cheever criticism from his earliest
    stories to *The Journals.* He has included "Later Criticism" of all novels
    and story collections and a transcription of Cheever's last interview with
    Robert G. Collins. Bosha's own twenty-page introduction to this rich
    volume is, after Robert Morace's 1986 critical survey, (see below), the
    single most comprehensive and intelligent assemblage of Cheever criti-
    cism in print.
Cheever, Susan. *Home before Dark.* Boston: Houghton Mifflin, 1984. A painfully
    honest biography by Cheever's only daughter, who is also a respected
    novelist. Insights into family conflicts and family history greatly help
    readers understand the importance of tradition for John Cheever and his
    genuine love for his children.
Donaldson, Scott. *John Cheever: A Biography.* New York: Random House, 1988.
    The definitive biography of Cheever. Donaldson is not only a superb bio-
    graphical scholar but also a first-rate critic of the relationship between the
    work and the life.

Book-length Critical Studies

Coale, Samuel. *John Cheever.* New York: Ungar, 1977. The first book-length
    study of Cheever's work. Coale's original and genuinely perceptive
    insights and analysis became the basis of Cheever scholarship.
Collins, R. G., ed. *Critical Essays on John Cheever.* Boston: G. K. Hall, 1982. An
    outstanding collection of a wide range of highly valuable essays on
    Cheever's work. Collins's introduction surveys, with genuine insight, var-

ious critical approaches to Cheever's work. The volume reprints fifteen representative reviews of the novels and short-story collections, several interviews, and seventeen of the best available critical essays, most of which were written specifically for the volume. See especially the essays by Burhans, Garrett, Kazin, Graves, Chesnick, Donaldson, Greene, Bracher, Slabey, Coale, Karl, Kendle, Rupp, Brown, Gardner, Waldeland, and, D'haen.

Hunt, George W., S.J. *John Cheever: The Hobgoblin Company of Love.* Grand Rapids: William B. Eerdmans, 1983. The longest, most comprehensive, and most serious study of Cheever's work. Father Hunt's uncovering of religious and mythic patterns is compelling and perceptive; his analysis of the novels is often brilliant and erudite and always clear and convincing.

O'Hara, James E. *John Cheever: A Study of the Short Fiction.* Boston: Twayne Publishers, 1989. A keenly intelligent treatment of about sixty short stories. O'Hara also analyzes a number of early stories that most scholars have overlooked. Part 2 includes some letters, interviews, and five of the best critical essays on the stories.

Waldeland, Lynne. *John Cheever.* Boston: Twayne Publishers, 1979. Waldeland covers, quite thoroughly, all the novels up to *Oh What a Paradise It Seems* and a substantial number of the short stories—about sixty-three. She includes in her discussions virtually all of the available reviews and criticisms and comprehensively synthesizes their various points of view.

Articles and Parts of Books

Blythe, Hal, and Charles Sweet. "Cheever's Dark Knight of the Soul: The Failed Quest for Neddy Merrill." *Studies in Short Fiction* 29 (Summer 1992): 347–52. A convincing argument concerning Cheever's conscious use of Grail materials.

Byrne, Michael D. "The River of Names in 'The Swimmer.'" *Studies in Short Fiction* 23 (Summer 1986): 326–27. A provocative analysis of Cheever's use of proper names throughout "The Swimmer."

———. "Split-Level Enigma: John Cheever's *Bullet Park*." *Studies in American Fiction* 20 (Spring 1992): 85–97. A thorough treatment of Cheever's mixed feelings toward American suburbia.

Collins, Robert G. "Beyond Argument: Post-Marital Man in John Cheever's Later Fiction." *Mosaic* 17 (Spring 1984): 261–79. Compelling analysis of Cheever's changing attitudes toward men, marriage, and homosexuality.

———. "Fugitive Time: Dissolving Experience in the Later Fiction of John Cheever." *Studies in American Fiction* 12 (1984): 175–88. An assessment of the pressure of time on defining experience.

———. "From Subject to Object and Back Again: Individual Identity in John Cheever's Fiction." *Twentieth Century Literature* 28 (Summer 1982): 1–13.

A thorough examination of problems involved in subjective/objective perceptions among some of Cheever's major characters.

Donaldson, Scott. "Supermarket and Superhighway: John Cheever's America." *Virginia Quarterly Review* 62 (Autumn 1986): 654–58. Insightful discussion of the despair in Cheever's vision of an overly technological America.

_____. "Writing the Cheever." *Sewanee Review* 98 (Summer 1990): 527–45. An informative discussion of the daunting problems involved in writing the definitive Cheever biography.

_____. "John Cheever." In *American Writers: A Collection of Literary Biographies*, edited by Leonard Ungar, supplement 1, part 1, 174–99. New York: Charles Scribner's Sons, 1979. A comprehensive treatment of all of the story collections and all the novels except *Oh What a Paradise It Seems*.

Edwards, Paul C. "Transforming Cheever: Three Failures in Reimagination." *Literature in Performance* 5 (April 1984): 14–26. Edwards finds attempts to transfer several stories into other media awkward and ultimately unsuccessful.

Fogelman, Bruce. "A Key Pattern of Images in John Cheever's Short Fiction." *Studies in Short Fiction* 26 (Fall 1989): 463–72. An imaginative interpretation of the various ways Cheever uses his recurrent aquatic images.

Gerlach, John. "Closure in Modern Short Fiction: Cheever's 'The Enormous Radio' and 'Artemis, the Honest Well-Digger.'" *Modern Fiction Studies* 28 (Spring 1982): 145–52. An insightful comparison of the way in which Cheever concludes two of his most popular short stories.

Hunt, George W., S.J. "The Vision of John Cheever." *New Catholic World* 228 (July–August 1985): 174–76. Hunt explores Cheever's essentially spiritual agenda and its connection to Christianity.

Johnson, Glen M. "The Moral Structure of Cheever's *Falconer*." *Studies in American Fiction* 9 (Spring 1981): 21–31. Johnson uncovers a number of religious allusions that create a moral structure for *Falconer*.

Magaw, Malcolm O. "Cheever's New Existential Man." *International Fiction Review* 17 (Summer 1990): 75–81. Explores Cheever's inherent existential position throughout a number of works.

Mason, Kenneth C. "Tradition and Desecration: The Wapshot Novels of John Cheever." *Arizona Quarterly* 43 (Autumn 1987): 231–50. A thorough examination of the way Cheever presents the fall of America through its loss of traditional values, a sense of history, and a sense of the sacred.

Morace, Robert. "From Parallels to Paradise: The Lyrical Structure of Cheever's Fiction." *Twentieth Century Literature* 35 (Winter 1989): 502–28. A convincing examination of the poetic basis of Cheever's lyrical prose. Included in James O'Hara's *Study of the Short Fiction of John Cheever*, 137–45.

_____. "John Cheever." In *Magill's Survey of American Literature*, vol. 1, 366–83. New York: Marshall Cavendish, 1991. A concise analysis of both Wapshot novels, *Falconer*, and five of Cheever's most popular stories.

O'Hara, Daniel T. "John Cheever's Contingent Imagination." *South Atlantic Quarterly* 91 (Summer 1992): 675–94. Explores Cheever's penchant for self-mythologizing and its relationship to the imagination.

O'Hara, James. "Cheever's *The Wapshot Scandal:* A Narrative of Exploration." *Critique* 22 (1979): 20–30. Shows the differences between the historical narrative of *The Wapshot Chronicle* and the more open structure of *Scandal.*

———. "John Cheever's Flowering Forth: The Breakthroughs of 1947." *Modern Language Studies* 17 (Fall 1987): 50–59. O'Hara theorizes over the sudden appearance of two of Cheever's landmark stories in 1947: "The Enormous Radio" and "Torch Song."

———. "John Cheever." In *American Short-Story Writers: 1910-1945,* edited by Bobby Ellen Kimbel, vol. 102, 26–42, of *The Dictionary of Literary Biography.* Detroit: Gale Research, 1991. A selective but thorough analysis of the emergence of Cheever's stylistic sophistication. Is especially perceptive on many of the critically neglected stories.

Reilly, Edward C. "Saving Grace and Moral Balance in John Cheever's Stories." *Publications of the Mississippi Philological Association* 1 (Summer 1982): 24–29. Explores the connection between Cheever's concept of grace and morality.

Stengel, Wayne. "John Cheever's Surreal Vision and the Bridge of Language." *Twentieth Century Literature* 33 (Summer 1987): 223–33. Perceptively examines the relationships between the images of bridges, dreams, and language in "The Angel of the Bridge."

Waldeland, Lynne. "John Cheever's *Bullet Park:* A Key to his Thought and Art." In *Critical Essays on John Cheever,* edited by R. G. Collins, 261–72. Waldeland defends *Bullet Park* against negative criticisms, convincingly showing it to be a pivotal work in Cheever's career.

Interviews

Donaldson, Scott, ed. *Conversations with John Cheever.* Jackson: University Press of Mississippi, 1987. This thorough collection of twenty-eight interviews, edited by biographer Scott Donaldson, contains all of the major interviews and a number of the early newspaper quasi-interviews from 1940 and 1948 from Cheever's hometown newspaper, the Quincy *Patriot-Ledger.*

Bibliographies

Bosha, Francis J. *John Cheever: A Reference Guide.* Boston: G. K. Hall, 1981. An indispensable guide to serious scholars and students of Cheever's work.

Coates, Dennis. "Cheever Bibliographical Supplement, 1978–81." In *Critical Essays on John Cheever,* edited by R. G. Collins, 279–85. Boston: G. K. Hall, 1982.

_____. "John Cheever: A Checklist, 1930–1978." *Bulletin of Bibliography* 36 (January–March 1979): 1–13, 49. Together with item listed above by Coates, a complete update on all the available scholarship on Cheever.

Morace, Robert. "John Cheever." In *Contemporary Authors: Bibliographical Series,* edited by James J. Martine, vol 1., 157–92, of *American Novelists.* Detroit: Gale Research (1986). A highly intelligent and keenly perceptive critical analysis of Cheever scholarship through 1984. Morace is one of the most reliable and scholarly critics of Cheever's work.

Trakas, Deno. "John Cheever: An Annotated Secondary Bibliography (1943–1978)." *Resources for American Literary Study* 9 (1979): 181–99. Some overlap with earlier listed bibliographies. Trakas does, however, find some obscure yet important sources. The annotations are helpful and succinct.

Index

The Author

Patrick Meanor is associate professor of English at the State University of New York, College at Oneonta, where he has served as chair of graduate studies in English for many years. He is the editor of *American Short-Story Writers since World War II* (1993), volume 130 of *The Dictionary of Literary Biography,* and the author of numerous essays on such literary and cultural figures as Aimé Césaire, Jean Genet, Bruce Chatwin, James Wright, and Charles Bukowski. He earned his B.A. and M.A. degrees under the Jesuits at John Carroll University in Cleveland, Ohio, and his Ph.D. at Kent State University. He lives in upstate New York with his beloved dog, Lucy, a sweet-natured vizsla.

The Editor

Frank Day is a professor of English and department head at Clemson University. He is the author of *Sir William Empson: An Annotated Bibliography* and *Arthur Koestler: A Guide to Research*. He was a Fulbright lecturer in American literature in Romania (1980–81) and in Bangladesh (1986–87).